ADVANCED PRAISE FOR *TICK TOCK*

"*Tick Tock* is a document, a community, a manual, a help line, a chorus of voices expressing the gamut of complicated emotions that accompany a person of a certain age contemplating the leap into parenthood. I wish this important book existed when I was at that crossroads, and am grateful for it today."

—MICHELLE TEA, author of *Against Memoir*

"*Tick Tock* reads like a wide-ranging chat with friends who ask 'What's *your* story?' These are human, lived tales that describe l and interconnected issues—political, social, and personal.

—JUDY NORSIGIAN and JANE PINCUS, co-founders o Our Bodies Ourselves

"*Tick Tock* challenges readers to rethink what parenting time in America from a wide variety of vantage points voices that are, in all their great diversity, eloquent, sha engaging. . . . Brilliantly framed and beautifully written.'

—ROSALIND PETCHESKY, PhD, Distinguished Profe of Political Science, Hunter College & the Graduate Ce University of New York

"As an over-40 mother myself, I appreciate how this groundbreaking collection marks momentous changes in gender roles, child-rearing patterns, and family composition."

—JOYCE ANTLER, PhD, Professor Emerita of Women's, Gender and Sexuality Studies at Brandeis University and author of *You Never Call! You Never Write! A History of the Jewish Mother*

"Honest, personal, and often downright funny, these brave parents provide insight, solidarity, and hope for any over 40 who are ready to love a child...and laugh and cry and wonder upon the universe every day for the rest of their lives. May it always be so."

—JESS P. SHATKIN, MD, MPH, professor of Child & Adolescent Psychiatry and Pediatrics, NYU School of Medicine

"*Tick Tock* is an exquisite, understanding, and inclusive examination of the unique challenges and joys faced by older parents. An unforgettable book—undeniably important and a pleasure to read."

—BEVERLY GOLOGORSKY, author of *Can You See the Wind?*

TICK TOCK

ESSAYS ON BECOMING A PARENT AFTER 40

EDITED BY VICKI BREITBART
AND NAN BAUER-MAGLIN

dottir
press

NEW YORK

Published in 2021 by Dottir Press
33 Fifth Avenue
New York, NY 10003
Dottirpress.com

FIRST EDITION
First printing: September 2021
Production by Drew Stevens
Cover illustration by Ashley Seil Smith

The poems by Elizabeth Acevedo are excerpted with permission from HarperCollins Publishers. Text copyright © 2018 by Elizabeth Acevedo.

Library of Congress Control Number: 2021938820

ISBN 978-1948340-458 (pbk)
ISBN 978-1948340-496 (ebook)

Manufactured in the US by McNaughton & Gunn.

Contents

PART III. DOES AGE MATTER IF I ADOPT?

PART IV. PARENTING AFTER FORTY

Introduction

In April of 2018, Senator Tammy Duckworth brought her ten-day-old daughter onto the floor of the Senate. This was historic, both because she was the first sitting senator to bring her infant to Congress and because Duckworth was fifty years old at the time.

Becoming a parent after forty is a growing phenomenon. While the general fertility rate in the US is at a record low, according to the Centers for Disease Control and Prevention (CDC), the number of births for women over the age of forty has increased every year since 1985.[1] Adoption by older people is becoming more common, too—actress and activist Mariska Hargitay adopted a child when she was forty-seven and Viola Davis adopted when she was forty-six.

And it's not just celebrities. In her article about older-parent adoption, Ann Brenoff reports that "over half (54 percent) of children adopted from the U.S. foster care system have parents over the age of 50 and 16 percent have parents over the age of 60." She quotes Adam Perlman, the executive director of the Evan B. Donaldson Adoption Institute, in saying that adoption by older parents is "a trend that's clearly happening."[2]

Regardless of the numbers, becoming a parent at this "advanced age" is not treated as "normal" in our culture. Gray hair or other physical signs of age mark and marginalize older parents in school or other parent-child community settings. Older parents report that they are often asked invasive and presumptuous personal questions about how their family was created.[3] While there's a long history of grandparents successfully playing a primary parental role, it hasn't seemed to change the stigma about becoming a parent once you enter or are past the fourth decade of your life.

Tick Tock asks the question: How old *is* too old to become a parent? This book is for anyone approaching or over the age of forty who is considering becoming pregnant, trying to become pregnant, thinking about adoption, is a partner of any of these people, or has already gone through any of these experiences. It includes poems and a narrative about being a child of older parents, as well as stories by people, ranging in age from thirty-eight to fifty-eight, who became parents after a birth (with or without reproductive technology), by being in a relationship with someone who is already a parent, or through adoption. These authors are racially diverse, and they come from different backgrounds and cultures. They are men, women, LGBTQ, straight. Many have encountered questions, comments, and judgments from doctors, friends, family, and strangers about their age as they try to become parents. They have felt stigmatized or chastised because they hadn't had children at an earlier age; they have often felt that something is wrong with them.

Tick Tock seeks to counter these negative attitudes while acknowledging some of the challenges for those who become parents as they approach or are over forty. As the stories in *Tick Tock* reveal, becoming parents later in life may mean facing issues of infertility, smaller families, less involvement of their own parents, financial burdens, and additional health issues as they age. It also brings great fulfillment and joy.

This book is divided into five sections. Each section focuses on a different aspect of being or becoming an older parent. While each story is found in the section that best matches the main focus of the piece, most of the stories overlap. As we redefine our perspectives on gender roles and age, we try to use age- and gender-neutral language whenever possible to be more inclusive. We use the phrase "older parent" while questioning the concept: Older than what?

There is a popular meme showing a woman's face with her hand to her forehead, looking very confused. The bubble over her head reads, "Oh no, I forgot to have children!" People who are approaching or over forty and hoping to become parents for the first time have very likely encountered the question, "Why did you wait?" which assumes it was a choice—rather than the complexities of life—that created the delay in becoming a parent.

Part I of the book presents some of the reasons people find themselves becoming parents nearing or after forty. Anthropologist Rayna Rapp relates this rise in the number of older parents to the changing gender roles of the last few decades. She explains that these changes are "linked to women being more educated—to the monetization of the economy where women must work outside the home to support children. . . . to the rise in the divorce rate—where there is more consciousness of violence and discord in relationships, where women have options to get out from bad relationships."[4] As Elizabeth Gregory suggests in her groundbreaking book *Ready: Why Women Are Embracing the New Later Motherhood*, the narrative of later parenting is a "happy tale of how much positive control women do now have over an aspect of their lives that ran roughshod over them for millennia."[5]

The narratives in *Tick Tock* demonstrate how changing gender roles and the nature of relationships affect the timeline for becoming a parent. For heterosexual women, the availability of contraception and abortion contributed to the ability to postpone becoming a parent or having another child. Traditionally, the order has been relationship first and then parenthood; for some of these authors, however, the "right" relationship took much longer than they imagined, and others decided to have a child without having a romantic partnership at all. For LGBTQ parents in the book, the process of claiming their sexual orientation took time, and in spite of some social changes, severely limited their parenting options.

Research into the reasons for delayed childbearing reveals that when women think about giving birth, they are generally well-informed and knowledgeable about the risk of "geriatric pregnancies," but they need to feel "ready" in regard to their relationships, their financial stability, and/or their health. Often, delayed childbearing is the result of circumstances outside of their control. Anna Louie Sussman, in her article "The End of Babies," goes so far as to say that our society has "become hostile to reproduction."[6] While our pronatalist culture encourages motherhood, it simultaneously makes it difficult for many to imagine developing a productive work life while raising children, and difficult to feel they can adequately provide for them. The lack of family leave, equal pay, and sufficient childcare hampers many women's dual role as parent and provider. In the '90s, the SisterSong Women of Color Reproductive Justice Collective developed the framework of reproductive justice that acknowledges the inequalities and inequities that affect becoming a parent and called for the human right to lead fully self-determined lives—to be able to "maintain personal bodily autonomy, have children, not have children, and parent the children we have in safe and sustainable communities."[7]

When some of the writers in *Tick Tock* came to the point in their lives where they wanted to have a child, they found that age had affected their fertility and the ability to follow through with their decision. Part II focuses on pregnancy—trying to get pregnant and being pregnant after forty. Reproductive technology has drastically changed this narrative. Those who have the resources try assisted reproductive technology (ART), most often in vitro fertilization (IVF). The CDC reports that the use of ART has steadily increased over the past decade, but ART treatments are not without risks, and they are prohibitively expensive for low-income people.[8]

A 2020 *New York Times* article, "What They Paid to Make a Baby (or 2)," highlighted five parents who were successful in using some form of ART. They were all over forty. With medication, procedures, blood work, egg donation, and surrogate fees, costs ranged from $21,000 to $107,957.[9] RESOLVE, the website of the National Interfertility Association, reports that only nineteen states have enacted laws that require some type of infertility coverage by private insurers.[10] With so many regulations, requirements, and exemptions for companies for religious reasons, most people wind up paying out of pocket. There is no ART coverage for people with public insurance.

Many women with resources can go through several rounds of treatments, only to be disappointed with the results. Recent CDC report indicate that for the thousands of ART cycles performed, only 36 percent result in births in women under thirty-five. The success rate depends on many factors, including the type of procedure and the age of the woman.[11] New research about male fertility challenges the assumption that this is only a female issue; it suggests that men, too, have a "biological clock." A couple's chance of conceiving begins to decrease when the man is older than thirty-five and drops even further when he is older than forty.[12] As some of the contributors here approached or passed the age of forty, they decided to stop the process of trying to get pregnant altogether.

Some of the authors in this collection did beat the odds by getting pregnant at advanced ages and having successful outcomes. Generally, people who get pregnant after forty are at increased risk of suffering diseases during pregnancy or facing complications during delivery. A study of 24,032 post-forty-year-old pregnancies found that women of this "advanced age" suffer an increased risk of emergency C-sections, forceps, and vacuum deliveries. In addition, women of advanced maternal age have a higher risk of adverse obstetrical and perinatal outcomes.[13]

Implicit bias around age and race can also lead to assumptions about whether to label someone "at risk" during the pregnancy. In a 2018 review, Hamideh Bayrampour and colleagues showed that being at risk is not just about physiological complications; it is about psychological and social phenomena as well.[14] For those over forty, being labeled "at risk" has a lot to do with a person's support network, their ability to control situations, and whether they have an established relationship or a planned pregnancy. These economic and social factors also influence who a person can choose as their medical provider, the care they get, and whether they will be treated as an individual, rather than a statistic.

There are strong indications that environmental, economic, and social factors—including systemic racism—contribute to risks and poor pregnancy outcomes for many women over forty. A 2017 article on pregnancy-related mortality in the US reports that while mortality rate increases with maternal age for all groups, racial-ethnic inequities persist; Black women have a mortality ratio 3.4 times higher than white non-Hispanics.[15] For people of color, racial discrimination over a lifetime can lead to tragic birth outcomes. Researcher Arline Geronimus coined the term "weathering" to describe racism as a cause for many Black people to be less healthy as they age, which greatly increases the risks of adverse maternal and infant outcomes.[16] In Dani McClain's extraordinary work on Black motherhood, *We Live for the We: The Political Power of Black Motherhood*, she "addresses the politics of mothering, namely, issues of power, position, and protection." She remarks that people of color are less likely to receive the services they need, "even when their insurance and income are the same as white people" and she encourages "self-determination in black parents-to-be."[17]

The authors in *Tick Tock* acknowledge the difficulties older parents face in trying to get pregnant, managing their pregnancies, and delivering healthy babies. Yet, each parent is grateful for the opportunity to become a parent; each story highlights the strength and resilience of the aspiring parents involved.

Part III focuses on older individuals who chose to adopt after the age of forty. Whether they went through ART and decided to stop, did not want to or couldn't go through with a pregnancy, or came to adoption after a major life event, these authors' journeys toward adoption were long, arduous, and potentially very costly. Adopting a child who is in foster care can cost anywhere from zero to a few thousand dollars, and the child will very likely not be an infant. A 2020 article in the *New York Times*, "What I Spent to Adopt My Child," sets the price tag for adopting an infant at up to $45,000 for a domestic adoption and even higher for an international adoption.[18] The cost, the amount of time it took to complete the process, and the difficulties these authors experienced around adoption depended on many factors: whether it was a domestic or international adoption, the age of the child they adopted, and, most definitely, their age.

Most domestic adoption sites state that the minimum age for adopting is twenty-one years old, and there is no apparent age cutoff for prospective parents. But in adoptions where birth parents select the adoptive home, "this means that there may be an age preference for younger parents who seem more desirable."[19] The Adoption Network website states: "In the majority of domestic adoption, the birth mother will choose the adopting parent(s). . . . If she has no problem with your age, the adoption can move forward. However, in domestic adoption, some agencies put a cutoff on an adoptive parent's age, usually at 40. . . . In international adoption, each country has age guidelines and restrictions. Many keep the age difference between the child and youngest parent at 40 years."[20]

For several white prospective parents in *Tick Tock*, regardless of whether they went through a domestic or international adoption, whether they used an agency or a private lawyer, or whether they were waiting for an infant instead of an older child, they found themselves with the prospect of raising a child of a different race and culture than their own. The opportunity to adopt a child is often the result of another person's loss due to personal, economic, and social factors. In her book *Beggars and Choosers: How the Politics of Choice Shapes Adoption, Abortion, and Welfare in the United States*, Rickie Solinger reminds us that, for women from poor countries, surrendering a child is most often not a "choice."[21] Domestically, Dorothy Roberts points out in *Adoption Matters: Philosophical and Feminist Essays* that inequities in the nation's public child welfare policies have resulted in a disproportionate number of Black children available for adoption.[22] Respectfully raising a child of a different race and culture was an additional challenge for many of the writers in *Tick Tock*.

Some adoption agencies acknowledge this challenge and run a workshop on cross-racial and cross-cultural adoptions, and many people decide they can't proceed with adopting a child of a different race after they learn what it entails. Others, like some of the writers in this book, take this on as a lifelong responsibility. In their book *Inside Transracial Adoption*, Beth Hall and Gail Steinberg emphasize that it "requires race-conscious parents who can find the courage to place their child's identity needs above their own discomfort and fears."[23] White *Tick Tock* contributors who have raised children of color remind us that in a racist society, their children have complex identity issues, in addition to the issues of being raised by older parents. With everything they face, the adoptive parents in this book emphasize the dynamic and life-affirming nature of their experience.

Part IV focuses on how advanced age can impact individuals and their children. Whatever the route to becoming a parent—birth, adoption, or through a partnership—being an older parent has its unique challenges. The contributors to this book often found themselves having a hard time just keeping up with their younger counterparts. They found themselves with different social references than other mothers with young children and often felt alone and isolated. Several writers lived through the era of the Vietnam War and through a time influenced by Simone de Beauvoir; the women's liberation and gay liberation movements; the Black Panthers; and the assassinations of the Kennedys, Dr. King, and Malcolm X—milestones and paradigms they may not share with younger parents. Several in this book talk about being mistaken for their children's grandparents. Some felt their children were at times embarrassed by their parents' age and appearance. At times, as older parents, they experienced a larger-than-normal generation gap between themselves and their own children.

While the differences in age between these parents and their children have strong emotional repercussions, a confrontation with their own mortality was among the most troublesome for these authors. Becoming a parent after forty is difficult but not impossible to imagine. However, thinking about a child being forty as they turn eighty or even ninety-five feels more unsettling. In spite of the fact that Americans are generally living longer, when thinking about how much of their children's lives they might not get to experience, older parents are once again confronting the odds.

Living longer, it becomes more likely that we face difficult circumstances: a child's death, a partner's illness or death, or an elderly or sick parent. The older parents who contributed to this book have experienced these challenges. The stories in Part IV highlight the resilience and confidence that age can bring to parents who face demanding situations. These stories demonstrate that those who become parents when they are over forty have many gifts to offer, especially the awareness of their own strengths and weaknesses and the insights that come from decades of living. The positive stories in *Tick Tock* as a whole underscore the inequities that exist in being able to successfully deliver healthy babies and raise healthy children when you are over the age of forty. These individuals could afford to try different methods of ART. They could find the best medical providers when they were pregnant; they had the means to pay for adoption services and international travel when necessary. These older parents had the opportunities, privilege, health, emotional strength, financial means, and family stability to make it work.

We've all heard that it takes a village to raise a child. This book demonstrates that in fact, as *Tick Tock* contributor Catherine Arnst says, "It takes a world." Older parents can have difficulty finding a community, a place where they feel they belong. Going against society's norms makes it more important for older parents to acknowledge their interdependence and to find or create their own communities of support. Part V echoes many of the themes that run throughout the book, but its main focus is on how older parents have formed support groups and created their own communities of care to sustain themselves and their children throughout their unique journeys. Some refer to the estrangement they felt from their own families' ideas about motherhood. Most did not have the benefits of the more traditional extended family, but they found support from their partners, friends, and, when necessary, they created their own groups in person and online.

The feminist and social justice movements of past decades laid the groundwork for confronting traditional social norms of the family. The increasing number of older parents challenges the notion of who can become a parent and when, and it exposes inequities around age, race, class, and gender. As Elizabeth Gregory suggests, "This choice to have children later is a huge shift for our culture . . . [and] will affect every aspect of your life and the lives of those who you love. . . . These changes already in place carry us towards a cascading set of changes on the horizon." By their very actions, contributors to *Tick Tock* call for a new narrative and for radical change, for attitudes and policies that can foster caring environments for all children, regardless of the parent's age or circumstances.

For those who are in the process of becoming parents over forty, we hope that *Tick Tock* will help make the process feel less ominous, if not easier. For those who have already become older parents, we hope this book will be seen as an appreciation of your life experiences. We hope this book supports people trying to get pregnant or going through fertility treatments, assists those over forty who wish to adopt, and affirms parenthood at any age.

PART 1
WHY DID IT TAKE SO LONG?

Life as an independent woman, in the States or in Lebanon or wherever, seemed not just doable, but appealing.

We Can Wait, But Are We Paying Too High a Price?

SALMA ABDELNOUR GILMAN

The late afternoon sun is glinting off a high-rise at the western edge of Central Park. We're on the floor, seven or eight of us, in a friend's Upper West Side apartment, drinking cold beer in cans, the stereo pumping '90s hip-hop, university bookstore paperbacks piled on the shelves. Life is new. We're twenty-two, twenty-three. A few of us know each other from college, others went to high school together in New York. One of the women I don't know turns to me.

"What are you doing in the city?" she asks me.

"Interning at a magazine. You?"

"I'm training to be a midwife."

A midwife. I silently, blankly, try to connect the word to something familiar. Eventually, I ask.

Babies. Midwives deliver babies.

I smile. I don't know what to say now. Or maybe I'm just numb from the beer. The Manhattan traffic hums out the window.

Nearly twenty years later, my cell phone pings with a headline: BRIGITTE NIELSEN IS HAVING A BABY AT 55! I'm on the subway to a quiet neighborhood in Brooklyn I never thought I'd move to. I click on the celebrity newsflash as the train rumbles over the Manhattan Bridge. All I remember about Nielsen is that she's the tall blond actor in a *Rocky* sequel I didn't see, but the headline has me with "baby at 55."

This sounds like good news to me. The story comes with the usual boilerplate paragraph about the risks of late pregnancy, the same language that shows up in every single article I've read about celebrities having babies after thirty-five. I skip over the paragraph. Enough with the fearmongering. Let's celebrate. Because if a woman can have a kid at fifty-five, that means we finally have more options than we've ever imagined—living the way we want, staying free for more than three decades of our adult lives, and then deciding if and when we want to have a family. We can actually do this. The dream is finally coming into focus. This is the world we deserve, I think to myself, clicking through the rest of the article as the train pulls up at my stop. A world where women can choose when to have a child. Where women who get pregnant can make their own decision about whether to have the baby, and women who aren't pregnant or even thinking about it yet can put off any parenthood moves until the time feels right.

What I don't realize that day, or don't let myself see, is that the celebrity-baby-at-fifty-five headline hides a more disturbing reality, one I'm all too aware of now.

In her novel *Motherhood*, Sheila Heti muses:

> The thing to do when you're feeling ambivalent is to wait. But for how long? When I was in my late thirties I thought that time was running short on making certain decisions. How can we know how it will go for us, us ambivalent women of thirty-seven? On the one hand, the joy of children. On the other hand, the misery of them. On the one hand, the freedom of not having children. On the other hand, the loss of never having had them—but what is there to lose?

If the woman wearing my faded tank top and jeans that afternoon on the Upper West Side could see me now, she would blink twice.

She would say I've surrendered to a lifestyle that traps women, a lifestyle we trick ourselves into thinking we want. At the time, I pitied my fellow college grad who wanted to build a life around helping women give birth. *Why doesn't she want to break free from all that?*

THE INTERNSHIP I DID that summer after college led to the career I'd set my sights on, to a journey that, for all its stomach-churning stress, steered me into the food and travel editor jobs I'd dreamed about. I hopped an international flight every month, went to all the new restaurants in town, rode the dating roller-coaster, listened to music and read novels for hours late at night, and mostly did whatever I felt like, or what I could afford.

Romance and adventure were on my shortlist. Babies, no.

Also, how could a person's body even do that—have a baby—I wondered? The question nagged at me during my twenties and lasted through the end of my thirties. I couldn't imagine the trauma women put themselves through. I had a hunch my body wasn't built to handle that and probably wouldn't survive it.

Even women I knew who were in no hurry to have a family seemed puzzled by my certainty that I didn't want kids. But fortunately, my parents didn't seem alarmed that I would deny them grandkids, probably because my younger brother had nothing against becoming a dad one day.

Not everyone shared my parents' laissez-faire policy. Our family's Lebanese relatives and friends, many of them based in Beirut and others in Europe and around the US, include plenty of free-thinking intellectuals and live-and-let-live types, but the what-do-you-mean-you're-not-getting-married contingent is strong. The closer I got to my mid-thirties, the more those inquiring minds wanted to know what I was up to in the romance department, and to help, to goad, to push me along.

One day, at thirty-six, a family friend who lived in New York called me up. She had an idea.

"I know a wonderful Lebanese furniture executive you should meet."

"No, thanks. No furniture executives, please." Whatever that even meant.

My cousin, who lived in London, called soon after. He had a colleague I should definitely go out with, a successful, well-traveled investment banker a few years older than me.

"Listen, he's not what he sounds like. Just have a drink with him the next time he's in New York."

I finally broke down and agreed to meet the furniture exec, the banker, and some of the other guys my worried minders kept sending my way. Those men generally seemed like intelligent, considerate people. But when trying to picture a future with them—even a second date—my mind would go blank.

What I could picture was a life that looked like the one a few older Lebanese women I knew were leading. They'd lived in Beirut their whole lives and stayed unmarried, instead pouring energy into their careers in academia or the arts. They traveled, hosted lively dinner parties, carved out their own space in the world. They fended off cultural pressure to go the marriage-family route and learned how to steel themselves in social situations where they'd get interrogated, judged, or just glanced at with pity. Some had wanted to get married someday but given up for one reason or another, while others, like me, had just never envisioned that life for themselves. One of those unmarried older women I'd always admired was the aunt I was named after, a director at a progressive school for girls in Beirut who made it her job to give her loving, unconditional support to everyone she knew. No judgments, no agendas, no advice to women to conform to traditional Lebanese ideas of what girls should do or think or feel or wear, or to conform to expectations of what they should grow up to be: good wives, capable moms, skilled hostesses.

I knew that if I never got married and never had kids, I'd have a lot of explaining to do on my trips to Beirut, though not to everyone. My aunt had died when I was in my twenties, but I felt hopeful. Lebanon is a cosmopolitan country with a highly literate population, and the young generation is making art and media that rips off the straitjacket and presents a reality that's more inclusive, more diverse, more feminist, more free—a world that visionary members of the older generation, including my older female role models, have been fighting for all their lives, whether silently or vocally. Yes, old-world norms are still going strong in much of Lebanon, but things are changing.

Life as an independent woman, in the States or in Lebanon or wherever, seemed not just doable, but appealing. Sure, I could imagine meeting the right guy one day and falling in love. The idea of an intense, lifelong romance appealed to me, too, just as long as we could skip the kid part and hop on a plane or stay up all night together, anytime we wanted.

IT WASN'T UNTIL the tip end of my thirties, standing on the verge of my fortieth birthday, that everything changed. That change didn't look or sound like a clock. As far as I could tell, I didn't have any clock, the kind that preoccupied most single women friends around my age and some of my male friends too. That change didn't sound like a voice saying, "Have kids now, before it's too late." The change looked like a funny, opinionated, heart-poundingly cute guy I'd started dating.

Fast-forward through months of on-again, off-again dating and heartache, through our gradually more intense relationship, and to the decision to move in together. With him, everything felt like an adventure. Even marriage and—well, whatever else—wouldn't feel confining with this guy; I had a hunch about this. He was too offbeat, too suspicious of artificial BS—or maybe it was just that I knew I was in love, and this time, it felt real. A voice popped into my head one morning as I was waking up and said, "Have a kid with this guy." The voice sounded like a stage whisper at first. When I pretended not to hear, it got louder. "NOW."

The sudden certainty caught me off guard. I kept it to myself. One night after he went out for pizza with a group of friends who have children, he came home and told me they'd talked about the schools in our neighborhood, and how it was a pretty good part of town for raising kids.

Within a couple of months of his pizza night, I was pregnant.

Our son was born halfway into my forty-second year, soon after we'd gone to city hall for our marriage certificate. Our daughter arrived a year and a half later. Somehow, we'd managed to conceive both babies without IVF or any other intervention.

It only took a month or two to get pregnant both times. The only explanation I have for this is what my mother told me when I went to college: "Be careful. We're very fertile in this family." Also, a friend gave me a copy of Toni Weschler's *Taking Charge of Your Fertility*. I'm convinced its specific tips I never got anywhere else on how to read my body's cycle helped me conceive as quickly as I did.

Things went more or less smoothly in my pregnancy until a few days before my daughter's birth, when I went for a routine check-up at my obstetrician's office. She looked at my blood pressure, then took my reading three more times. Up until now, I'd had no issues, but on this day, my blood pressure was sky-high. She immediately sent me to the hospital for monitoring. When my first preeclampsia test came back negative, the doctors on duty called for another test to make sure. I went into labor before I could take the second test.

Luckily, my doctor was on top of the situation from the moment she saw my blood pressure spike. But too many women's symptoms don't get noticed in time. Preeclampsia can kick in before or after birth, and the sudden rise in blood pressure can cause organ failure and death if it's not treated quickly enough. The complication usually starts after the twentieth week of pregnancy, and the risk rises with maternal age.

Our friend and upstairs neighbor, Vee, also suffered from preeclampsia when she gave birth this spring to a beautiful baby girl. Vee is an African American woman in her late thirties who works in the music industry and stays fit, but she almost didn't survive the birth. Her blood pressure shot up a few days after she gave birth, and she had to rush back to the hospital, leaving the baby alone with the dad. Her midwife had noticed that her feet looked swollen, even when Vee didn't realize anything was wrong. Her partner texted us late one night, terrified, to tell us Vee had gone into the ICU. One harrowing week later, she finally came home. If no one had recognized Vee's swollen feet as a warning sign, her baby would have likely never seen her mom again.

TOO OFTEN, whether new moms survive their pregnancy and childbirth is a matter of luck. Too many women die in childbirth, not because of untreatable medical emergencies, but because of inattentive staff, miscommunication among doctors, and issues related to structural racism and socioeconomic prejudice in hospitals. So does it take a certain amount of courage to add another risk factor like age, even if it's a relatively small risk, in a maternal health system that's so badly in need of repair? I hate that I think this way now.

WOMEN CAN, should, and do have more options now for becoming mothers later in life, but too often we don't get the information, the medical care, or the support we need to make that promise real.

The more I learned about the seemingly arbitrary, luck-of-the-draw obstacles that stand in our way, the more I wanted to stand on a street corner and yell. Instead, I started a website. A website is a form of yelling—quiet yelling. I called mine Crunch Time Parents, after women like me who were having kids or thinking about it at crunch time—or what the medical profession charmingly still calls "advanced maternal age." I wanted to advocate for parenthood after thirty-five and to back it up with data, to show that babies in our late thirties or forties are a viable and even desirable option—but that making the option a reality means taking a close look at the impact of hospital protocols, societal inequities, and specific health factors on women's outcomes. It was time to fight the stigma and the fear around "advanced maternal age," to address gaps in the maternal health system and make sure women are better-informed about our choices.

Before the site went live, I gathered up all the information I could find about the number of women having kids after thirty-five these days and what the outcomes look like. In general, the data suggested that women who wait face a rosier outlook than we've been told when it comes to getting pregnant.

As the psychologist Jean Twenge writes in *The Atlantic,* much of the hype about how hard it is to get pregnant after thirty-five is based on French studies dating back to the seventeenth century. More recent studies she cites show that women aged thirty-five to forty who have sex twice a week during the most fertile days of their cycle face about an 80 percent chance of getting pregnant, odds only a few percentage points lower than what women in their twenties and early thirties can expect. Those odds sound pretty strong to me, or at least better than what we've been led to believe.

We're also lucky to live in an era when we have so many choices if we want to try options beyond natural conception. Advanced reproductive and fertility treatments, from intrauterine insemination (IUI) to in vitro fertilization (IVF) to egg-freezing and beyond, are constantly improving, and new treatments, tests, and options are coming out seemingly by the week.

For my website, I put out the word that I was looking for women who had given birth after thirty-five or were trying to, and who were willing to talk to me about their experiences. The general theme I picked up on is how fortunate we all felt to be moms. Some had gone through several miscarriages first, others had multiple rounds of fertility treatments before conceiving, and others, like me, had gotten pregnant soon after they started trying—and, in some cases, totally by accident in their early forties. A bunch of women admitted that when they were younger, they would've resented the shackles of parenthood and missed out on the joy. I nodded.

While I know plenty of women in their late thirties and forties who got pregnant fairly quickly and had healthy babies, I am now more aware of women who never could, even after spending tens of thousands of dollars on fertility treatments. I talked to several women who felt crushed by it all as they neared forty-three and beyond. None of their efforts to get pregnant naturally or otherwise had panned out, and they had to stop fertility treatments for financial or health reasons. Many didn't have the money to pay for any assisted reproductive treatments in the first place. The heartbreak of trying and failing to get pregnant, of running out of time, shouldn't have come as a surprise, I suppose. But it was sobering to find out how much women have to spend to even have a chance at giving birth if natural conception doesn't work out. Is it the same old story—that only the rich can win better odds than what nature doles out?

EVERYTHING IN ME still wants to tell my young women friends that they can wait if they want to. They can live full lives and honor any hesitation they might feel about becoming parents too soon. But recent surveys show that more than half of college students—both women and men—have no idea when fertility starts to decline and hold unrealistic ideas about fertility treatments. As young people reach puberty, it might be time to consider giving them an agenda-free overview of fertility as it changes through the years and teach them about the factors involved in having babies at various ages. Broaching the fertility subject in schools would be incredibly controversial—even the most basic sex-ed curriculum is still controversial in the US—and it would be complicated, since the information would have to get updated frequently and delivered without the "have babies young or forget about it!" hype that Sylvia Ann Hewlett notoriously perpetuated in her book *Creating A Life: Professional Women and the Quest for Children*. But should we start a broader conversation about how to educate our youth about fertility—and about the issues that can impact maternal health and childbirth in our society—starting as early as it makes sense to do so? At puberty, or in college, or at our annual gynecologist visit?

Now I know what I would've missed by not having kids. I don't want anyone who might like to have a child someday to bump up against the reality that they've run out of time. While I don't have any answers yet about how women can live with the freedom and equality we deserve and stay healthy and solvent if we decide to delay parenthood, I'm optimistic that we'll discover solutions. No doubt that will mean electing well-informed and committed candidates to office, people who are up to speed on maternal health and devoted to fixing the inequities.

Women may never be able to have kids as late in life as men can, and most of us may not even want to, for our own sake or for our kids' sakes. But before long, with any luck, we really will be able to tell women they can wait until their forties or longer without gambling on their life plans or their lives. And it won't just be about pregnant celebrities making headlines in their fifties.

Through a quirk of fate or through a twisted sense of divine humor, I turned out to be the lesbian vegetarian daughter of Southern Baptist deer hunters.

Out of the Closet and Out of Time
LAURA DAVIS

Sometimes, when I'm drifting in that murky twilight space between consciousness and sleep, a scene plays out before my eyes. It's sepia-toned and eight-millimeter-grainy, the way my dreams often are, but it's also as emotionally crisp and sharp to me as the day it happened. We are outside by a flower bed at a nursing home on a summer day: my mother, my grandmother in a wheelchair, my youngest child, me. Arranged in a half circle in the warm sun like a fragile crescent gently arcing between past and future, ordered by age, we pose together: my mother's strong hand on her mother's frail arm, my sweet daughter leaning her head on my shoulder. It's so vivid, it's as if someone took our portrait, a picture of the four of us alongside a graceful, laughing shadow only I can see. Sometimes I wish I had that photo; sometimes I don't.

My grandmother had my mother, her first child, when she was just shy of twenty years old; she would go on to have four more. Twenty-two years later, my mother had me and then soon my brother. We are close-knit, we are southern, we are small-town, and through the generations, our family has often balanced precariously on that line between the lower-middle class and all that lies beneath it. Unsurprisingly, we have a lot of blue collars, but also more than a few scholars. All of us have been well-trained from childhood in the idea that family takes care of one another from birth to old age to death. That's why, in the weeks after my grandmother hurt herself, my mother stayed at her side constantly, and why I was there to help my mother.

There was nothing new about this; this same scene had played out many times before (sometimes even at the very same facility)—when I watched my grandparents take care of my great-grandparents, and then my parents taking care of theirs— so I don't know why this day jolted me so painfully, except that I was especially exhausted that afternoon, and my grandmother was emotional and frustrated at her lack of progress, and my mother looked thin, which she always does at times of stress. I knew she'd been so busy that she probably hadn't been eating as much as she should, and as I was standing there tiredly by those flowers, I kept thinking, *We just need one more set of hands.* And that's when the math rolled out before my eyes as the breath left my body in a painful *whoosh.*

I ended up as a far older mom than I ever wanted to be because, either through a quirk of fate or through a twisted sense of divine humor, I turned out to be the lesbian vegetarian daughter of Southern Baptist deer hunters. I know, right? Don't worry, I think it's funny too. Every now and again I think even my parents do, although I'm not sure they would admit it.

In my experience, most straight people who talk to me have at least a vague understanding that being a queer person impacts my life as a parent in the present day. However, I find that very few realize how the past upheaval of my coming-out process (particularly in the US South, particularly in a fundamentalist church, particularly in the era in which I did so) mightily constrained when and how I would be able to have my children in the first place. Thus, straight people rarely stop to think about the tangible ways that a difficult coming-out experience can easily derail a queer person a decade or more from the business of finding a partner and having children. In my case, those lost years meant all the difference between what, according to my doctor, would have been a fairly easy conception when I was younger, and what actually happened: years lost on the expensive, excruciating roller-coaster of infertility, miscarriage, and the multiple rounds of IVF that finally led to the birth of my first daughter when I was thirty-eight and the second when I was forty-one.

Recently, a young mother walked out to my car beside me after we dropped our children off at preschool, and she said, rather enviously, "It must be so nice that you chose to be an older mom; you're so settled in your career. You know exactly who you are." In a lot of ways, she wasn't wrong. Those things are true, and they are nice. In fact, I'm beyond grateful for those things every day. Where she missed the mark is her assumption that being an older mom is a choice I made: it emphatically wasn't. The question posed by this book, "How old is too old to become a parent?" is a good one, even though I don't have a good answer to it. However, I think an equally important question is whether an older parent became one by choice or because of some barrier that made the clock run out a little differently than they really wanted. And if older parenthood isn't always a choice, that means a lot of us are still working through our grief about it, even in the midst of all the joys it can bring.

That grief was exactly what I felt with my mother and grand-mother at the nursing home that afternoon, a grief that I didn't know until then could literally physically hurt. What suddenly clicked for me in that instant was that if I was forty-three that day, my mother sixty-five, and my grandmother eighty-five, according to the traditional age most women in my family and culture have their kids, my almost, could-have-been, would-have-been, should-have-been daughter—that laughing, graceful shadow who suddenly leaned in there beside me, as real and as close as if I could touch her—probably would have been twenty-one or twenty-two that day, plenty old enough to be that beautiful, much-needed set of hands. My actual daughter had just turned one. If I had followed suit and had a daughter who was twenty-one, she likewise would have been just old enough to have her first, wouldn't she?

The thought of that made me turn away quickly, so that no one would see that much to my surprise, I was crying. All I could think in that moment was, *Oh my God. We are missing a whole person who could have been here. I have cost my family a whole person.*

If you had kept the film rolling on the nursing home scene that day, in a few moments, you'd have seen my wife, who is in her fifties, pulling up in our minivan, pushing the bifocals that always annoy her up onto her head, and lifting out our oldest child, who soon stopped my weepy reflections about imaginary grown daughters because she was talking ninety miles an hour about whether a certain dinosaur belonged in the Jurassic or the Triassic. (Don't ask me. I'm an English teacher and have no clue. I just nod wisely a lot so she thinks I do).

So that's us. We're old(ish) lesbians with two kids we adore but who never, ever sleep. The other day, we spent about eight hours debating whether we should get long-term care insurance now, before my wife turns fifty-six and the price goes up, or whether we can wait until our youngest is out of daycare because, as teachers, we sure as heck cannot afford both of those things at once. These are our scintillating conversations these days.

It was my wife, by the way, who, upon reading the previous paragraph over my shoulder just now, made me add the "ish" to the word "old." I don't really argue with her much about anything since she's pretty critical to the parenting enterprise around here, not least since she recently reached what I have long considered the holy grail of older parenthood: at IHOP, she can order our children chocolate smiley-face pancakes off the kids' menu *while simultaneously qualifying those pancakes for the senior discount.* I'll pause to let you take that in and be suitably impressed with how well I married.

As you're hopefully able to tell, we have a good time around here. We laugh a lot (because what else are we going to do?), and like most parents of any age, we feel that our kids are the center of our universe, and there's nothing in this universe or any beyond it that would make us trade them for anything. And yet it's exactly this overwhelming, otherworldly love for my daughters that makes me most mourn how many fewer years I am likely to have with them than my mother and her mother had with each other. I know I would have been just as sad about losing those years if my wife and I had intentionally chosen to be older moms, but I realize more and more that there is an extra element of anger and grief for me, tied to the fact that I *didn't* choose this—would *never* have chosen this—but that my culture's response to my queerness set so many extra hurdles in my path that the age I was able to have children was delayed beyond anything I knew how to control.

To be honest, I resent those lost years. I hate them. It makes me so angry, that very real amount of time and energy it took to assert my identity over and over to a family and a community who wanted me to be someone else; to wade through countless conversations, trying to reassure and explain things to my loved ones; to find a way forward with friends. What was most emotionally exhausting was the time and energy it took to repair my relationship with my parents, which had imploded on big gay impact. Not to mention how much more time it took me, as a lesbian in the late '90s/early 2000s, to find a suitable partner to parent with at all, since there were significant (and sometimes even dangerous) barriers to asking someone for a date in those days, in a small town in the South before widespread use of the internet. My straight friends simply did not face (or even think about) these types of obstacles as they unconsciously and breezily utilized the privilege of meeting plenty of eligible partners through church, family, friends, and social networks. Meanwhile, the one other maybe-lesbian in my tiny town and I just kept sitting on the sidelines, looking at each other doubtfully.

As a mother in my forties, this is the thing I have had to struggle with most—my grief over how this all took so much *time*. These aren't abstract concepts. For me, these things are easily measured in real hours I spent, real days I lost, real moments that interfered with me doing what my friends were doing: dating, self-exploration, hobbies, marriage, pregnancy, parenthood. Those were really long years, and I have had to mourn most for what they stole, not just from me, but from my children: more years together. My straight friends have grandchildren now. I look at them and envy how they have had twenty or more years with their children—to watch over them, to help them, to nourish and cherish them. And now they glow in photos with new grandbabies to snuggle. What I wouldn't give for those almost-twenty extra years with my daughters.

For that matter, what I wouldn't give for them to have that much more time with my mother and her mother. Just this morning, in fact, I watched our three-year-old giggling on FaceTime with my mom and my grandmother, and I found myself, as I often do, begging the universe for more time, whispering my mantras: *Please let my grandmother live long enough for my youngest kiddo to turn four, so that she might have a chance at remembering this woman who delights her so. Please let my parents live as long as my grandparents, so that they'll be there for the graduations, the weddings, the family beach trips.* I worry about these things all the time, and I mourn how my wife and I might never live long enough to see our own grandchildren, much less our *great-*grandchildren.

I think this anxiety hits me more as someone from a blue-collar culture in the South, where it is the unquestioned norm to have your children young. My more urban friends don't think I'm so old to be a mother, and so I tell myself I'm not. But to my hometown friends and family (and even to myself), I am as much an oddity as a forty-four-year-old with a toddler and a kinder-gartener as I am for being queer, maybe even more so. I love the children I have and the ages they are; I love my wife; I love so many things about being a queer woman. I am a better person and a far stronger, wiser, more grateful, and more empathetic mother because of those lost years, and I certainly have a well-earned sense of humor because of them too. I am proud to have become the person and mother I have grown into, encompassing forty-plus years of complex identities: queer, southern, feminist, blue-collar academic, chief pancake eater. And yet, daily, even if no one else ever sees or knows, I'm also engaged in a simultaneous lament of sorrow and bittersweet regret over precious time lost. Those shadows are always there—that imaginary grown daughter I pictured so vividly that day, helping me and my mom and my grandmother. The other (very real) child I met only through ultra-sounds one long first trimester, only to watch him falter, fade, and die at the beginning of the second because my eggs were too old to have divided correctly enough to give him a chance at this beautiful, messy life. This, too, is parenting over forty, or at least it is for me.

Currently, I work in a department of interdisciplinary scholars, where several colleagues study reproductive justice, and down the hall a bit farther are a few who study LGBTQ issues. I find myself amused as I sit in my office literally in between them, wondering if they realize that I embody an intersection of their two fields. It strikes me as ironic that reproductive justice work and work by queer scholars is usually separated like this, when, in my experience, my reproductive rights were always entangled with my lack of LGBTQ rights. I wish there was more written about how a lack of safety, marriage rights, or even mere acceptance as a queer person can lead directly to a loss of reproductive freedom. I wish I'd had more queer foremothers to teach me how to come to terms with my identity, come out to my community, find a partner, figure out the emotional and legal challenges of finding a sperm donor, and leap the medical and financial hurdles of getting pregnant without simultaneously running out of reproductive time the way I did. But of course, those foremothers didn't have those experiences to share with me because so many of the queer parents a generation or two before me were fighting even harder problems, often losing their children completely if they were able to come out at all.

Thus, I tell myself that things could be worse, and, without question, I know that is the truth. I have the precious children I ached for all those years, and no one is trying to take them. I'm old enough to know that nothing is guaranteed to anyone of any age, and that makes me, as a mom, determined to wallow with joy at every part of this experience. I will eat all the pancakes, I will learn all the dinosaurs, and I will try to pretend we are too young(ish) to need long-term care. I will reflect tiredly with my wife over coffee that if our children continue to stay up in twenty-four-hour shifts, hey, we will have had just about as much awake time with them as if we'd had them ten years before we did, and we will laugh and laugh the way only truly delirious parents of young children can. But then, two seconds later, I will again let myself mourn, and I will find myself thinking, still, about how things might have been different if I had lived in a culture that hadn't convinced me, my parents, and my friends that being gay was so terrible.

What if they (and I) had only needed a day, or a week, or a month to work through my being queer? What if *coming out* never again meant *running out* of so much else—out of time, out of eggs, out of years? What if?

*I felt at times as though
an army of little men in boots
with sharp cleats were running
laps nonstop on my uterus
and ovaries.*

OTM (Old, Tired Mommy): Not What I Planned
LINDA WRIGHT MOORE

U p until twenty-six, my life followed the outlines of what I wanted and expected for myself—and what was expected of me.

College: check.

Early career success: check.

Marriage: check.

Next up, of course, would be a baby or two. I assumed this would just happen, easily and soon enough, because, well, that's just how life seemed to be when I was young: smooth, mostly on track, with goals and accomplishments regularly attained, even if—on occasion—there were speed bumps that forced me to revise how I navigated toward my objectives.

Take my first marriage, the One Big Mistake of my life. It was over by the time I was thirty. By then, I had four local TV news gigs in three cities under my belt, and I was making my first major career transition. I became a journalism professor and newspaper columnist in Philadelphia and continued doing some broadcasting and production work. Thirty-eight years later, I'm still here.

Along the way, I met my true love, and when I married again, the biological gong was clanging. It was time for babies, but the babies didn't come. With a basal thermometer in hand, I tracked my temperature in tiny, tenth-of-a-degree increments, watching for the small spike that meant ovulation was imminent. Though my devoted new husband, Acel, was cooperative, months went by, but still no pregnancy.

Life went on. We bought a house. I envisioned swings in the backyard and contemplated which room would be best for the baby. But still no pregnancy.

By this time, I was thirty-eight, considered nearly ancient in terms of motherhood in the late 1980s. The infertility industry was still relatively new, exotic, and for someone my age, often unsuccessful. The initial consultation, the infertility "workup," took place in an office located almost in the country. The drive there led past a beautiful tract, a working farm with stables and worn, split rail fences. *It will work*, I'd tell myself during my frequent visits to the clinic. *It must work . . . but what if it doesn't?* Then a deep breath and a scan of the landscape. *It is so lovely and peaceful here.*

When I first met the infertility specialist, Dr. Berringer, I liked him immediately. He was unassuming, young, and slightly bald with kind eyes. I sensed that he understood the emotional turmoil roiling beneath my tight smile and intense gaze. He slowly explained the in vitro fertilization process. There would be hormone injections I'd have to give myself at inconvenient times, locked in my office between classes at Temple University. The preparation would be followed by egg harvesting and fertilization, then implantation a few days later. The prospect filled me with dread and anticipation. I hated needles, but I knew what we wanted. If my husband, a Type I diabetic since his early twenties, could cope with insulin injections and multiple needle pricks to measure his sugar daily, then certainly I could step up to this process. I had my eyes on the prize: a baby. So I shook Dr. Berringer's hand, clutched the prescriptions he'd written, and hurried off to the pharmacy. Round one on the IVF merry-go-round was about to begin.

Several weeks and multiple injections later, I returned to the clinic for the egg harvesting process, not knowing what was in store. For starters, gentle Dr. Berringer was nowhere to be seen. Instead, his partner, Dr. Applegate, would do the egg extraction procedure. She was brusque, square-jawed, and unsmiling, and she skipped the pleasantries. No small talk or soothing encouragement from her, just silence. As I climbed up on the exam table, I glimpsed the instruments on the side stand: gleaming, sharp, and seemingly very long. I was tense, cold, and soon in agony.

"Mrs. Moore, I need you to lie still, please," Dr. Applegate said with a hint of disdain, as if admonishing a wriggling toddler.

"Yes, okay," I mumbled feebly as tears ran down the sides of my face into my ears. "I am trying." I clenched my jaw, tried to relax, and finally it was over. Elsewhere, sperm was "collected" from my husband, poor baby, doing his business in a little room into a sterile container. Next, eggs and sperm were united to party in a lab we never saw, and, like magic, there was the beginning of a baby: embryos. In fact, lots of them. The final step was the return of the fertilized eggs to my uterus—quite a painful process, like the awful egg extraction.

Afterward, cold and exhausted at home, I pulled up the blankets and stared at the ceiling, wondering if anything good could come of such unpleasantness and pain. I had my doubts. After all, I had had a miscarriage during my first marriage. I remembered the spring morning when I woke up and discovered that the bed was wet. I slid my hand under the covers into a pool of . . . I looked at my hand, then screamed. Blood was everywhere. It was not that time of the month. And there was a lot of blood. No pain, just blood. I don't remember getting there, but we hurried to my gynecologist's office.

He was calm and matter of fact: the bleeding had stopped, so probably a miscarriage, he said. There was a test—an ultrasound, perhaps. So long ago, I don't recall. After the test, he said, "Yes . . . a miscarriage, possibly an ectopic pregnancy." So it was good, he said, that it "ended itself early." I was only twenty-seven or so and relieved I wasn't going to bleed to death. I hadn't even been trying to get pregnant, really, so it never occurred to me that this scary episode might foreshadow a problem like infertility. I had never even heard that word back then.

My mother had had two miscarriages, one before me and one before my brother. I could remember her using the black telephone on the little table in the hallway to call a neighbor, Mrs. Rose, for help, when I was all of three years old. I wondered, *What if the problem here is me?* But my determination was still strong, so I girded myself for IVF, round two.

WAITING TO REPEAT another in vitro effort, the shadow of infertility followed me each day. As I drove to work, I'd glare at anyone pushing a stroller or baby carriage. I was not alone here. Three of my closest friends from college were in the same boat on turbulent seas; each of us was married, and by our mid-to-late thirties, all three of us had confronted infertility. Years later, we would speculate that there was something in the Palo Alto water that did us in—a bit of dark humor that became an inside joke between us. However, infertility among a handful of African American women might be more than just a sad coincidence: national statistics from a 2002 study show that married Black women have nearly twice the odds of infertility as married white women.

NONE OF THIS was on my mind as I chased my baby dreams in earnest after my second marriage in 1989. At thirty-eight, I certainly didn't think of myself as old. Like many of my Baby Boomer contemporaries, I'd gone to college first aiming to get educated and become a self-sufficient working woman; marriage and parenthood would follow. Our careers had claimed our peak years of fertility, but we didn't notice. The Pill had enabled our sexual freedom and abortion was legal, so unwanted pregnancy was not an issue; fertility was taken for granted. Our mothers, in contrast, had married and had children well before thirty. They frequently worked as teachers or perhaps nurses—careers they could suspend or tailor to the priorities of child-rearing and homemaking. They were women who lived with what Betty Friedan called "the problem that had no name," a search for meaning to their existence beyond the roles of wives and mothers. And they raised their daughters to chase bigger dreams of having it all: marriage, children, and serious careers.

And now, here I was. With my career and marriage in place, I was searching for the personal fulfillment and completion I believed a baby and family would bring. It had never, ever occurred to me that this might be challenging, rather than automatic.

My husband and I both considered it important. We had even spoken about adoption as a possibility, recognizing how many African American children were growing up in homes or foster care, without the stability and security that loving parents could provide. I knew how common it was for Black children to languish in and "age out" of foster care when adoptive homes couldn't be found for them; a close friend actually managed a city program that supported foster children on the cusp of adulthood, helping them to learn skills as basic as balancing a checkbook, renting an apartment, and applying for a job. As we went for our second IVF try, the adoption option was already on my mind.

That second IVF cycle was inevitably less daunting than the first, but the road to be traveled was still difficult. Dr. Berringer was still very gentle and kind, and his sidekick, Dr. Applegate, was still cold, perfunctory, and distant. This time, the hormone treatments generated a bumper crop of fourteen eggs, all of which were fertilized with my husband's sperm, then incubated for a few days into embryos. When it was time for the implantation, I was a bit surprised to hear the plan was to implant all fourteen fertilized eggs in my uterus. For a moment, I envisioned a cartoon of myself exploding with children as Acel ran to the hills to escape the mob, but then the real point came home to me: this was a long shot, so the strategy was to aim the full arsenal of maybe-babies at my body, in the hope that one might take hold.

After the first IVF attempt, I tried to ignore the hormonal upheaval taking place in my body: the tender breasts, irritability, and close-to-the surface emotions. It was all very much like a giant case of PMS, though I don't recall that the term existed back then. I felt at times as though an army of little men in boots with sharp cleats were running laps nonstop on my uterus and ovaries, but I tried to think positively.

When I went back to the clinic for my pregnancy test, I cheerfully told the nurse who drew my blood that I had given the name Abigail to one of the embryos but stopped after that. The nurse looked a bit stricken, so I said no more. I went back to waiting, which was the hardest thing of all. With mega-doses of hormones coursing through my ovaries and psyche, I was teary and shaky and certain for a second time that I was swollen and emotionally edgy because I was pregnant.

But I wasn't. Not the first time, not this time, and there would be no third time.

My insurance would have paid for one more round of IVF, but I detested the process and understood now that the odds were not in my favor. I felt as if I would disintegrate if I went through all that hope and pain again. Instead of exploding with babies, I envisioned being shattered into a million pieces and vanishing altogether, like flakes of stardust, or perhaps ashes.

I bid farewell to Abigail, my embryonic never-child, and cried. Acel and I talked and agreed to turn thumbs-down on a third round of IVF. We decided to adopt. I was thirty-nine when we started the process, and Acel was ten years my senior. But happy hearts beat young: we were now on a more certain road to parenthood.

Adoption begins with the paperwork phase. We filled out form after form, including a background check for criminal activity and child abuse. We were required to ask friends to write references. I've always wondered what they might have said about us. Maybe something like simple and straightforward, like, "Linda and Acel are a great couple and will be wonderful parents," or how the yearning in my eyes made them sad. I never saw the letters, of course, but we were "approved" to pursue adoption.

Finally, the time came to find her. It was always to be a baby girl, since Acel had a son already in college.

One evening, we sat with our assigned social worker and she showed us a photo album. There may have been a few children on the first few pages—I don't really recall. But when I saw her, I stopped scanning. "Tell me about her," I said, my attention glued to the bright eyes and half smile on the tiny face looking out between the slats of a crib. I felt like she was saying, *Come, please, and take me home with you.* Something drew us to her. There was an instant connection. We knew she was the one—our one.

The social worker explained that now that we had identified a child, it would take up to a year before the placement was made and the adoption could be finalized. Why so long? I'd just taken a new job; I'd be busy settling into my new gig and preparing for the baby's arrival while we waited. I didn't do a lot. I avoided bringing the crib we selected home because I didn't want to "jinx" the adoption process.

It turned out to be a short wait. Instead of a gestational nine months to plan, or the full year the adoption agency had predicted, I had three weeks to prepare. When we arrived at the adoption agency, we were joined by my parents, who'd driven down from their home in Cincinnati to be present for the birth of our new family. I recall being nervous, but with an overlay of joy.

Then I was holding her in my arms for the first time. She was beautiful, cherubic with fat cheeks and loads of curly hair. She was so much more than I could see in the few snapshots—our only connection until now.

My baby girl, Mariah. She was named after my grandmother. I fell in love instantly.

Mariah was a fabulous sleeper; she loved naptime and slept straight through the night without waking up. I like to say what I suspect she was thinking on that first evening home was, *Gee, my new mommy is old! I need to let her get her sleep.*

And so she did.

JUST AS THE "gestation" of my new family was a quick few weeks, my maternity leave was also brief—about two and a half weeks. The stress of being a working mom suddenly became evident to me; the five o'clock exodus of all the mothers in our newsroom was something I had never noticed when I was fancy-free and childless, but then I joined them at the elevator, ready to charge out into rush-hour traffic to pick up our kids on time and avoid the hefty late fees charged by daycare centers.

Despite the pressure of balancing the demands of work and marriage and now a long-sought-after child, this was a deeply satisfying time in my life, made more so because I wasn't so young. Having had many good years of adulthood free of the obligations of parenting, I found being a mom delightful and satisfying—an adventure. Even as Mariah left infancy behind and developed into a busy little person with an array of activities and requirements of childhood, such as soccer practice, piano lessons, and more, I mostly enjoyed the ride.

However, it was lonely at times. Acel was fifty years old when Mariah arrived and set in his ways: his journalistic habit of working late or shooting the breeze on the phone or over a cocktail with colleagues through the evening didn't mesh well with the schedule of a toddler, or of a ten-year-old with homework and hair to be done each night. This reality led me to dub myself a "married single parent," a position familiar to many women (and some men).

Today, my baby girl is twenty-eight years old, and I am sixty-nine and able to reflect on the good side of being a "grown-up" parent who brings maturity and tolerance to the task of child-rearing. While I don't doubt that I would have been a good mom at twenty-eight, at forty I was probably a bit less likely to fumble and stumble than I might have been when I was younger. Being a seasoned mom was a plus, particularly during the wild, boundary-stretching years of adolescence: when you've seen and done it all yourself, your child's developmental hurdles and she-nanigans are not so surprising, though they are still cause for consuming adult beverages and lying awake at night, wide-eyed with worry. As older parents, when there are bumps in the road, we can generally navigate our way to solutions. It isn't always easy, but we've already traveled many miles of life's journey and learned a lot in the process, which helped us guide and nurture Mariah.

Mariah always seemed okay with having "older" parents and being an only child. However, she did, for a time, have an imaginary friend. She often signed greeting cards with her title, the "O & O"—one and only. Today, she sometimes reflects on how we let her get away with stuff, but she also admits she didn't dare try to pull some of the stunts her friends tried because she was too scared. To that, I say, great—well-done, Linda and Acel!

Of course, by today's standards, we could be considered relatively young old parents. With the advent of technology that can successfully bank sperm, freeze eggs and embryos, and enable surrogacy, women now have the choice men have long enjoyed: the capacity to procreate well beyond traditional childbearing and parenting years. A recent example is television newswoman Tamron Hall, who was a student in the broadcast performance course I taught at Temple University. In April of this year, she gave birth to her first child through in vitro fertilization at age forty-eight, using her own previously frozen eggs and her husband's sperm. While I'm not certain that motherhood (or fatherhood) at any age is reasonable, I say more power to the pioneers venturing into this unexplored terrain. If forty is the new thirty, and seventy-five is the new sixty-five, perhaps attending the college graduation of your child (not your grandchild) at seventy is just fine.

Our most difficult time as a family came during the seven and a half years Acel was paraplegic, wheelchair-bound, and chronically ill, requiring extensive rehabilitation, physical therapy, and home care. It tested our marriage and my stamina as I continued to work full-time and also provide support to my elderly parents, who lived nearby. Mariah was in college then, learning to be independent and find herself, while her father and I were occupied by the challenge of his declining health. I am proud of the way we all remained calm and carried on as best we could through that time.

ACEL LIVED TO SEE Mariah graduate from college in 2013 but died two and a half years later. One year after that, my father passed away, then my mother two months later. The losses have been tough for both Mariah and me, but again, we've carried on. As a widow for nearly four years, I am learning—late and at last—how to live alone, how to find happiness flying solo. Being an "older mom" and an adoptive mom has been a wonderful ride—exhilarating, exhausting, and challenging in magical and unexpected ways. It was not the path I planned, but it is what life delivered. Fast forward: my daughter is an adult now and pursuing a deferred but long-held dream of becoming a surgeon. She and her partner are engaged and will marry next year. Her proud mommy happily supports her efforts and plans. Mariah is all grown-up now, but she will always be my baby, which feels exactly right—just like I planned.

PART II

PREGNANCY AND BIRTH AFTER FORTY

Colleagues—both nurses and doctors—would comment on those crazy women who wanted to have a child after forty-five, not knowing that I was one of them.

My Road Trip to Fertility
MARTINE GUAY

I am a fertility nurse practicing in Montreal, Quebec. But first, I am a proud mother of four. I had three children in my twenties and thirties. I had them "spontaneously," as we say in my field of work (which makes it sound like we were reproducing like rabbits). And three years ago, I had a fourth child—not so spontaneously.

When I was first pregnant at twenty-five, did I ever think I would do it again in my fifties? Of course not. My own mother became a *grandmother* in her fifties, and I probably thought I would too. When my sister had her first child at thirty-seven, hers was considered a "geriatric pregnancy," a medical term still in use but less frequently than "advanced maternal age." Like most people, I thought that childbearing years ended around forty-five, with exceptions in one's late forties. But life can be full of surprises.

When my fourth child was born, I was fifty-eight and his father was forty-eight, which makes us an unusual family. More so if you add the fact that his father is of Indian descent and born into a Hindu family from Mauritius, and that I am Caucasian born to a French-speaking Catholic family here in Canada. But nowadays, there are many different family units and configurations, all of them pretty unique.

I often say that my last pregnancy did not last eight and a half months but rather eight and a half years. So let's go back a decade or so, to my late forties.

At that time, I had started a new chapter in my life, having just moved in with Anshu, my second common-law spouse. (In a province where only half of the couples marry, common-law relationships are . . . well, very common!) He was thirty-five at the time and had no children, although he loved kids and they adored him. My own children were independent by then, the youngest one being almost eighteen. Then I started to look into ways of starting a family with my partner. To be honest, he thought I was a little crazy, considering my age. He kept telling me that when he decided to be with me, he had known that that meant he would never have children of his own, and he had come to terms with that. Well, I wasn't convinced, and I kept exploring various avenues.

Until then, my reproductive journey had been uneventful. Like many women of my generation, I started taking the Pill when I was seventeen. I stopped when I wanted to get pregnant at twenty-five, which happened after only three months of trying. Two other easy pregnancies followed, each of them three years apart. After using an IUD between pregnancies and not liking it, I went back on the Pill after my third pregnancy at the age of thirty-two. I was lucky enough to never have had to decide whether to abort an unwanted pregnancy. I am definitely pro-choice, and I live in a country where abortion is legal, available, and free, but it is not a decision I would have liked to make.

After spending twenty-three years together, my first spouse and I separated—not by my choice, but these things happen. Therefore, I found myself single again at forty, which I thought was pretty old at the time. I was convinced I would never be in a long-term relationship again and was approaching an age where my doctor was no longer comfortable prescribing the Pill for me. Following her recommendation, I decided to have my fallopian tubes tied and felt quite relieved afterward: I was free to have a healthy sex life without worrying about getting pregnant again.

Two years later, I met the man who would become the love of my life. I was forty-four; he was thirty. We played volleyball together and became friends. After a full season of volleyball and post-game beers, we became much more than friends for a summer, and then for life. I felt it was unfair to him that because he fell in love with a woman my age, he would have to forego parenthood when it was obviously his calling. So I looked into having my tubal ligation reversed.

Because of my age, I could not have that surgery done in Canada, where such a procedure is covered by public healthcare. One fertility doctor answered my email bluntly: "After the age of forty-three, the only option would be egg donation." I remember being truly shocked—I was a nurse then, but I'd never heard of anyone doing egg donation. It sounded like something out of a sci-fi movie or novel, too *Star Trek*-y for me. But I wasn't ready to give up.

I found an American doctor who specialized in tubal ligation reversal and who agreed to do the surgery. At that point, my hormonal results were quite good, and I was still ovulating regularly. In my family, menopause tends to come late; therefore, I was convinced I was still fertile and could get pregnant spontaneously after this procedure. So I planned a trip to North Carolina, pretending to attend a nursing conference with a friend, as my partner had just started a new job and could not take time off to accompany me. I was going to keep it a secret from the rest of my family, but a few days before leaving, I decided to tell my children, on the off chance that something went wrong with the surgery or anesthesia. Each of them reacted differently, according to their respective personalities. Overall, they respected my decision, although they all thought I was crazy for doing it.

On our way to North Carolina, I received a text message from my oldest daughter, the one who had been the least enthusiastic about my project: *I wish you a great "road trip to fertility" and hope all goes well!* That message literally made my day.

We met with the nurse and the doctor the day before surgery. I don't remember his name, but I remember he said, "Who am I to decide whether or not you should try to get pregnant just because you're fifty? You are still ovulating, and your uterus is fine." The trip and the surgery were successful.

For the following two years or so, we followed all the recommendations and tried hard to get pregnant. My period came late a few times and we hoped we were pregnant, but we weren't. Meanwhile, we considered adoption—a process that is strictly regulated in Quebec. International adoption is only legal in a few countries, each having their own regulations and selection standards. Because of my age and the fact that I already had children, we did not qualify in most of these countries, except for one, which unfortunately was not accepting any applications at that time. As for domestic adoption, there are very few in our province; free access to contraception and abortion has had a direct impact on the number of young women who carry a child to term to then give it up for adoption. And then in order for a couple to adopt a healthy infant, they must be added to a waiting list of seven to eight years. As for fostering or fostering-to-adopt, this option was open to us, but my partner did not want to take in a child and get attached to her only to have to let her go. I even considered moving to India, where by virtue of his lineage and parentage, we could have adopted after living there for a few years. But because of my age, we would only be allowed to adopt a child older than three years of age. Adopting a child who had spent her first three years—of utmost importance when it comes to attachment—in an Indian orphanage was not something we were ready to do.

Having had to rule out adoption, we considered embryo adoption or donation (well, actually, I did, as my partner wasn't too keen on this alternative), which was not an option in Canada at the time, but I knew it was done in India. Since I was planning a trip to South India anyway, I contacted a fertility clinic there and explored that possibility. They gave me a list of blood tests and scans I should do ahead of time and medications I should buy; I would then be able to have the procedure done within two weeks while staying in Mumbai. Accordingly, I went to see a fertility doctor in Montreal to get his opinion and to see if I could get those tests done in his clinic. He said they could certainly do it but quickly added, "Wouldn't your husband prefer to have a child genetically linked to him, using his sperm and donor eggs?" I remember being surprised he would suggest that because I thought that at fifty-two, I was too old for IVF. At the time, the publicly funded IVF program had just been launched, and most Quebec fertility clinics had set the age limit for egg recipients to fifty. Not this doctor. I remember him saying this whole age limit for women was sexist, as nobody would bat an eyelash if I was thirty-eight and my husband was fifty-two—I liked that. Technically speaking, I was a "woman of reproductive age" as provided by the act and regulations, since I had not yet hit menopause, and therefore I qualified for three IVF treatments, as did all Quebec women at the time (that program was abolished in 2015 due to budget cuts; its reinstatement in 2020 only allows for one IVF treatment). By then, egg donation did not seem as sci-fi as before; it became a viable option to me because I had done everything I could to get pregnant with my own eggs, and I had even been considering embryo donation. Time had also passed—this was three years after that doctor had first mentioned egg donation, and it takes time to assimilate such a notion. We started to look for an egg donor.

At the time, there were no egg banks in Canada, as the law prohibited paying a woman to do egg donation. In this context, only altruistic donation was legal. Naïvely, I had thought I could ask my daughters, but this, too, was if not legally unacceptable, then morally unacceptable, as mothers might pressure and manipulate their children into donating their gametes. Then I remembered that in the past, two of my younger girlfriends—both nurses—had separately mentioned the possibility of giving me some of their eggs if I ever considered IVF one day. I reached out to them, and they both said they would think about it; in the end, they both declined. It was disappointing, but it wasn't the last time we were to be disappointed.

One day at work, a friend—also a nurse—mentioned that she had been conceived thanks to fertility treatments. Thinking that this part of her history might make her likely to consider donating her eggs, I asked her about it when we were alone in the lunch-room. She didn't say no; she said she would like to think about it. Two months later, after returning from my trip to India, I brought it up again. This time, she said yes.

We then embarked on the long path toward egg donation/IVF. The process involves blood tests, intravaginal ultrasound scans, psychological assessments (for both the donor and recipient couple), consent forms to be signed, hormone injections, and more scans. And then came the egg collection, finally, done under anesthesia. She was a little groggy and disappointed when we heard that only five eggs had been collected—much less than we had hoped for, considering her young age (twenty-seven). I thanked her profusely, she left with her antibiotics and painkillers, and I went home, awaiting the lab call that came the next morning.

Only three eggs were mature enough. In the end, there was only one healthy-looking embryo that made it to day five, the day it was transferred into my uterus. And that was the first time I heard that well-known saying in the fertility world: all it takes is "one egg, one embryo, one baby." Eleven days later, I went back to the clinic for a pregnancy blood test in the morning, and I received the call in the afternoon: we were pregnant.

I know now that IVF treatments don't always lead to a pregnancy, but ours had. It's hard to describe how happy we were. Two weeks after the positive pregnancy test, we went to the clinic to do a viability ultrasound, and there it was: a heartbeat, or rather a flicker. Pure joy.

The next week, I told my mother, my children, and few close friends that I was pregnant. After I explained the whole IVF process through egg donation to my mom, I remember her saying she was happy for us, but I mostly remember her asking me, "But won't you feel like an incubator, nesting a baby that's not genetically linked to you?"

I was a little hurt, but I tried not to show it, realizing that the whole technological aspect of egg donation was way too sci-fi for my eighty-year-old mother. My children said they were happy for me and for us, as did our friends. We even told my parents-in-law in Mauritius via Skype. They were surprised but very happy to hear they were finally going to be grandparents.

The following week, I started to bleed. I went to the clinic for an ultrasound, which confirmed I was having a miscarriage. That day was one of the worst days of my life; I knew that when my partner came home from work, I would have to tell him the sad news and that it would send him from seventh heaven to the depths of despair. I cried myself to sleep that afternoon, and later, we cried together. We had been so happy for those three weeks.

We asked our donor if she would do it again; she thought about it and agreed to do it, but not right away. A few months later, we tried a new protocol and got five embryos. One fresh embryo was transferred; the other four were frozen. I got pregnant again and miscarried again, around seven weeks of gestation, same as the previous time. Before attempting another transfer, my doctor ordered more blood tests to rule out coagulation issues and a hysteroscopy to make sure my uterus was healthy with no scar tissue, no fibroid, etc. That summer, we did two more transfers of two frozen embryos each time; both proved unsuccessful. Our doctor felt that we should look for another donor, since our first donor's eggs and my partner's sperm seemed incompatible.

We didn't feel like looking for another donor at this point. I was fifty-four and my partner was forty. We felt that after two egg donation cycles, four transfers, and two miscarriages, we had given it our best. We considered moving to Mauritius to be close to his parents and maybe applying for adoption there as residents, but that project fell through. We both went back to university as part-time students and concentrated on other projects. We had no regrets, but a great wave of sadness kept washing over our hearts.

The following year, my doctor called me and asked if I had read this new study out of Columbia University regarding good outcomes with pregnant women aged fifty to fifty-five; when they were healthy to start with and did egg donation, their results were just as good as with women under forty-three. We thought about doing it again. We considered buying frozen eggs from Spain, which ended up being too expensive; we found a donor through our clinic but she changed her mind after all the biomedical tests and the psychological assessment were done and paid for; we even tried finding one on the internet (we did, but she was asking $5,000, which was against the law in Canada). These disappointments added to the previous ones, and we felt there had been enough grieving. By the end of 2013, a full five years after we first began our road trip to fertility, we closed that chapter of our life for good. Or so we thought.

In December 2014, out of the blue, a friend and colleague of my partner's asked him why we'd never had children together, seeing as she knew he loved children very much. He told her our story, and right away, she offered to give us some of her eggs. She said, "I've had three kids. I don't need those extra eggs." By then, I was working as a fertility nurse, and I knew that we now had more hurdles to overcome: I was soon to be fifty-seven and she was thirty-seven, so we were both older than the respective recommended ages for recipient and donor by the standards of most clinics. My original doctor still had a more relaxed view about age limits, but his clinic no longer had its full license, and he and his colleagues had to rent another clinic's facilities to do their egg collections and embryo transfers. I asked for a meeting with that other clinic's doctor in order to convince him to allow my doctor to proceed and pleaded my case convincingly (his words, not mine)—I quoted the Columbia study; pulled out my chart, showing I'd done all the required tests (EKG, heart echo, pap test, mammography), and argued that if I had been forty-two and my husband fifty-six, there wouldn't be any problem, right? He had to agree I had done my homework, and, in the end, he gave his approval. I remember literally jumping up and down in the elevator, ecstatically happy.

We were very lucky to have found another generous friend who would agree to go through the whole IVF process and thereby allow us to try to become parents. She responded well to the treatment but found the egg collection procedure more painful than expected, as it was done without general anesthesia in this clinic. Four embryos made it to day six, and two fresh ones were transferred that day. I got pregnant and miscarried again. Before going in for our last transfer, I underwent another hysteroscopy and endometrial scratching; I also had osteopathic and acupuncture treatments, feeling I should leave no stone unturned.

Three days after the embryo transfer, I started experiencing nausea, which I'd never had in any of my (six) pregnancies. My doctor said it was a good sign, and I wanted to believe him. When I did a repeat ultrasound at ten weeks and everything looked fine with one healthy embryo growing normally, my doctor said, "You know you can relax now and start believing in this pregnancy, right?" I did, and we did.

My pregnancy was relatively uneventful, except for a bit of

spotting at nineteen weeks (my vigilant doctor sent me for an ultrasound immediately, which confirmed that everything was fine, and that we were having a boy!), and modified bed rest as of twenty-six weeks of gestation. When we reached the end of the first trimester, we told family and friends about the pregnancy. They were surprised, as most of them had assumed we had given up on the baby project—surprised, but mostly happy for us. My mother, my siblings, and my children were concerned about my health—and so was my partner, for that matter—but I really felt fine right from the beginning.

Rohan was born on April 4, 2016, weighing in at seven pounds, twelve ounces after thirty-eight weeks of gestation. As he cried like most newborn babies do, we cried for joy.

Four years later, we still tell each other how lucky we are to have him in our lives. We thank both of our donors on a regular basis, usually around Mother's Day. They've both seen him a few times. The second donor's children call him their "almost-brother," and they love it when we send pictures of him. Grateful doesn't begin to express how we feel toward them both.

This time around, it was a long road trip to fertility: one surgery, three IVF treatments with two different egg donors, six embryo transfers, and three miscarriages before we reached our final destination. But at the end of that road, we are so happy that we persevered through our journey, that we had the resources and capacity to continue onward and consider ourselves the luckiest people in the world.

Here are my final thoughts about age and pregnancy: there is still a stigma associated with older parenting, and even more with women of advanced maternal age. I see it in my fertility nursing practice; I even hear it occasionally from nursing colleagues. But I heard it more often when I worked in the neonatal intensive care unit (NICU), where colleagues—both nurses and doctors—would comment on those crazy women who wanted to have a child after forty-five, not knowing that I was one of them. IVF treatments are still taboo in some circles, and even more so when it comes to sperm and egg donations. I contributed to that taboo by not sharing my experience with those colleagues, which I recently realized while working on my master's thesis on this very topic. This is why, while I was reluctant to talk about my pregnancy while I was living it (I posted nothing on social media, for example), I now talk openly about my advanced maternal age experience with colleagues, friends, acquaintances, even strangers. I have been invited to do so on the radio, on television, in magazines, and now in this very book, and I am doing it to help break down barriers, taboos, and stigma. My experience as a fertility patient for all these years, and as an egg-donation and advanced-maternal-age parent, has made me a better nurse, and a better fertility nurse in particular. I am more accepting and less judgmental of other people's choices and lives.

You may ask: How old is too old? I would counter: Who am I to judge?

She looked sort of like us, northern European, and her photographs demonstrated a penchant for dressing in costume—pirate lass, fortune-teller, clown.

Old Mom
SARAH DOUGHER

The first time a stranger called me the grandmother of my own child, I was in a midwestern airport, hauling my two-year-old to a connecting flight. I was purchasing a bottle of water; the baby was having a tantrum. I put her on the floor to let her shriek and flop around, as you sometimes have to do, and calmly made my purchase. The clerk gave me a sororal smile, leaned over the counter, peered at my snotty creature, and said, "Grandchildren are a handful, that's for sure. I've got four of my own!"

I smiled and said, "Yep, a real handful!" Then I picked up my daughter, who arched her back like she was possessed and shrieked "NO!" again and again as we walked out. The clerk's misunderstanding of my relationship to my kid is one that will be repeated for the rest of my life, I'm fairly certain. This is one of the consequences of having my first child at forty-five, and my second at forty-nine.

You can be a grandma at thirty-eight. You can be a mom and a teenager. Saying that I have small children makes me seem younger to people. People have children during a wide age range, but our cultural conception of the correct age for a new mother is somewhere between twenty and forty. Someone might think I'm fifty-ish, but when they see me breastfeeding, they dial it back to forty-five. Because I've never been a younger mother, I can't say what is different about being an older one. I can say that I did not seriously consider children until I was in my early thirties. I had the privilege of easy access to birth control, as well as to abortion, had I needed it. Not having a child when I was younger allowed me to focus on the things I wanted to do then: I got a doctoral degree, for instance. I traveled, lived communally, and toured as a musician.

My initial plans for children with my then-girlfriend were disrupted by a breast cancer diagnosis at thirty-five. Getting a form of cancer that doesn't hurt except when excised has a different impact than other, more sudden and exhilarating brushes with death. It exacerbated what felt impossible—that I would never live long enough to parent children successfully in a loving partnership. As I was dependent on this same philandering partner's health insurance for treatment, my approach to mortality was shot through with trade-offs; I could stay with her, keep the insurance, look away when she fucked other people, drink myself to sleep, and pretend I'd had a healing night's rest. Instead of compelling me to live each moment with a clear-eyed zest for life, I was a lackluster cancer battler. My alcohol dependence increased as my friends and family tried to rally me from deep depression. My drunkenness was an inarticulate demand: *Recognize my suffering! See me!* But no one could see my cancer, and my physical debilitation and drinking were read as a moral failing. I had radiation treatment on one cancerous breast and five years of the estrogen suppressant tamoxifen. Eventually, at forty, I was in remission and I quit drinking.

My children are the result of a partnership I never thought I would be so lucky to have, with a man whose commitment to family matched my own. On our third date, when I was forty-one, we determined we'd have children. By the spring of my forty-second year, I was making notes in a book about "Clomid mood swings" and "Follistim"—the drugs that stimulate follicles to produce multiple eggs per cycle. The reality is that even between forty-one and forty-two, your reproductive odds drop sharply, and your egg supply is low. We optimistically started with intrauterine injection, which basically just saves the sperm part of the trip to the fallopian tubes. After this failed, we ratcheted up quickly to IVF, and my notes became more dire: "anxious," "aching," "weepy," "overwhelmed," "thirsty," "dumb," "headache-y," "spaced-out," "crampy," "sleepy," "fragile," "gassy," "tender," "bloated," "insomniac," "crazy." As unpleasant as this all was, it was less horrific than my life as a drunk cancer victim had been. When you do IVF, you think you are going to be the miracle person whose eggs just needed a little prodding. I learned I am no miracle person: after two IVF rounds, we decided to pay someone young for her eggs, a process gently mislabeled as "donation."

Through an agency, we chose a person whose family history did not include breast cancer, alcoholism, or mental illness. She looked sort of like us, northern European, and her photographs demonstrated a penchant for dressing in costume—pirate lass, fortune-teller, clown. The reasons people value extremely good-looking, high-achieving egg donors seem strange to me, but the whole thing was very strange, so we thought we would choose someone who at least liked to have fun. We didn't know why she wanted to get paid for undergoing a physically uncomfortable, time-consuming, and, in the scheme of things, not-that-lucrative process. Platitudes about helping others with the gift of life? Maybe to pay for community college? Or to buy the best fortune-telling costume of all time? This mysterious blond person had a crucial part in making our family possible, but I know her just from blurry snapshots on the egg donation database. She could just as easily be that person with the baby crying the next time I board a plane.

I know that I am more patient and tolerant of both my own foibles and the shortcomings of others than I was when I was young, and this is a very useful trait as both a parent and a person. I care a great deal less now about what others think of me, but I care very deeply about the needs and opinions of my family. I'm more concerned with regular practices related to health and well-being, and I prioritize this. I have very limited time to myself, but that time is exceedingly well-spent.

How others gauge my fitness for parenting is really their concern, based on their own biases. If they choose to look upon the choice as unfair to my children, who will eventually (as we all will) become parentless, they need only look to the experiences of people whose parents are already out of the picture because of fundamental disagreements, addictions, or tragic circumstances. Sometimes, for millions of reasons, parents and adult children don't get along to the point of estrangement, and yet these people often thrive and make excellent parents themselves. How we lose and gain family is never ordinary.

Motherhood has ushered in a sudden, unexpected connection to other, much younger women with kids. I am a college professor who works in public high schools teaching in a dual-credit program, so I am in regular contact with young people. This new, specific closeness I feel to younger moms in my classes is not something I verbalize to them; it is, however, something I try to support structurally. I don't need to understand the details of their lives, but I want to use what small power I have to give them options—I can be in touch by email when they can't come in; I can lend them the computer and encourage them to write about their experiences in the context of our class. I try to use my role as their teacher to help them value the work they are doing as moms, and to let them know I see that work, and I see them too. Maybe this identification is something like what the shop clerk felt when she treated me kindly at the airport. (Sometimes when I tell this story, friends remark that I should have gotten angry about her assumption. "How rude!" they say. Other times, my friends will reassure me that I don't look at all like a grandmother. But what, really, does this look like after all?)

It was only this, I remind them: I was pegged for what I am, an older woman. Hers was a verbalized example of the ways in which we all use visual, socialized cues to size each other up and operate in the flow of received ideas of gender and role. To interrupt that to say, "No, I'm not her grandmother, I'm her mom," would have rejected the kindness the person thought she was offering. Do I have a responsibility to let the clerk know that older women can be excellent mothers? This must be proven only to my children. Do I have to represent and call her out on her assumptions about femininity or reproductive fitness? This would only cast unneeded doubt on the support she was trying to communicate, trite and pro forma as it was. I choose to hold onto the kindness of this woman, not her misreading of the situation. Is it really on her that reproductive science is not cheaper and more widely accessible, or more common? Is it her fault, after unloading *Cosmopolitan* and *Shape* magazines all day, that she might have conventional assumptions about age, reproductive capacity, and vitality? That she might view my slightly androgynous, cardigan-wearing, and graying form as a "grandma?"

I came to understand the airport incident as a consequence of my unique path: I will be misread and my experiences will be assumed, unseen, unknown. Contained within this path is an opportunity to experience deep empathy and connection. In that harried airport moment, when I put my child down on a dirty floor and let her scream and cry, making everyone uncomfortable, it didn't matter what people thought about me or my role in my family. For her part, the clerk's comments suggested to the other people (who were likely uncomfortable or irritated by us) that it is difficult to care for a screaming child, and that a screaming child is not out of the ordinary. She signaled that she knew this was a challenging situation for any person, and that she saw my work. Grandmother or not, I was seen.

I'm sure the press will never blow up this story: "lonely fiftysomething man faces the fact he'll never have kids."

The Terrible Math
ELLINE LIPKIN

A few days after my son was born, finally home from the hospital, I bolted awake in the middle of the night. The world was slipping out from under me. It was a feeling unlike anything I had ever known. Yes, my hormones were running a course they had never run before; yes, my body was trying to sleep while my ears attuned themselves to the sound of an infant's breathing. When tears started falling from my eyes, I realized what had suddenly hit me was the knowledge that one day, my son's life would continue on—without me. If things went as expected, I would die, and he would go on. There would likely be wide swathes of his life I would never know. That this had never occurred to me—not even in relationship to my own parents—was startling. Perhaps I couldn't have known how to imagine what this meant until he was born. I began to do what I called "the terrible math": if I had a "normal" life expectancy, how much of his life I would get to see? It was a calculation I realized would only get harder with the passing years. I wished again my one wish—that I had started trying to have a child earlier. I now wanted every precious bit of time we could share.

My first calculation with "the terrible math" occurred when trying to get pregnant in my early forties, when every month brought a new accounting: "if I get pregnant this cycle, the baby will be born before the end of the year," or, "in time to meet our public school registration cutoff," or, "before the trip we've planned," or . . . or . . . or. I was never oblivious to the grim fertility stats for women over thirty-five. As a writer, I abhorred cliché, yet it felt like I had become one. I had finished my PhD program at thirty-seven, and after a long relationship ended, I'd begun to date in earnest, hyperaware of my own biological clock, especially as those around me began to freely comment on its countdown. At one point, during a routine gynecology visit, the doctor began a lecture so fierce about my dwindling odds for conception, I almost asked if she had a man in the next room who could come in and "service" me, since, hey, I was already undressed from the waist down. Why waste a second more? I babbled about needing a full-time job, the security of tenure, not being settled yet—things that professional women are told to attend to, even as they are simultaneously scolded (as I was) for doing so. I left the appointment with a lab order to have my follicle-stimulating hormone (FSH) tested, and I increased my time perusing dating sites.

During those years, I began to notice a curious phenomenon that made my blood boil. I was largely getting clicks and likes on my online dating profiles from men easily ten to fifteen years older than me. At first, I didn't want to be ageist or make any assumptions that I wouldn't be compatible with someone in another stage of life or even generation, yet what rapidly became clear to me was that many of these men, who hovered around fifty, felt a lightning-bolt need to settle down and "start a family." They weren't so much seeking partners as they were seeking women who were (as I came to call it) the "next available womb." Hence, women who were their age-mates, presumably in peri- or full-on menopause, were useless. The assumptions built into this calculus about a woman's reproductive worth enraged me. It was another way in which a woman's "market value" was tacitly—or not so tacitly—measured and weighed.

But what caused me to pound out blunt, angry emails was the assumption that *they* were exempt from any age restrictions in their baby-making, while I knew my own biological clock (a phrase I came to hate) would expire. I remember asking one would-be suitor if he really thought it was a good idea to be turning fifty and have a child in kindergarten. Another shared his logic that becoming a parent past sixty would coincide well with his retirement, so he would have more time to spend with his child. When I asked if he thought he would live to see his grandchildren, he insisted it was only the next generation that he cared about.

In more recent years, the concept of "advanced paternal age" has slowly taken firmer hold. A white paper on the National Center for Biotechnology Information website states: "There is no clearly accepted definition of advanced paternal age. A frequently used criterion is any man aged forty years or older at the time of conception." The paper goes on to cite various statistics regarding advanced paternal age and its association with "increased risk of new gene mutations."[1] In an April 2009 article in the *New York Times* titled "Your Old Man," author Lisa Belkin writes about how new studies show that children born to older fathers "have, on average, lower scores on tests of intelligence than those born to younger dads." But the lines that made me want to sit up and shout "so there!" were these: "French researchers reported last year that the chance of a couple's conceiving begins to fall when the man is older than 35 and falls sharply if he is older than 40." Later in the article, Belkin quotes Dr. Dolores Malaspina, a professor of psychiatry at New York University Medical Center, who says, "The optimal age for being a mother is the same as the optimal age for being a father."

Ha! I wanted to shout, except that news, counter to the perception that men are okay to keep reproducing because they can keep generating sperm (albeit, poorer copies), has never been heralded by the press the same way the precipitous drop in women's chances has been. What Belkin gets to at the end of her article is how scientific evidence that men, too, have a ticking biological clock could undermine the socially accepted open-ended timeline for male procreation.

If a new understanding of blending one's career trajectory with family hits a man at twenty-seven rather than forty-seven (the magic number, I found, when it seemed to dawn on unmarried men: "hmmm, better get on with this wife and kids thing"), how could this change social expectations as they cross with biological imperatives? Would childcare finally be a priority in the workplace? Or paternity leave? Would different patterns of career-climbing set in if a thirty-five-year-old man knew his chances at fatherhood would decline if he waited to procreate?

I'm sure the press will never blow up this story—"lonely fiftysomething man faces the fact he'll never have kids"—in the way it uses similar narratives as a cautionary tale meant for younger women not to wait too long or be too picky. What's also galling is the propensity to hear humorous smirking at "late fatherhood" ("he's still got it in him!"), in contrast to the more common judgment of "older women" starting a later-in-life family. "But it would be a satisfying start if men had to pause and see age as part of their biological equation, too," says Belkin, in her exploration of the social effects of this data.

In another *New York Times* article, "It Seems the Fertility Clock Ticks for Men, Too," author Roni Rabin comments, "It's a touchy subject." She writes, "Some advocates, however, welcome the attention being paid to the issue of male fertility, saying it is long overdue and adding that it could level the playing field between men and women in the premarital dating game." Later in the article, she cites Pamela Madsen, founder and executive director of the American Fertility Association, who says, "I don't see why everyone is so surprised. Everyone ages. Why would sperm cells be the only cells not to age as men get older?"[2]

All of this news cited in well-documented—if undersung—studies cheered me. But they didn't change the attention I was getting from men I still deemed too old to be my partner.

Fast-forward to meeting my current husband, both of us on the cusp of turning forty. We met, we married relatively quickly, and I started charting my morning temperature as we began "trying" (a euphemism that made me wince) before we tied the knot—not so easily accomplished when we lived in separate cities. On our honeymoon, which we delayed so we could each finish our semester's teaching, I found out I was pregnant at age forty-one. I was thrilled but cautious. By the time I got to a doctor's office at nearly ten weeks, I knew the pregnancy wasn't viable. Thus began another long period of "terrible math," counting out how long it would take to miscarry, reset my cycle, and wait the suggested few months before trying again. The grieving that accompanied this loss had no timeline. Now over forty, I also knew there was no time to waste. We consulted with a reproductive endocrinologist—three, actually—and began the expensive, frustrating, and painfully never-covered-by-insurance venture into reproductive technology.

Getting pregnant once and then miscarrying felt like a tragedy; when I had a second miscarriage, it was worrisome; and the third made it clearly a pattern. What I also figured out by then was that for a woman over forty, factoring in the time it took to get pregnant (several cycles), the time spent miscarrying (several weeks), then waiting to try again meant the months stacked ominously against the dismal actuarial charts for conception and—more significant to me—carrying a baby to term. If it took six months to get pregnant once more, it was easy to calculate how I'd tip over from one set of stats to another and then another and then another, each progressively worse.

In an article in *Los Angeles* magazine entitled "Baby, Please," author Monica Corcoran Harel recounts her own fertility journey after crossing the threshold of forty. After citing career-climbing as the primary reason she delayed, she comments, "In recent years any warnings delivered to women about their waning fertility have been labeled sexist at best and an insidious attempt to scare ambitious young women out of the workplace at worst." Harel interviews her own fertility doctor, who says of the culture in Los Angeles, "I see women who are 42, but everyone tells them they look 32, and they do. I have to convince them that Botox can reverse their crow's-feet, but I can't do that with their eggs."[3]

I was thrilled to be pregnant at forty-four and to become a mother at forty-five. Yet I know there is a reckoning that those who start parenting post-forty have to face, however publicly or middle-of-the-night it occurs. I'm sure the words "advanced maternal age" are somewhere on my medical chart, but no one has ever said them to me directly. When my reproductive endocrinologist commented that my ovaries seemed "robust" for being over forty and my FSH not too bad, I remember feeling a wave of pride. Yet when I sat at my infertility support group meeting every month, it became clear that the common assumption that women who wait till forty to conceive can do just fine wasn't always the case. Seeing over-forty friends or acquaintances walk around with their babies' chubby legs dangling from Ergobabies strapped to their chests encouraged all of us; even one anecdote of someone much older and more challenged "succeeding" would buoy us, though it did nothing to refute the actual odds.

Especially hard-hit in this group seemed to be the women who believed waiting would work out for them, only to find it didn't— the clock couldn't rewind, and self-recrimination piled on top of fury made for a bad emotional mix. I could see that for women who had been consistently met with success and achievement, it was a blow to realize this was a challenge that they couldn't study hard enough to make happen, or orchestrate, or delegate, or command. Infertility is cruel in many ways, and some weeks there were more twentysomething women at the group than fortysomethings. Many in their twenties felt ostracized, felt they were singled out for failure when told the stats were all in their favor. For those of us above forty, we wrestled with blame (from ourselves and others) while trying to tip into the tiny percentage of successful stats and to not be in the majority for our age group.

What I found I couldn't voice to these older would-be mothers was that while the "but you could be hit by a bus tomorrow" argument applied across the board to all parents, young or old, I think there's a head-in-the-sand approach to ignoring the reality of risks that do increase with age, like disease and other ailments. And the most poignant aspect of this reality is the potential of leaving a child sooner than expected or burdening them with caregiving at an age before they might be mature enough to do so.

When a cousin got engaged to a man of fifty-five (sixteen years older than her) and planned to have a child, I sent her an article I remembered seeing in the *New York Times* entitled "He's Not My Grandpa. He's My Dad," which plumbs some of the issues particular to children born to "later-in-life" fathers—typically the product of a second, younger wife. There is a frank exploration of the sobering life expectancy stats, tempered with the usual "but [the younger child] keeps me young!" or the optimistic "that's why I'm motivated to stay in shape" kinds of comments. But some dads don't fare so well. Author Thomas Vinciguerra interviews the widow of Tony Randall, who became a father at seventy-seven (wife, twenty-six), and died at eighty-four, leaving behind two children, ages six and seven. His widow tells the reporter she has "some strains of guilt" about her choices. Her thoughts are echoed by another widow, Lori Cohen Ransohoff, who was married to a man forty-one years her senior who left her with two young children. "He was so healthy I just took it for granted. I never thought that far ahead. Looking back, I realize that was foolish. Now I tell my daughter, 'Maybe you shouldn't marry an older man,'" she comments.

One father in the article dubs his clan "SODS" (Start-Over Dads), most of whom are fifty and up when they meet their newborns. They reckon with the age gap between themselves and their children, with how mortality is a specter less easy to ignore. But there is often the expression of joy in having reached a professional pinnacle that means they can relax a bit more, work less, and enjoy their children, something an adult "first" child caustically reflects upon, who remembers her father never had time for her, as he does now for her half-sibling, who's young enough to be her own child. "It's so pleasant," said Dr. J. Allan Hobson, seventy-three, a former Harvard Medical School professor of psychiatry and father of twin ten-year-olds Andrew and Matthew. "My success as a scientist depended on my neglecting my first set of children. Now that I'm retired, we have a lot more time together."[4] Not a comment a first set of kids might want to hear.

While I never naïvely thought that fertility stats were not to be heeded, or that I would magically be exempt from their dire prediction, I simply didn't find the person I wanted for a partner—parenting and otherwise—until the end of my thirties. I am thoroughly aware that had we met sooner, I would likely be the mother of another child—maybe two—and the thought haunts me nearly every day. I live with what waiting meant for me: the lack of a sibling for my child, the size of the family we won't have, and the ever-rooted wonder about how much of his life I will get to see. We have talked about adoption as a way to expand our family, and when I realize how long it could be before a child would be placed with us (and before that adoption could be permanent), I calculate another variant of the "terrible math:" unless we adopt an older child, my husband and I would fall squarely into the demographic of older parents whose time with their children is even more curtailed.

My own reckoning never seems to end. I'll be fifty-five with a ten-year-old, I'll be sixty-seven when he graduates college. Will I get to see my own grandchildren? Not likely, if he waits as long as I did to have a child. I'm deeply grateful that, at age seven, he's now old enough to retain memories of the grandparents he still has. The sense of ghost children my husband and I would have had if we weren't the ages we were is ever-present. One perspective is that it all comes down to some poetic wondering anyway: we never know what's behind the next curve or how long our luck will hold out.

Sometime in the midst of those Suzuki classes, my periods stopped.

Mourning the Loss of Fertility
LINDA CORMAN

When I turned forty, I mourned that I would never have children. I was unmarried, not dating anyone steadily, and had decided against braving single motherhood. Mourning consisted of acknowledging to myself that I most likely would never be a mother, and allowing myself to feel the sadness, a feeling I normally would have run several marathons to try to avoid. It also consisted of my confiding in my stepmother about my deep disappointment on a visit to her and my father during the summer of my fortieth birthday.

My stepmother, with whom things had never been particularly warm, said, "I still hope you can." She seemed genuinely sad. Twenty-seven years later, I still remember that moment as perhaps the one, in our twenty-three-year-long relationship, when I felt true compassion and empathy between us. I think she even choked up.

The following fall, I met the man I married two years later. Shortly after we decided to get married, I said I wanted to start trying to get pregnant right away because there was a good chance it would take a long time, if it was possible at all. Within a month of him agreeing to this, my period didn't arrive on time. After waking up on a Saturday morning several days after it still hadn't started, I went for my usual run, feeling crampy and thinking that might dispel the cramps. About halfway around the Central Park Reservoir, my usual route, it dawned on me that I might be pregnant. Suddenly, the fearless athlete in me began worrying that if I kept running, I'd jiggle the embryo—if there really was one—to death. I stopped running, then, remembering stories of runners keeping at it well into the late stages of pregnancy, I started up again. Then, a few hundred yards later, I abruptly halted once more.

By the time I made it to a drug store to buy a pregnancy test kit on the way home, I felt like I was in a surreal fantasy. After wandering around the store, hoping to find a kit on a shelf, I realized they were behind the cashier with the condoms, and I was going to have to ask for one.

My hands shaking, I managed to pee on the thermometer-like instrument, and there was little suspense. It turned pink almost immediately. I wondered if there was a mistake. I reread the directions. They said false positive or negative readings were possible. But—yikes! I called my fiancé, who was hanging out with his thirteen-year-old daughter (by a previous marriage). "So soon?" he said, in his inimitable concise way, calculated to protect his daughter from getting the news just then. She'd had plenty to deal with already, having only recently been informed we were getting married.

My first pregnancy went without a hitch, except for some unnecessary hysteria when even some of the finest doctors in the country (courtesy of my doctor brother-in-law) missed that some unexplained bleeding was simply a hemorrhoid, and a late delivery—two weeks after my due date, my obstetrician said I should be induced because the placenta tends to break down faster in older women. Being induced was painful, but my son was born vaginally, and he was and is a dream come true.

So, naturally, having had one perfect child, I wanted two. That had really been my dream all along, so if I hadn't had to give up half the dream, why couldn't I have the other half as well?

Much as I wanted to have a second child, I didn't get around to broaching the idea seriously to my husband until about four years after our son was born. We were both working, money was tight, and reconstituting a family was challenging. It was hard for either of us to imagine how we could do it. But as another decade marker of my life loomed, I knew it was then or never. I decided I wanted to throw myself headlong into icy water, damn the consequences.

I was goaded by the presence of a fifty-year-old mom in my group cello class, required of parents of children studying Suzuki cello so they could help their kids practice. Our group of four moms and an instructor, which a neighbor of mine dubbed "the Yo-Yo Mas," met every Friday night for several months. Of this group, three were pregnant: the instructor and two students, one of whom was the fifty-year-old. We all joked that playing cello was a fertility drug, and every session began with a report on how the expectant moms were doing. *Certainly if the fifty-year-old can do it, so can I at a mere forty-eight*, I thought.

Then, sometime in the midst of those Suzuki classes, my periods stopped. I couldn't believe it was the end. I was healthy; I'd had a completely healthy child with an uneventful pregnancy at forty-four. Of *course* I had more time.

When my obstetrician gently told me I might be in menopause, she sent me to a specialist to find out for sure. The specialist—I can still feel the fury I felt toward her—coolly and clinically told me I was done. I was out of eggs. "You're lucky to have had one," she said. You don't have to go to medical school, or just about any school, to know that this is not the thing to say to a grieving woman.

My second round of mourning about the end of fertility blanketed me during a trip to the Netherlands shortly after the visit to the specialist. There's a picture of my son and me in one of the rooms of the Hotel de Filosoof, a wonderful bed-and-breakfast in Amsterdam, where each room is dedicated to a philosopher and painted a relevant color. I think of our having stayed in the black room (Nietzsche), but the picture shows us in quite a bright, cheerful room (Spinoza?). Only I was in an existential morass.

Twenty years on, I feel only a grain of the grief. It is astonishing to me that it's possible to emerge from such pain and to barely feel any of it any longer. From this vantage point, it still seems desirable to have had another child, but no more possible— from a practical point of view—than it seemed then. The other day, a new gynecologist I was trying out was taking my history and asked when I'd gone into menopause.

"Forty-eight was on the early side," she remarked.

"Thank you!" I blurted, experiencing her remark as affirmation that I had been robbed. I briefly recounted how I'd been disappointed not to be able to have a second child, and that was that.

Why does my growing belly, paired with my older face, signal open access to inquire about really personal matters?

A Phantasmagoria of Pregnancy and Birth Beyond Forty

JULIA HENDERSON

It is nine-thirty in the morning. I have managed to drop my eight-year-old off at school and arrive at my appointment on time. Thank goodness I remembered to go online last night and make a booking; the lab waiting room is already full. I stand in line behind a man who smells like garlic and antiseptic. *Oh god.* My stomach churns. I pop a piece of gum in my mouth; it helps a little. I try breathing deeply—bad idea, garlic. I try to cover my nose with my hand inconspicuously while I scope out the location of the washroom and the closest garbage can. *Twenty steps to toilet, five to trash receptacle—okay.* I hold my clean hair over my nose and breath in the smell of shampoo, fighting the next wave of nausea. Finally, I'm at the front of the line. I hand the girl my health card and requisition and note that she is pregnant, too, young and pregnant. She looks up at me with shining eyes and glowing skin. She resembles a fresh, ripe, glorious peach. I chew my gum a little harder. "Room two," she says. I breathe and chew my way to room two, then hoist myself into the chair. There I sit— exhausted, anxious, sick—and this is only the beginning.

I am here to check my hormone levels. A home pregnancy test has confirmed I'm pregnant—again. But I'm forty-three and a half, I've had four miscarriages, and I'm here for the second day in a row to see if my hormone levels are rising or falling. I'll soon know if there is a chance this baby will make it. A lab technician comes in, her hair in pigtails, an assortment of beautiful tattoos on her arm. I see she's pregnant too. *Are you kidding me? Is this some kind of strange torture chamber of youthful fertility?* She looks down on my dazzling gray roots (I'm not supposed to dye my hair till after week ten) as she sorts through my chart and a variety of labels and tubes.

"Name," she says. I tell her. "Can you confirm your date of birth?" There it is: the dreaded question. My body shrinks as a wave of sickness swells.

"July 14," I choke out, "1970." I feel my cheeks flush as I utter the year. *What is this?* I think. Embarrassment at having failed so many times to have another child? Or some deeply ingrained ageism causing me to feel embarrassed at demonstrating (by virtue of my pregnancy) that I'm having sex at my age?

I cringe again as I see the surprise on the lab tech's face. "Wow," she says. "Good for you!"

As a University of British Columbia PhD student doing research at the intersections of theater, performance, and cultural age studies, I found myself fascinated by my experience of pregnancy at an older age. While I was deeply curious about my feelings and interactions, at the same time I found it impossible to influence most of them, especially certain feelings of being out-of-time-and-place. I felt a disjuncture between my internal age identity (youthful), how my body felt (tired, sore, no longer young), and how people reacted to me (interpreting me as a broad range of ages). The blood test I described above was but the beginning of SO MANY medical procedures during this pregnancy: lab tests, scans, probes, medications. Each time, I felt equally if not more embarrassed to utter my birthdate in order to confirm my identity. I was ashamed at my own embarrassment, but at the same time, I couldn't overcome it. The recurrent thought seeped into my consciousness: "I would have done this so much better when I was twenty-five!"

Compared to my first pregnancy eight years prior, this pregnancy and birth were extremely medicalized. With my older son, I'd had a minimal number of tests. This time, I had many. First there was the abovementioned hCG test to confirm pregnancy. Hurray, the levels went up! Then I had to take progesterone until the tenth week. (My husband said it made me taste like Bitter Yuck, the stuff you put on furniture so your dogs don't chew it.) I also had to increase my thyroid meds—since my older son was born, I had developed hypothyroidism. With this came monthly blood tests to confirm my TSH levels were okay, since thyroid dysfunction can cause miscarriage. Ultrasounds weren't so bad, and I had many. My obstetrician became my friend. She would hold my hand in the early days while the lab tech at the Recurrent Pregnancy Loss Clinic checked to see if there was still a heartbeat. Every time I saw the little flicker, I would cry with relief.

My attitude toward all the tests had changed too. During my first pregnancy, I didn't really want them; I was fearful certain tests would harm my baby. This time, I welcomed them all. I now saw most medical treatments and procedures as helpful, and I was willing to do anything it took for this baby to arrive safely into the world.

Once I made it past eight weeks (the point at which I had miscarried three times), it was time to think about testing for genetic abnormalities. I had had amniocentesis with my older son—even eight years prior, at the age of thirty-five, I was considered to be of "advanced maternal age" and at higher risk for chromosomal abnormalities and birth defects. My husband was older, too, ten and a half years my senior, but apparently it was my age that was an issue, not his. Now there was a new test, NIPT (noninvasive prenatal testing). It could be done as early as ten weeks and had no real risks; I could just have a blood sample sent off for analysis. The only trouble was it was expensive—eight hundred dollars was a lot to lose if I miscarried again soon after. But my husband's mother offered to pay, and we decided to go for it.

So back I went to the lab, which now had three young, glowing pregnant staff members, to offer up my arm and my birthdate again. The test was easy—just another tube of blood, much less scary than "amnio." But the three-week wait time for the results was excruciating. For three weeks, I held my breath, sometimes quite literally—I would wake in the night gasping for air. I would dream of giving birth to giant tadpole-frogs and dogs that wouldn't stop crying.

Finally, the test results arrived: I was having another boy, and he was chromosomally typical! I had made it past one more milestone. I hugged my obstetrician friend and wept with relief, dripping salty tears all over her blue hospital scrubs.

Understandably, I was nervous to tell anyone I was pregnant. I had miscarried before and the experience had felt much worse when everyone knew, since it meant dealing with everyone else's emotions and going through the labor of repeatedly explaining what had happened. I was also reticent to reveal my condition because of the stigma against motherhood in academia. I was beginning the fourth year of my PhD program in Theatre Studies. Although I had one child, I had been able to keep up the pace required to excel, had received some top-notch scholarships, and was considered a student with a lot of promise. I felt the faculty's excitement and investment in me. Yet I knew this investment was tenuous, dependent upon my keeping pace.

On one of my first-year essays, the professor commented on a statement I hadn't supported well, writing, "This smacks of motherhood and apple juice." Clearly, motherhood was not highly valued here; it was equated with bad research. I was also on the mature side as a PhD candidate; slowing my progress could limit my chances of a tenure-track job. I waited until my twenty-week detailed ultrasound showed that my baby had no congenital defects before telling anyone at school I was pregnant. My classmates were excited. My supervisor, a woman about my age and with a child of her own, was also extremely supportive. Others expressed their congratulations, but I sensed a general deflation in how other faculty members saw my prospects as an academic. Performance anxiety crept its way into my nighttime fantasies. I began to dream of showing up for class inappropriately dressed, having lost my notes. My slides would fail to work, I'd scurry around, lost, and undersea creatures and fantasy animals would materialize in my audience of students. In my slumber, I envisioned dog-babies or lizard-babies falling out of me as I taught and sloshed across the stage in a humiliating wave of sticky, bloody failure.

Exhausted from ongoing poor sleep—a result of my arms going numb, disturbing dreams, and the nighthawk baby dancing inside me—and from mild anemia, I decided, with the support of my obstetrician, to take a medical leave. I had worked up to thirty-eight weeks with my first son, but this time, I lacked the stamina. One bonus of taking leave was that it meant my scholarships, which would've expired before my baby was born, would be put on hold, and so I would be eligible for maternity leave benefits through this funding. My research did not involve live human or animal subjects, so I "unofficially" continued my work at home, resting and taking naps as I needed them. However, it was hard to focus. My body was tired, and my mind was fearful. My obstetrician referred me to an obstetric mental health clinic to help with anxiety.

In talking to other older mothers, I discovered my sense of anxiety was common. Many older parents have put in years of emotional, physical, and financial investment. Many have had multiple losses or years of infertility. Some have devoted a large amount of money to fertility treatments. Above all, the sense of running out of time is pervasive, the ever-present biological clock ticking like the crocodile on Captain Hook's trail, poised to consume him if he trips.

Among the battery of tests I underwent, my obstetrician friend referred me for heart evaluation. When my first son was two years old, I had developed three different heart arrhythmias, and not only had they exhausted me, they had also prevented me from getting pregnant, since the drugs I needed would harm a fetus. I had undergone three successful ablation procedures over two years before I could try to conceive again. Now, during this pregnancy, it was important to double-check that all things cardiac were still okay.

The results came back showing I was fine, but the team's precautionary recommendation was that I deliver at the hospital equipped with an adult cardiac care team and in a delivery room with all the specialized cardiac equipment. That meant I couldn't deliver where my obstetrician friend worked, and I had to see a different obstetrician who had privileges at the hospital with the cardiac team. I asked her what would happen if I went into arrhythmia while in labor. She said it depended on what kind of arrhythmia, but if it was PSVT (paroxysmal supraventricular tachycardia) like I'd had before, I would likely be given adenosine. (Adenosine is a drug that flatlines your heart for about five to ten seconds and essentially allows it to reboot. They place the cardiac paddles under you before administering the drug "just in case," and a team of about six people proceed to stare intently at the monitor, waiting to see what happens.)

For anyone who's had adenosine, it is the longest, most uncomfortable ten seconds of your entire life. It feels like several elephants are standing on your chest while your insides are being squeezed into your brain to the brink of exploding. Despite all reassurance, I couldn't imagine that something so effective at flatlining my heart would not also flatline my sweet baby's teeny-tiny ticker. The thought of having adenosine while in labor was overwhelming and horrifying to me. Dismayed to think this might be my baby's first experience of the world, I burst into tears. The obstetrician was stunned and became flustered. She mumbled something about it being hard when a patient actually knows what drugs do. After an awkward attempt to comfort me, she exited the room, leaving me to heave my giant turtled body off her table, unassisted. Now I had more fodder for my dreams: my dozing became filled with visions of ticking time bombs in my chest and scenes of doctors yelling at me to push while my body would not move or speak. The flatline sound would sneakily infiltrate my nightmare and grow in intensity until it felt as though it was suffocating my brain.

One of the most surprising aspects of having a second baby at an older age was the unsolicited questions and advice I received. Had I forgotten this with my first son? Had I been so delighted, naïve, and curious that I didn't mind? One day, when I was not yet visibly pregnant, I sat in my GP's office as my older son played with the toys in her waiting room (the appointment was actually for him). An elderly woman sat beside me and watched him play for a while. She then turned to me and said, "I don't know why people have only one child. It's not fair to them. It's irresponsible. Why do people do that?"

Completely taken aback, I stifled my tears and decided to be truthful. "Well, I was on heart medications so I couldn't have more babies for a while, and then I miscarried four times."

That gave her pause for a moment. "Oh, well, that's okay then," she continued, "but I don't understand why other people choose it." I came to dread medical waiting rooms.

Another time, as I counted down the minutes to see my obstetrician, the woman beside me noticed my older son's age and asked if he and the baby had the same father. When I said yes, she asked if my pregnancy was an accident. "Is it an 'oops baby?'" she laughed.

My closest friends knew the truth. But other friends wondered the same thing, and many did not hesitate to ask. Why would people automatically assume that because there was an age gap between my boys, my pregnancy was unplanned?

On the contrary, several young friends proclaimed how inspired they felt by my pregnancy: "I'm going to focus on my career now and have babies in my forties too," one declared. She cited numerous celebrities who were also having babies in their forties. I kept quiet, unsure of how to respond, fearful my emotions would overwhelm me. The media makes it look easy. The news gives the impression that everyone can do it. However, I knew from my obstetrician friend that a large percentage of her patients having babies over the age of forty were doing so using donor eggs or embryos. Conceiving unassisted after age forty is not a realistic "choice" for many people. I was lucky I could still get pregnant easily, but I couldn't seem to reach my pot-of-gold baby at the end of this rainbow. I felt torn between a sense of responsibility to provide these young women with the truth, a desire to avoid talking about my personal experiences because they were too raw, and a wish not to crush anyone's dreams.

Besides these young cheerleaders, other strangers felt free to openly ask a range of probing questions. They queried whether I'd had IVF, how old I was, if my husband wanted this baby. I found myself wondering, *What is this strange phenomenon? Why does my growing belly, paired with my older face, signal open access to inquire about really personal matters?* A conversation with a friend was even harder. She told me that she'd wanted more children, but that she and her husband had decided it would be unfair to the baby because of how old they were. "You have to really think about that, you know. We wouldn't be around when that baby grew up," she expounded. She meant no harm; she'd intended to identify with my desire to have another child. But I was the same age as her, and my husband was considerably older than hers, so it was hard to escape suddenly feeling irresponsible for choosing to have another child.

At the same time, my dreams continued. Larva-like babies evaporated from my clutch. I misplaced my dog-baby again and again and awoke in a panic. Shadowlike men followed me in the dark and choked me as I tried to scream but could summon no voice.

However, two days before my due date, I learned that my dreams and fears did not inform reality. I had made it through labor to the pushing stage. Everyone kept telling me how second babies practically fall out. My son, however, had not received the notice that second births were meant to be speedy affairs. I labored, unmedicated, for about twenty-eight long and exhausting hours. Finally, I requested an epidural (and wondered why I'd waited so long), my midwife broke my water, and they gave me meds to speed and strengthen the contractions. Now, after twenty minutes of pushing, my little boy was about to emerge.

I held my breath and pushed, pressing my feet against the birthing bar and pulling on a twisted sheet as though I was hauling myself out of the water on a water ski towrope. His gooey pink head emerged up to the bridge of his nose, and his wide eyes blinked open—there, he stopped and looked at me. I was his first sight!

At this point, my midwife gave a signal, a nurse pushed a button and said something about *code pink*, and suddenly a bunch of medical staff flooded the room. I didn't know what was happening and barely had time to think. "On the next contraction," my midwife's calm voiced coached, "give it an extra hard push."

I could sense a hidden tension in that calm, so I bore down and pushed with every ounce of strength in my being. I summoned up all the years of longing and aching and channeled that emotion into a volcano of power. I pushed like a warrior, like an Olympian at the end of her race, like a female Hercules, and finally that little baby, my second son, popped out. They scooped him away to be suctioned. I held my breath till I heard his cry, noticing the huge team of people surrounding us. It took longer than I expected, and a flicker of panic brewed in my belly. But then it came: a cry so pure and clear and strong it echoed through the centuries. He was finally here: safe, healthy, powerful.

We named him Hart—Hart of my heart! His wide, curious eyes looked around the room. "Behold," he seemed to be saying, "I have prevailed!"

Baby Hart and I spent the night in the hospital and went home the next day. I have never before felt such gratitude as I felt toward all those who made it possible: all of the medical staff who paid close attention and provided excellent care; my obstetrician friend and my midwife, who went far beyond the call of duty for me; my husband and older son, who stood by me all the way; my friends and family, who provided excellent support; and my brave baby, who had the strength to arrive safely in this world. For all of this, I will be endlessly thankful.

As much as I experienced stigma, skepticism, and judgment, I also experienced extreme generosity and kindness. I recovered more quickly than from my first birth, and Hart was a very chill, relaxed baby. My bad dreams stopped. Breastfeeding was easy, my milk came in fast, and, by six weeks, he was in the 95th percentile for weight. Once I was past the pregnancy, I found having an infant took about ten years off my social age, and my own age identity shifted too. I felt young, pretty, vital, lush. This time around, I felt no pressure to go to exercise classes or to attend baby groups. This time, I knew how quickly babies grow up, and I recognized that I should savor every delicious, drool-soaked, diaper-filled moment.

One of the main differences about becoming a mother after the age of forty is that it is often the climax of what has been a very long and arduous physical and emotional journey. I think older parents are often acutely aware of how lucky they are. They often have peers who haven't had the same good fortune. As opposed to my first pregnancy, when I found the loss of independence painful, this time I was focused on gratitude.

My husband, Milt, was working a jigsaw puzzle at the dining room table when I told him I felt pregnant.

Giving Birth after Fifty

PHYLLIS COX

A few months ago, a friend who lives in central Florida mentioned to me that she'd read an article in her area newspaper about a woman who, at age fifty, had given birth to a naturally conceived baby. The article had caught my friend's eye because she knew that almost twenty-seven years before, the same thing had happened to me. She'd never read or heard of such a story in the news before, and neither had I, although I'd lived a very similar experience. Thinking about the article took me back in time to late January of 1992, when I found out that, to my complete surprise, I was indeed pregnant.

A close friend from college had been visiting us that weekend to celebrate her fiftieth birthday, which was a huge milestone for both of us. Both Bette and I were half a century old! (I had celebrated my fiftieth birthday the previous August.) After Bette left and I was lying down for a short nap, resting up from the busy weekend, I felt a persistent kind of bumping and thumping in my lower abdomen. At first I thought it was just a bubble, but it wouldn't go away. The only other times I could remember feeling anything like it were when I'd been pregnant with each of our three daughters. *That couldn't possibly be the cause of this soft bumping*, I thought. *I haven't had a period for over two years. I'm positive I've gone through menopause.* But the bumping felt familiar!

My husband, Milt, was working a jigsaw puzzle at the dining room table when I told him I felt pregnant: not nauseated or even unusually tired or unable to wear my regular clothes, although they were beginning to feel a little tight. *Too much birthday cake*, I'd thought. Being practical and mathematical, he said I should go and buy a home pregnancy test and take it, just to be sure I wasn't pregnant—and to be doubly sure, I should get two tests.

The first test I took showed positive results, but I couldn't believe it and neither could he. But when the second test showed the same result, our doubts disappeared.

We decided I had to get to an ob-gyn as fast as possible. My dear friend and confidante, Cindy, recommended her doctor as the very best choice we could make, but the receptionist told me the earliest appointment I could get was two weeks away. We couldn't wait that long! So, my husband called again and said, "I don't think you understand. My wife is almost fifty and a half years old! She needs to be seen *now*." We went for our appointment the following day.

The doctor who saw me was kindly and almost grandfatherly, but we felt comforted that he also seemed knowledgeable, experienced, and wise. He confirmed my pregnancy that day with his own lab test, and he scheduled a sonogram, an amniocentesis, and other tests to determine the condition of our baby. All tests produced positive results and let us know that after three daughters, we would be having a son—and he would be arriving in about four months. We'd be producing a baby in what seemed like half the regular time.

Our emotions ran wild—a mixture of shock and disbelief, concern, and confusion, but joy and thankfulness that our little boy seemed to be developing just fine.

My husband and I bounced questions back and forth. What to do next? When should we tell our girls? Maybe after just a little time to get used to the idea ourselves? How long until my pregnancy would really show on my size-ten body? Would I be able to keep teaching evening classes at our local high school for the rest of the spring semester? The baby's due date was right at the end of the school year. How would our friends react? Would they think we were crazy? Would they think it was funny? Would people worry about us?

We told our girls first, all together. Ellen, who was twenty-two and a senior in college, seemed relieved and not totally surprised. She said that some of her close friends had told her that I seemed to be putting on weight, and that she might need to talk with me about it. Clare, sixteen and a junior in high school, said there was no way she would push her new brother around town in a stroller because people would think she was his teenage mom and that we were adopting him to raise for her. Ann, age eleven, asked, "Will Mom be all right?" Having a new little brother that none of them could have ever imagined any more than their parents could have seemed unreal to them just then, but they began to warm to the idea and to think it just might be exciting.

As for our friends, we just didn't say anything to many of them. The four months went by fast, and loose shirts and jackets and other kinds of layers hid the baby bump. The coolness of the spring weather made all of those layers comfortable as well. (Maybe people thought—as Ellen's friends had—that I was developing a body image problem, but they were just too tactful to mention it.) My husband, Milt, and I are both only children, so we had no siblings to tell, and none of our parents were still living except Milt's mother, who had dementia. We wished that our parents could've been able to share our surprise baby with us. They would've loved him so much.

Time flew by. Before we knew it, Dr. McLean was telling me to celebrate Memorial Day weekend quietly that year and to come in for a Caesarean section the morning of Monday, May 26. He recommended the C-section because of my age, although

I'd been healthy the whole time of my pregnancy, both known and unknown. At age fifty-going-on-fifty-one, I was a high-risk patient.

Our confidence in Dr. McLean never wavered and one of the nation's best children's hospitals was next door to the hospital where our son would be born, just in case he needed special care. We checked into the hospital just as the sun came up that morning, and by 10:00, we were taking turns holding our son in our arms—a miracle of miracles. We had no other words to describe his birth. He did well from his first moment of life, never needing any special care from the excellent neonatal unit next door, although he was examined there meticulously.

Next, he needed a name. We hadn't picked one before he was born because, somehow, he seemed unreal to us until we finally saw him. Now we put our five heads together to choose one. Each of our three daughters has the first or middle name of a parent or grandparent, so we decided to continue that tradition by naming him after my husband and my father—both of whom conveniently have the name Milton—as well as after my husband's dearest friend Tom (Thomas). His sisters really wanted him to have a name of his very own, however, so we gave him three names—Milton Christian Thomas—and we all started to call him Christian, which over time has shrunk to Chris.

At the end of our week in the hospital, Chris and I came home, and from then on he was just there, a new member of our family, surprising to many. We had to introduce him to those who hadn't known he was coming or at least hadn't indicated that they knew. Cousins, friends, neighbors, people who we only met or knew casually, and people who knew us from work met Chris over time, and we all settled into being a family of six. Most people were encouraging to us, saying that although they would never want to start raising another child at our ages, they were sure that if anyone could do it, we could—and that we would be just fine.

We made no newspaper headlines, but in our small town, we became well-known as the couple who had a new baby—naturally—at ages fifty and fifty-three. By being special himself, Chris made us special too.

In the fall of 1992, Dr. McLean invited us to an assembly of incoming medical students to meet them and answer their questions about our experience of giving birth at our advanced ages. Chris attended with us so that the students could see us all together—not a traditional combination of parents and child. We also visited Dr. McLean and his wife in their home several times, and in some ways, he became a grandfather to Chris, as well as the doctor who delivered him. Chris's birth had made him feel special as well; it had been a kind of capstone to his medical career. I also met with students in a writing workshop at our local university, answering as best I could any questions they had about late-in-life birthing and parenting.

Gatherings like these have helped all of us to see our experiences from many perspectives. The students entering medical school asked questions about the physical challenges of my pregnancy and the postpartum period. *Was I unusually tired, especially in the last trimester of my pregnancy?* I didn't remember being more tired than usual. *Was having a C-section a strain on me, since it was major surgery?* I did remember the nerve pain being severe as the stitches healed, but the discomfort was temporary. *Was postpartum depression a problem?* I was fortunate not to have had it.

Some members of the group asked whether it had been especially hard to schedule a newborn into our family life, along with a preteen, teenager, young adult, and two parents over the age of fifty. I answered that although things didn't always go smoothly, each of us helped as we could, trying always to be flexible and to respect each other's priorities. They wanted to know whether I was embarrassed to appear suddenly among friends and associates with a newborn and whether I felt embarrassed explaining how and why I had him. I told them I truly enjoyed introducing him as an amazing and wonderful surprise to his father and me. For our family, learning has been going on now for over a quarter of a century. The baby boy we brought home in 1992 is now a grown man with a degree in economics, working in corporate technology. In the years between, Milt and I have revisited familiar parenting experiences—from loss of sleep with a new baby through taking turns as parent helpers in preschool, volunteering in elementary school activities both in and out of the classroom, driving to cross-country and swim meets and often working after we got there, having groups of boys in our home for sleepovers or parties or just to hang out and hoping that everything, including the boys, would be intact when they left. Have there been times when we were tired and wished for more of the energy of our younger years? Absolutely. But we've been thankful for the experiences of those years and the wisdom they built, along with the patience they developed to see us through.

Chris's own experiences growing up in our family have definitely been unique. At times, he must have felt that having in some ways four mothers was three—or even four—too many, that he and his dad were too outnumbered for comfort. At other times, he must have been glad for the love and support his sisters so generously added to his life. And when each of them married, he gained another brother to identify with, to do "guy things" with, to bring balance to his life. Now he's a youngish uncle to three nieces and a nephew, ages almost two to fifteen, adding yet another dimension to his life, just as he's added so many dimensions to all of ours.

I asked him recently what it was like growing up with older parents. Being tactful, he said the pros outweighed the cons because he's had parents who are loving, patient, wise, helpful with life's questions as he's encountered them, and supportive when he's come upon rough patches. The only con he mentioned was that his dad and I are technologically "unsavvy." I'm guessing he knows we are "unsavvy" in other ways as well—that we're often out of step with his culture—but he's too diplomatic to say so.

Transitions have been challenging for Chris, especially from high school to college and from college to the work world. It may be that as older parents, along with his sisters, we haven't given him freedom to develop the confidence he needs. Now as he grows fully into adulthood, we're seeing his self-reliance strengthen, along with his determination to make good decisions.

He never comments to his dad and me about realizing that he'll have fewer years with us than his sisters, who were born when we were so much younger, or his friends, who were also born earlier in their parents' lives, although the thought may very well enter his mind. Milt and I have been very fortunate to have good health so far, and we try to preserve it with a healthy lifestyle. Milt turned eighty five months before Chris's last birthday (age twenty-seven), and I just turned seventy-eight. We cannot help seeing time shortening for us. When Chris was born, we had no idea how much time we would have with him. Each of these past twenty-seven years has been such a gift to us, so we look forward to each year yet to come with joy.

PART III

DOES AGE MATTER
IF I ADOPT?

Everything was out of my hands. Smoking was the least of it.

Growing Roots
SARAH WERTHAN BUTTENWIESER

The beginning of our family becoming an adoptive family seemed to have a lot to do with hair: mine, in my early forties, was going gray; my husband didn't have all that much of it; and our three boys had enough to pull into ponytails, although they preferred to wear it out.

My gray wasn't a few strands or even a flamboyant streak. It insisted itself upon my dark hair, inseparable. I'd dyed it for years, and I'd decided to stop for reasons that spanned expense, time, environmental consciousness, and concerns that the chemicals presented a health risk I no longer wanted to take. Vanity, too: I thought I looked older with too-dark hair on increasingly pale skin than I would with gray. But I worried that no birth mother would want an older (early forties), gray-haired adoptive mother to raise her child.

Amongst myths and stereotypes about adoption, the most prevalent is that women who choose adoption are very young "teen moms." I'd imagined that I might well be old enough to be my daughter's birth mother's mom, possibly even older. Not only would I be old enough to be her mom, with gray hair I'd *look* like her mom—or *even older*.

We did face a hair problem. Several social workers told us many prospective birth mothers were put off by boys with long hair, so we swapped in photos with the boys' hair pulled back. We awaited a daughter who, we joked, would have short hair (she does not).

Rather than a teen-mom scenario, our daughter's birth mother was in her early forties, which made ours an unusual match. The social worker, Deb, said, "Caroline doesn't want a cookie-cutter suburban family and likes that your boys have long hair. It is pretty certain she's carrying a girl, and she has an ultrasound this week to confirm." She added, "Caroline hasn't had any children. She felt like this was her last chance to have a baby, but by the time she discovered she was pregnant, she was no longer with the birth father. She didn't have the funds to terminate her pregnancy and wasn't prepared—financially, logistically, or emotionally—to raise a child. But she wants an ongoing connection." Our family wanted an open adoption too. To be born to one mother and go to another seemed like a fissure. I hoped relationships with the birth family would smooth things out, like grout between tiles.

This baby felt like a last chance to me too. I was over forty, and my pregnancies had been nausea-filled, which took a toll on me and my family. My husband, Hosea, wasn't as keen as I was to add another child, although he was willing, with some justified fears about raising four children. He certainly didn't want us to endure another of my pregnancies. Plus, after having given birth to three boys, the odds I'd carry another boy were high. I selfishly wanted a girl. I didn't want to dress her in pink, but I didn't *not* want to dress her in pink either.

Relieved not to be too old to be Caroline's choice, I was still nervous. So was my husband, who was in his late thirties at the time. We spoke to Caroline the Sunday after Thanksgiving on different phone extensions. I huddled under blankets, chattering with nerves. Blankets did nothing. Caroline spoke quickly, her voice raspy and nervous. To our shared relief, we all liked each other enough to want to meet. She offered to visit the following Sunday, interested to see our house and meet our children—and us.

A week later, Caroline's car pulled into our driveway. "You could have a horse here," Caroline said. (We later learned that her mother had a horse farm.) "We're a quarter acre shy," Hosea replied. "A friend tried."

Our son, Lucien, guided our house tour. Our other son, Ezekiel, said hello and returned to reading on his bed. I wondered whether the house was too big or too messy, too casual or too fancy. In the living room, I cut slices of chocolate chip banana bread. Lucien took one and went off to play. Hosea poured tea. He'd grown up in England and Caroline's parents were English, so tea was a common bond.

"Did Deb tell you I smoked?" she asked. I took a sharp but shallow breath. We shook our heads. I'd never smoked, but I'd tortured myself over diet soda and white flour when I was pregnant. "I've tried to stop, but it's more like I cut down." That's what I'd done with soda.

"Quitting is hard," I murmured, hoping I didn't sound as if I'd entered a red zone between judgmental and freaked out. Everything was out of my hands. Smoking was the least of it.

Our conversation in the living room echoed the one over the phone a week earlier: how the ex-boyfriend had refused to help pay for an abortion and hadn't offered financial assistance toward her pregnancy or for a baby, how he didn't "believe" in adoption but hadn't stepped up, how she wouldn't want a baby to go to his family's apartment, where three generations were living in two bedrooms and the grandmother was left to deal with many children. Mostly, we listened and asked questions. Why did she think he was opposed to adoption? Caroline wondered if this was a cultural belief; he was Jamaican. She posited that it was about ownership, as in, "No baby of *mine* is going to another family," emphasis on mine.

"He doesn't care what I want," she said, sounding more hurt than angry. "I'm the one who's pregnant."

We nodded. She was the one who was pregnant. Had I known her earlier in her pregnancy and known she'd wanted an abortion, I could've helped her find one and pay for it, because I'd worked within the networks of abortion funds in Massachusetts, which helped women obtain funds for the procedure. I thought about how she was pregnant and how all choices were hers to make, but how strange it was for me to believe so strongly in her agency over her body and, simultaneously, to want a specific outcome—bluntly, that outcome being "to raise her baby."

Before Caroline left, we became awkward—to shake hands or to hug? We hugged. The relationship between a birth mother and an adoptive mother is complicated by the fact that power is unequal, and yet each party needs the other. The birth mom has the ultimate power; she's pregnant with the baby. There's only that one baby, and until the birth mother decides whether to opt for adoption placement or to parent the baby herself, that baby is hers. That same baby is the baby an adoptive mother wants. I wanted that baby. But once the decision/placement has been made, the adoptive mother arguably has more power—ostensibly, she is set up to raise the child financially, logistically, and emotionally. And then, once she legally becomes the child's mother, that other mother—the one who gave birth to the baby—is relegated to a more nebulous status, as if her contribution ends soon after a baby's birth.

And yet despite the fact that the major and immutable act of giving birth does not repeat or continue, it endures in so many ways. Think of the family resemblances, neuroses, preferences, and mannerisms biology dictates. That was one reason we'd hoped the relationship with Caroline would be more than a portal to family medical history.

We discussed who'd be there during labor: I'd attend the birth and Hosea would occupy the waiting room. At the time of the baby's birth, my husband would be thirty-nine—the age I was when we'd had our last boy—and I would be forty-four. That wasn't the number that made me feel old, it was that I'd be fifty when that baby started kindergarten.

Saskia was born with a head of dark, sleek hair that never fell out and grew curly in toddlerhood. By preschool, her hair was long, then buzzed after an unfortunate lice incident, and then long again. For much of elementary school, the ends turned ombre in the summer sun.

After Saskia was born, there was concern that the birth father wouldn't agree to adoption and might ensnare Caroline into a custody suit. Given that possibility, however remote, Caroline held onto her parental rights rather than sign papers to cede them at the customary four-day mark. But we brought Saskia home. Our adoption agency and their lawyer gave us guidance to document that Caroline remained connected and involved, in case the adoption failed due to the birth father's objection. His name wasn't on the birth certificate, and protocol demanded he receive a certified letter and the birth notice go into his local paper, a lengthy process. So we waited.

And waited.

If there was any silver lining to the elongated limbo we shared, it was that we saw Caroline and members of her family often during the first months of Saskia's life. We bonded, all of us, against the threat of this man destroying everyone's family plans. Instantly, awkwardly, we became family due to a tiny person who couldn't even talk.

Seven endless months and two threats to contest the adoption later, the birth father's parental rights were terminated by a judge. Despite the birth father's objections, he did none of the necessary work to gain standing (no DNA test, and he never contacted the Department of Child and Family Services).

We were all so relieved that things could move to the conclusion we'd all wanted: adoption. But it wasn't only joy and relief we felt. According to Deb, to cede parental rights at four days is wrenching—and "to sign at seven months is excruciating. It was about the hardest signing I've ever done. Caroline loves Saskia; she knows her. Saskia's so real, it's much harder," Deb told me. It was hard for us—hard for me—to know Caroline had to do something so painful, and that we got to be happy about it. And about three months later, I had to call her to say the adoption had been finalized.

"That's great!" she said, with what sounded like a labored burst of enthusiasm. "I have to get back to the horses." Elated as I was, relieved as I felt, I experienced deep sadness at her sadness. Had I not known her well, I wouldn't have begun to fathom how painful this adoption business was.

Our friendships formed long before Saskia could talk. Caroline held Saskia during early visits (she didn't want to change her diaper or feed her). As Saskia grew, Caroline played board games, tickled, and painted fingernails with her. Before Caroline moved from our shared state, we arranged a few visits where they had an adventure and I waited at a nearby coffee shop. One time, during an ice-skating show just across from the hospital where Saskia was born, I braved the lobby there to exorcise ghosts. It was eerie, nearly empty on a Saturday. I ate some chocolate and drank some tea amongst the big plants and muted colors. As I sat there, I thought about how fortunate I was that Saskia came last in our family and came when I was old enough (mature enough, I hope) to share her in these ways. The person I was at thirty-two, the age I was when I welcomed our first child, probably would've felt that Caroline's presence challenged my identity as a mother. By the time Saskia was born, I already knew I was one.

Although our friendship is fueled by Saskia, it's now mainly carried out between Caroline, Hosea, and me. We text. We're Facebook friends, so when I post photos of Saskia, she sees them and I can show Saskia photos of Caroline and her beloved horse.

Caroline and I arrange visits when she's visiting her family. She sometimes calls to discuss something she's struggling with or to request a little extra help. What was hard in her life—financial instability and not feeling like she has a definite path to security—didn't change after Saskia's birth. I wish it would. Sometimes I worry that's a desire I have more for myself, to be assured she made a good choice and was rewarded with security and satisfaction.

When Saskia turned eight, she asked, "Why did Auntie Cece decide on adoption?" While it wasn't the first time Saskia wanted to know, up until then I'd been able to satisfy her with my answer, which was that Auntie Cece wanted her to have two parents and siblings to grow up with, especially since she could stay close to Saskia too.

Later, talking with Caroline, I said, "I wanted to let you know Saskia would like to talk to you about why you chose adoption."

"What do I say?" she asked. I repeated what I'd always said.

We scheduled a visit. She called a couple of times, anxious. I worried Caroline might decide against coming. But we did meet up at a pizza place between our houses—and then Saskia didn't ask her after all.

This afternoon, when the mail came, there was a pink envelope addressed to me. Inside was a Mother's Day card, with a sentiment of wishing happiness to people most important to me, sent not by one of my college-age children or sisters or mother, but by Caroline. I'd sent one her way, too, and this year, our daughter—the one she gave birth to and the one I am raising—wrote inside, "Happy Mother's Day! I love you!!" Now eleven, she drew a tiny sketch of the two of them, then added more hearts, and with my reminding her, signed her name.

I'M GRATEFUL BEYOND WORDS that our connections have endured. Despite stories of these ties fading or fraying or breaking in open adoption, that hasn't been the case for us. We gained an entire family through Caroline and Saskia.

While I can't speak to how she feels, I think Caroline believes she made the best choice, and the longing or sadness that lingers is outweighed by her sense of connection and gladness that her girl—our girl—thrives. A word I've contemplated infinity times over since I first saw Saskia in the labor room is "bittersweet." It applies, perhaps, to all our connections with one another. The friendship I have with Caroline often feels weighted with it—not melancholy, not regret, but awareness that the tie binding us together was predicated upon her loss. I can't help but hang onto my guilt that I was the luckier one.

"When your child becomes a teenager, whether you admit it to yourself or not, you begin a long process of saying goodbye to them.

"La Llapa": A Father Again at Forty-Five
JIM SHULTZ

My wife, Lynn, and I spent the first year of our marriage as volunteers in an orphanage in the Andean foothills in a city named Cochabamba. We were about to depart on a work project in apartheid South Africa when a set of magical events occurred, which led us to adopt a little girl from the orphanage—the one who was more interested in organizing crayons than coloring with them. When we returned from South Africa to finish our adoption, we would have to bribe a judge with a sixty-dollar gold ring in order to set the court date for our adoption of five-year-old Elizabeth. By then, Lynn was thirty-two and I was thirty-four. It was April 1992.

Three years later, well-resettled in San Francisco, we adopted another one of the children who'd been part of our year in Bolivia, a seven-year-old named Miguel. During the weeks after his arrival in the US, you could always tell when he'd entered a room because the lights would go on and off like a theater call for the end of intermission. He was fascinated by the wide variety of US light switches. His various unsupervised science experiments also included testing the effects of an electric curling iron on a plastic shower curtain and taking apart his desk in his first-grade classroom.

It was through experiences like these that we were introduced to parenthood: the antics of young children rather than the sleep patterns and dirty diapers of an infant. Our joys as parents were such that as Elizabeth and Miguel hit middle school and were no longer tiny but preteens, we knew we wanted to do it all one more time, but this time with a baby. We wanted to do it once from day one, disrupted sleep and dirty diapers included.

As with many other couples, we spent a few years in our late thirties counting the months that went by with no pregnancy, in spite of our best efforts. We also knew we didn't want to raise our third and last child in the race against clock and calendar that seemed unavoidable in the US. My life as a father was marked by afternoon-upon-afternoon of missing the Muni train that would get me to after-school pickup on time. We were both tired of seeing our children for only a few hours in the evenings in between weekends.

In October 1998, we moved back to Cochabamba for what was supposed to be a year. I wrote a book about our lives there, *My Other Country: Nineteen Years in Bolivia*, and as the title implies, we stayed not one but nineteen years.

In Bolivia, our efforts at pregnancy continued with no success. We discovered that a doctor in Cochabamba was very adept at the procedure known as IVF, and we gave it a try twice. (Because Cochabamba is a small place, this meant that the nurse who took my sperm sample both times was also another parent in my son's sixth grade class. I could have done without that.) But our efforts at IVF failed, and we moved quickly to Plan B: adoption.

We were luckier than other couples in this regard. First, we never faced the prospect of being childless—we had two children, whom we loved. Second, adoption was not some sort of scary prospect or one we disagreed on; we'd done it twice. And so as Lynn approached her forty-third birthday and me my forty-fifth, we once again dived into the tricky landscape of Bolivian adoption.

We filed our request with the court, asking for a baby this time, a girl. We were quizzed by a Bolivian government psychologist in her early twenties, unmarried and with braces, about whether we were truly capable of being parents. We were tempted to explain that if you are raising two teenagers at the same time and have not gone out of your mind, that makes you qualified.

Then we waited. We waited nearly nine months, the normal human gestation period, for the legal gestation period to run its course. There was certainly no shortage of abandoned babies who needed to be adopted in Cochabamba. The local orphanage, where our older children had also begun their lives, was overflowing. But the government just never got to the paperwork required to make them adoptable, and instead they languished in an institution.

Then, on a cold Bolivian winter morning in July, the judge finally called us into her court to announce that she'd matched us with a baby and that we could meet her that same day. In the long reading of her official file, she was fourteen months old and had been abandoned at just a few weeks old by a young mother who'd left her with a fruit seller in the market and never returned. This was not an unusual thing for desperate, single teenage mothers in Bolivia.

During our anxious ride to the orphanage, a miracle happened (or perhaps it was just bad typing), and the baby girl suddenly became just eight months old upon our arrival. We waited, all four of us, in a small room set aside for just these epic first encounters of baby and family. Lynn and I had a million thoughts racing through our heads as we waited for the first glimpse of our child-to-be, not the least of which were about how our teenage son and daughter would react to a baby who was a stranger.

The orphanage staff brought her in wearing a new pink dress and a tiny bow in her black hair and handed her to Lynn. Her small hands and dark eyes focused on one of the oversized buttons on her new mother's purple sweater. We took turns holding her and took her for a walk around the small playground, where toddlers battled for time on the swings. Elizabeth and Miguel were in from the first moment.

After about ninety minutes of this, we were gently nudged to return her to the orphanage's baby room, where thirty-five babies shared thirty-two cribs lined from end to end. We left her with our first gift to her: a small stuffed bear with a rattle in its stomach.

For the next week, we were allowed to come and see her every day to feed her, change her diaper, bathe her, and be observed by the same young psychologist with the braces, which was how Bolivian authorities checked to determine if we were up to the job. Apparently they determined we were, and after a second visit to the courtroom and some more reading-aloud of papers, we were officially entrusted to take her home. We named her Mariana, reclaiming the name that had been my grandmother's as a girl until officials at Ellis Island decided that Mary was more suitable in America in 1906.

Our two dogs, a mother-and-daughter pair of black Labs named Simone and Little Bear, were deeply curious about this small new human we'd brought home. They were patient as she made the happy discovery that her tiny fingers precisely matched the holes in their cool black noses. Later, they worked out an arrangement between them that involved Mariana getting her face licked in exchange for tossing food onto the floor. This was the start of an unending love affair between a small girl and animals, which has led to her dream as a teenager of one day becoming a veterinarian.

As older parents, we've had certain experiences that other parents don't get to have. For example, when we took Elizabeth on a tour of US colleges during her junior year of high school, we were the only family also pushing a baby stroller. We also had a very long run—more than twenty years' worth—of putting out cookies and milk for Santa.

When your child becomes a teenager, whether you admit it to yourself or not, you begin a long process of saying goodbye to them. (A wise friend of mine once told me that adolescents are actually programmed to help you through this process by becoming less pleasant to be around.) Nonetheless, it becomes very difficult to not have thoughts like, *Oh my gosh, in two years she'll be off on her own.* Looking ahead again at an open runway of seventeen more years of hide-and-seek, birthday parties, learning to read, Christmas mornings, first ride on a bike, and all the other moments to come—that gave us great joy.

And the reality of it has given us great joy as well. It is almost a truism that in a later round of parenting, we learn to take it in more fully, to be less nervous and more appreciative of each moment. All of that has been true. Mariana and I invented a game called "bus running" when she was three, which was what we yelled out in the mornings as we raced, laughing, to catch the dilapidated mini-bus that took us down the hill to her preschool. We learned to stop—even at the expense of being late—to carefully study the giant mound of ants that lived along our run there. Sometimes we brought them food. Later, when we moved to the countryside and her kindergarten was a beautiful and blessed ten-minute walk down a tree-covered dirt road, we always made time to climb the adobe wall that looked like a dragon and for her to pick a purple wildflower to take to her teacher. The older you get, the more you appreciate that things end, including childhood, and so you sacrifice haste and punctuality to squeeze it for its sweet juices. If you're smart, that is.

Yes, I spent the last decade surrounded by friends who are in their fifties and liberated of their children as a day-to-day responsibility, and I have watched them travel or take up new hobbies or post a multitude of Facebook photos of a life of new freedom. And I envy them not at all. I was deeply happy that my sixtieth birthday coincided with Mariana starting high school. I am deeply grateful to still be "doing" the parenting thing.

Am I less physically energetic at sixty-one than I was at forty-five, when my older children were the age my youngest is now? Sure. I have not once given her a bloody nose in a ferocious game of one-on-one basketball, as happened on more than one occasion in my first time around as a parent. Yes, maybe we instead spent more time sitting together, eating breakfast on our Bolivian front porch as she commanded, "Tell me a story about Elly and Miguel when they were little." She grew up aware that her family had had another time before her, a time when the other kids had their turn being small, and she wanted to assemble the details in her head.

I think there is a deeper sweetness to the experience of older parenting, not because the child is different but because *you* are different. I spent all my years as the father of young children as a weekly volunteer in their classrooms in two different countries. To celebrate the birthday of Mariana's fourth grade teacher, a very patient woman, I stood atop a desk and read *Green Eggs and Ham* aloud in a variety of accents—Russian, Indian, Brooklyn. In the middle of it, Mariana blurted out, "Do it in the language Maddy speaks!" referring to a coworker of mine from the UK, who spoke in English but with a thick posh accent. Why on Earth would I have ever traded in such a moment for the alternative joy of taking up golf or learning to paint with watercolors? I got to stand on a desk in my daughter's class and thrill her by reading in the voice of a Spice Girl, "Would you eat them with a goat? Would you eat them on a boat?"

In Bolivia, there is a slang phrase—*la llapa*—which refers to that extra tomato or apple or banana the woman selling produce in the market might give you as a small bonus after buying from her. Now our little "llapa" is sixteen going on seventeen, just like in that song in *The Sound of Music*, and I am bracing myself for the third goodbye, the one that will leave us, finally, as "empty nesters."

But then the fates rescued us once more. On the eve of my sixtieth birthday, our daughter Elizabeth—the girl who once organized crayons in a Bolivian orphanage—gave birth to our first grandchild, a spunky little girl named Isabella Rose. Lynn, Mariana, and I came to the US for what was supposed to be six months for the birth and the beginning, with the plan to return once again to Bolivia. Instead, we stayed. We transplanted ourselves to the unlikely small town of Lockport, New York, which sits astride the Erie Canal, so close to the border that you can almost see Canada from your house.

Once again, the long runway is open with years ahead of birthday madness, watching the movement of bugs, discovering new flavors of ice cream, and reading Dr. Seuss in strange accents. Life without a small child in its midst? I can't imagine it. I don't want to—and I don't have to, because now I will do it as "Gapa."

I didn't wait a long time to have children; it took a long time to have children.

States of Mind
JUDITH UGELOW BLAK

I became a mom for the first time at forty-eight, the second time at fifty. "Why'd you wait so long?" nobody who knew me asked. For my family and circle of friends, the answer was obvious. My relationships had never been longer than three months—that is, other than the one-year relationship I had with Jimmy in my twenties. No, the focus had always been on the husband. Always the husband. That was my mother's take and secretly, my worry. My friends saw too many of my very long string of unrequited, turbulent, long-distance love affairs to even wonder when I would get around to children. And the men I'd been involved with . . . well, I don't think even one of them ever considered me the future mother of their children, but let's not go there.

I am embarrassed to admit I hadn't been superconscious about birth control. I never lied about it; the men (and I think I can say definitively didn't supply their own condoms) never asked. Not an admirable quality on my part (nor theirs), but that came out of the hippie, pre-AIDS era I matured in. Nonetheless, no pregnancies. So, at thirty-eight, feeling my biological clock ticking away, I panicked and decided to switch strategies: child first, husband/boyfriend/whoever later—if ever.

At thirty-eight, I was no longer in Manhattan, where I'd lived alone for thirteen years. I'd moved to a shared, family-oriented house in Aarhus, Denmark. I belonged to a diverse, intimate community created during the three previous years, when Dane after Dane came for vacation stays in my New York apartment. I housed musicians, social workers, teachers, nurses, activists, and newspaper reporters. I wound up knowing the color toothbrush of more people from Aarhus than that of all my friends in the country, making it easier to move to Aarhus than any other city in the US.

In Denmark, biological clock still ticking away, I talked options over with my Danish girlfriends—options I don't think would've been so easily talked about with my girlfriends in the US. There was the get-drunk-in-town-and-pick-up-a-guy-and-get-him-into-bed option. There was the rent-a-lover-for-a-night option, though I'm not sure the pregnancy part would've come with the deal. There was the artificial insemination option. There was the adoption option, but in Denmark, the process was protracted and didn't favor single parents. And there was the ask-a-male-friend-to impregnate-me option.

My friends convinced me the last option was optimal, since I could theoretically pick someone whom I could be happy with as a father if he wanted to be a father. I had to search, but I found a man I knew slightly who came with good references and was willing to father my child. His ex-wife—and this could only happen in Denmark—convinced him to take on the role because it would give their two preteen daughters another sibling. Ironically, he and I wound up falling in love, getting married, and, over eight years and with every conceivable aid—past-life regressions, no-coffee/no-alcohol vitamin therapy and diets, reflexology, counseling, acupuncture, visualization, meditation, quitting the job, artificial insemination, and then two types of IVF—failed to conceive a child. We were told my eggs were too old.

From the start, my husband categorically dismissed adoption as an option. By 1996, he dismissed it even more because Denmark limited the age difference for adoption between parent and child to forty years. I was forty-four years old, which would make the youngest child we could adopt four years old. That was a no-go for my husband, and I suppose it would also have been for me, had he not been so opposed to it. It didn't matter anyway, for I was done focusing on me. I was tired of watching the calendar and the time, tired of the disappointment each time the pregnancy stick failed to show more than one line, tired of trying so hard. I just wanted to drop all this and move on.

In 1998, I found a two-month self-development program in the US called *Living the Dream* and thought this would help me find a new dream to replace my lost motherhood one. With forty others looking for greater connection and meaning, I dug into issues of love, marriage, money, children, and work. This didn't lead to too much healing, but I had a fun time trying. I got the *Boss from Hell* award, learned how to "moon," flirted with homosexuality, went for moonlit walks in the mountains, dared to get angry, learned how to tolerate people I couldn't otherwise tolerate, and basically hung out with a completely different crowd than I was used to.

Ironically, though, this led me back to children. My new dream was to help families with children with autism set up home-based programs. My husband, in the meantime, had softened on the adoption option. That didn't matter; I was now beyond that. So we moved to the US, where I trained as a child facilitator—someone who could model for parents how they could join, build relationships with, and teach their children. Among the skills I had to learn was falling in love with a child upon meeting.

Over the course of almost two years, I fell in love and said goodbye to more than one hundred children. At some point, that sense of enrichment got replaced by loss. I started again to want my own child. I wondered how I would feel waking up at seventy without children.

I once again called on my Danish girlfriends, my go-to advisers, who were now parents and grandparents of teenagers. With a social work background, they seemed relatively free of social constraints to help me explore the challenges of parenting at my age. They questioned whether I understood what lifestyle changes this would mean. I replied, "Of course I do," with that conviction we have when we don't know what we don't know. After all, I had done my share of travelling to Brazil, Pakistan, Israel, and Mexico; I had gotten the travel bug out of my system. I had done my share of staying up all night and sleeping wherever the night found me. I was ready for a change. They knew I didn't know what I was getting into, but the disconnect between their experience and my naïveté couldn't be bridged. At the end of our discussions, I was sure motherhood was my next chapter.

So, my husband and I acted, and it went fast—whirlwind fast. Eight months later, we'd adopted our first son; he was five days old. Two and a half years later, we adopted our second son; he was nine days old. At fifty-three and fifty, my husband and I had two beautiful, bouncing boys: Clint at two and a half years and Thor at six months.

As warned, life changed more dramatically than I'd anticipated. I was exhausted from not sleeping and being "on" constantly. I was smelly from having too few showers. I was hungry because the boys got fed first, and then something else had to be attended to, and I would forget to eat. I no longer did yoga. Everything became about the boys.

That included nursing the boys. I had read in *Mothering* magazine that a child's suckle could produce the prolactin hormone needed to produce milk. That was back in 2000, when not so much information was available. Since I was a fan of attachment parenting, I decided this was for me. But it didn't work. I was told it was likely because of my age and that I hadn't previously borne a child. That didn't stop me, though. I found an apparatus for mothers having a hard time bringing their milk in—a pouch that contained the milk and had a thin tube that got threaded over the nipple. When the baby latched on, the milk came from the bag, not the breast. The baby didn't know the difference.

I did this in public. I got stared at, and now I'm guessing it could've been for any number of reasons: I was doing this in public with no regard for whether this was allowed or not, I had this strange little plastic bag of milk hanging from under my shirt between my breasts with a tube running over my breast, and I might have seemed unusually old to be nursing an infant. Who knows what was going on in others' minds? I laugh now, thinking about how provocative this must have been. I remember already feeling too old then to care what other people thought about it.

Otherwise, age didn't seem a factor at the start. I was in love with my boys. Like any honeymoon period I had ever experienced, nothing fazed me. Floating on a cloud, I could conquer all. In fact, the challenges at the start related more to our different skin colors: their dad's and mine, white; the boys', Black. Everywhere I went, and it seemed like *everywhere*, strangers felt compelled to ask about the boys. "Where did they come from?" "Where were they born?" These were tiring questions that constantly reminded me we weren't an ordinary family, unnerving questions that reminded my boys (who were soon old enough to realize these questions weren't asked of other families) that we weren't an ordinary family.

I became disdainful and fearful of public spaces. I wanted to protect my boys from different treatment. "Not ordinary" was fine; that strangers should be our constant reminder was not. My anger compelled me to script an answer like, "In the hospital, stupid." In my less reactive moments, I wished for the courage to ask in return where their children had been born or where their children had come from. But cleverness wasn't the answer to this dilemma— it wouldn't stop the onslaught of questions. Here was where my age didn't serve me better. This was a new domain for me, and I was clueless. My strategy was to prepare the best I could with my practiced responses.

I thought I was prepared when an older woman in the checkout line at the local Price Chopper turned to look at me pushing the wagon with two-year-old Thor, dressed only in a diaper and sitting in the child seat. I was ready with my new I'll-show-you answer. Then it came: "How old is your granddaughter?"

Well, I was beyond flustered—so flustered that I replied, "He's my grandson. I mean, I mean—" That was the first verbal reference to my age since becoming a family. I didn't feel old, nor did I really look or act old, I thought. But obviously, someone—this woman—saw me as old or older.

All these questions made me even more conscious of wanting to surround myself with diversity in general: if not other families with a mix of colors specifically, perhaps one that embraced atypical family constructions, like two dads or two moms. Why not? I suggested moving to a more diverse community like West Medford, a town not far from my sister in Massachusetts. My husband felt less compelled than I did to do something about it; I think not growing up in the US affected how he saw race as something divisive. The upshot was, we did nothing. Even after we separated in 2005, when my husband moved back to Denmark when the boys were five and two, I didn't have the courage to do this on my own. I thought myself selfish and cowardly, but also just too old to start over.

Though the boys had many friends in school, making play-dates was a little more challenging—not because the community was driven by a black-white divide. No, the challenge came from younger mothers who seemed to want to hang out with other younger mothers. I didn't blame them. Me being in my fifties and them in their twenties and thirties meant our world views were different. I had grown up in the hippie era with Vietnam War protests and Kent State student killings; SDS and the Black Panthers;

Gloria Steinem and Simone de Beauvoir; the assassinations of the two Kennedys, Dr. King, and Malcolm X; the abduction of Patty Hearst; and the typewriter and rotary telephone, while these mothers seemed so much less naïve and inner-focused. Age and differing world views seemed a good enough reason to stay separate, but it didn't benefit the boys, and I was lonely, and now I was on my own.

Since my focus was my boys, I worked hard to become part of the "group" and had to keep working hard to stay a part. This meant ignoring parts of me so I could feel and act more like someone born in the seventies, born post-protest and feminist era—which made me feel even lonelier. But if a successful community for the boys meant being a mom who fit in, I did what I needed to do and feigned interest, which wasn't entirely put-on. In time, some of my relationships with these younger mothers deepened and became mutually meaningful friendships for which I was grateful. Age disappeared as a limiting agent.

At times, the parenting tasks were divvied up according to our differing capabilities, like the time my friends Heidi, Annie, and I took the kids swimming. That is, Heidi and Annie took our three older ones swimming, while I minded the three younger ones still in strollers. Heidi and Annie played like dolphins in the pool while I lullabied the younger ones to sleep, one by one. My "grandmother" role suited me fine—I was good at it and relieved not to be in the pool.

In 2009, the boys and I moved to Denmark to be closer to their dad. The boys were eight and six, and I couldn't really parent them on my own. My community in the US had been nice but simply not strong enough to give me the support I needed.

In Denmark, the challenges with younger mothers followed, but there was a greater tradition for community parenting: my boys often ate dinner and slept at friends' homes, even on school nights. That community, together with a loving commitment

from my ex's family, who babysat and took the boys on outings and for weekends, gave me the reprieve I was looking for.
Besides, my community of Danish friends was still intact, and that
delighted me.

Today, at sixty-six, I no longer feel spunky, no longer look
young. I have lost that is-she-or-is-she-not-older look. That is my
take on me. I belly-laugh (and celebrate) when sixteen-year-old
Thor says his friends think I am in my forties. "You keep yourself
young," he says, to which I send him a kiss. I am grateful, though,
that I no longer have to keep pace with the young mothers. I
am grateful for being able to retire from that club and rejoin my
older girlfriends, whose children grew up a while ago. Don't get
me wrong—my new girlfriends and I have created a history that
is bound by our children. I need not diminish those friendships
in the process of rejoining my generation.

So how old *is* too old? It depends on who you ask: the state,
the community, the children, me. It wasn't my intention to be an
older mom. I didn't wait a long time to have children; it *took* a
long time to have children. The journey I've described wasn't the
dream I started with, nor was it the path I envisioned along the
way. I've garnered a sensitivity to age, color, diversity, family construction, childless families, parenting styles, and to the impact
of the question.

My younger mother-friends remind me time and time again
that age is a fluid concept. Without exception, they counter my
complaints of how tired I am from all the mothering with the reply,
"I know what you mean." Youth doesn't protect even those younger
mothers from the "senior moments" of forgetfulness, fatigue, or
disappointment, and neither does youth own the rights to the pure
bliss of motherhood. The tiredness I feel, though, cannot really
be compared with the tiredness a younger mother experiences,
as much as she might think it's the same. In a time when friends
my age are intentionally or unintentionally slowing down, I don't

get that choice. That's not me—not yet. Though I feel like I am hitting the wall in the marathon, I must keep going; I still have a duty and will spend much of my retired life still mothering. I am not complaining here. This was my choice at forty-eight, and at sixty-six, I still like it.

Because every mom who gave birth has a bloody birth story to tell, and damn it, she's going to tell it.

25% Pure Gold
BARBARA HEREL

I became a first-time mom at the age of forty-five by way of domestic adoption. I am now fifty-five years old with a ten-year-old. I find there is a lot of common ground between me and the thirty-five-year-old mom with a ten-year-old. We both stay up at night, worrying about the same things: the bully on the bus, whether or not a month without gum is too harsh of a punishment, and will my kid grow up to be a productive, compassionate member of the human race or the kind of person who takes up two parking spaces. Things like that. Aside from the audible crack of my knees as I bend on the playground, or the flush of a full-on, full-bodied hot flash, I don't feel any older than she does. Turns out, we're both wonderfully, equally forgetful about names, appointments, and why we walked all the way downstairs only to walk upstairs again to remember why we walked downstairs in the first place.

Helpful hint: just grab toilet paper.

Not to say that I've found motherhood to be "timeless," that there are no differences in coming to motherhood later in life. It's a fair bet that most fifty-five-year-old women do not have kids going to summer camp. The moms my age, the ones I went to college with during the Reagan administration, are now planning their children's weddings or becoming grandmas, and I can't help but feel out of step with them. The college gals are planning another one of their out-of-town trips, which always sounds all sorts of me-time-wonderful, yet doesn't exactly work for me as the Keeper of the Ten-Year-Old Schedule. But it's more than that. This particular parenting time, where my daughter likes me for the most part and, at the very least, eventually listens to what I say, will be fleeting. A long weekend is just too long a time away from her and my husband. Let's face it: if I'm going on a trip sans child, it's going to be with him. Our couple time has consisted of short-lived encounters and platonic embraces ever since we became parents. I know my girlfriends know all this because they've already experienced it. Still, feeling out of sync and missing out on connecting with women with whom I have a shared history doesn't feel all that good.

The big difference fitting in with the thirty-five-year-old moms is that I didn't give birth to my child. My husband and I turned to adoption in my early forties when my ovum began clamoring, "We're tired and cranky and not reproducing anymore—let's play bingo." Now, at fifty-five, there's not a peep out of them; a clear case of one-and-done. But my younger-mom friends, who are sporting plump, lustrous eggs that are screaming wildly to get this party started *again*, are talking about having child number two or three, so it's back to those bloody birth stories all the time. Because every mom who gave birth has a bloody birth story to tell, and damn it, she's going to tell it.

I don't begrudge any mother their hard-won battle. However, as a mom who actually wasn't a mom at the time of my daughter's birth—merely a hopeful one doing my best to balance feelings of detachment and excitement as I waited in the hospital lounge while her actual mom was giving birth—these no-holds-barred birthing conversations always make me feel like an outsider. And woozy.

I distinctly recall sitting in a circle on the library floor with fellow members of the New Moms Group, now new friends thanks to our shared new-mom status, our little cherubs tucked between our legs, anxiously awaiting our turn to introduce ourselves and our "cutie pie" or "sweet boy" to each other. I felt my otherness swiftly and deeply, as new-mom friend after new-mom friend recounted the birth of their little peanut from the first contraction to the gelatinous afterbirth. When it came to my turn, I tentatively held up our homemade adoption-profile book and overenthusiastically and nervously rambled on, saying things like, "Our daughter's birth mom loved our adoption book. I was afraid she would think we were too old, hahaha, I'm forty-five and my husband's forty-seven, but she just felt like we were 'the ones.' We were there for our daughter's birth—not in the room, mind you, hahaha, but in the waiting room, and we love her, our daughter's birth mom—oh and our baby, too, of course, hahaha. We talk and share pictures and we make plans to go back and see her . . . yeah, so that's us."

I sat silently out of sorts, foolishly convincing myself that it wouldn't always be like this. That these mom conversations would evolve as our babies grew. That soon we'd all be laser-focused on potty training, relentlessly regaling in tales of near misses and outright urinary disasters. But no. Be forewarned that labor and delivery stories are forever for the telling, especially when Mom is trying for baby number two. Happily, on the non-bloodied side of things, the library is also where I found moms just like me— adoptive and older. I always thought I'd have to consciously seek out my compadres, but I've come to learn that we adoptive and older parents are everywhere. In fact, there are two adoptive families with two older moms right in my own neighborhood, no special effort required.

Bloody births aside, I only ever envisioned myself with one child, but my husband always thought he'd have at least two kids.

I'll admit that when our daughter began begging for a baby brother or sister (I was about fifty at the time), it did make me falter. But all I needed to do was a quick calculation to quickly put things into perspective. Being in my fifties with a newborn or young child? The truth is, when you're an older parent at the get-go, you only keep getting older.

Just how long do I have? I'm fifty-five; my husband is fifty-seven. My parents are eighty and in good health, yet have experienced health issues over the last few years that are now noticeable, giving me more than a glimpse of new aging realities for them and possibilities for me. Thankfully, they live close by and have been—and continue to be—active, doting grandparents. But nagging speculations do crop up. In twenty-five years, will I be a doting grandparent, or will I be dead? Or, maybe even worse, will I be a burden to my thirty-five-year-old daughter? These thoughts don't come to mind when you're trying to conceive or adopt. You're in the "I want a baby!" stage and you're consumed with this longing, just like any other wannabe mom or dad.

IT'S ONLY AFTERWARD that these questions arise—when you become a parent, when you're madly in love with your baby, when you're whispering solemn pledges during the 3 a.m. feeding to always keep her safe from pain and harm. When you know that there is so much pain- and harm-inducing stuff out there that's out of your control. This is when it first dawns on you that you might not be around for as long as you need to be.

Damn.

There is no other choice for me but to embrace my parenting journey as a card-carrying AARP member—which offers lots of good family fun discounts, by the way—as a mom in menopause with a daughter who's not yet in puberty, yet is highly aware of tampon commercials and often exclaims, "That's not happening to me!" So while she and I won't be arguing over who took the last tampon, I have no doubt that between us, we'll have enough synced-up hormonal upheaval to keep things lively.

Listen, no matter how old you are, parenting is hard. Ninety— no, 80; no, maybe now 75—percent of the time, parenting is hands-down pure torture. The mistakes you make, the self-doubts that follow, the monotonous daily grind, the other parents. . . . But the other 25 percent?

Pure. Gold.

There is nothing I'd rather be doing in my sixties than planning my girl's sweet sixteen party, visiting college campuses, or exploring new countries with her. I'm keen on seeing what will "stick" as she gets older—tae kwon do, tennis, golf, something else? And I must say, I heartily look forward to discovering all the many ways I will no doubt unintentionally and intentionally embarrass her. In fact, this is what keeps me vibrant: watching life unfold through my daughter's eyes and keeping that feeling of pure gold going. Being a parent is the best-kept secret for staying vital.

*The problem was that
our son did need help that
the intervention team could
not process.*

Too Old for Cartwheels: Reflections from an At-Risk Family

JULIE BUCKNER ARMSTRONG

The parenting class painted a beautifully inclusive picture. *If you adopt a biracial baby*, the social worker said, *then you become a biracial family. If your teen comes out, then your family becomes LGBTQ.* My partner and I committed fully to this rainbow vision. Our application to adopt a Florida foster-care child stated that age, gender, orientation, and race mattered less to us than the ability to bond. We were over forty (my partner forty-five, myself forty-eight), college professors, economically and emotionally stable. We wanted to give a child who would not typically have such opportunities a good home, a college education, and a chance to travel the world.

Ten years later, our rainbow vision sometimes seems more like rose-colored glasses. We did not consider that adopting an at-risk child would make us an at-risk family.

Because we were later to parenting than our peers, my partner and I thought adopting an older child would help us "catch up." We wouldn't look like our new child's grandparents. Better yet, we could skip the diaper phase! Our child would arrive continent, conversational, and sleeping through the night. The eight-year-old we eventually adopted did indeed bring those qualities—along with big brown eyes; tousled blond hair; an open smile; gifted intelligence; a voracious desire for attention; a nonstop potty mouth; ADHD; PTSD; and a habit of breaking furniture, walls, and windows. We soon figured out that traveling the world would not meet our new son's needs. Instead, we learned to navigate the social workers, guardians ad litem, and Medicaid doctors of the welfare state.

Rather than mainstreaming with our peers, we found ourselves increasingly marginalized. Many of our child-free friends, happy with their carefully curated bungalows and cocktail hours, did not know how to accommodate our troubled boy. Neighbors called the police when his tantrums got too loud or called us, horrified, when he ran down the street in bare feet, yelling, frustrated over trying to learn to tie shoes at nine. We frightened the parenting set's normativity notions with what we call the "foster care taint." Playdates meant tactful invasions into our son's past: "Was he . . .?" friends and family asked, trailing into silence before uttering words such as *molested* or *abused*, which they dared not speak. Well-meaning teachers and counselors slipped us copies of Foster Cline and Jim Fay's *Parenting with Love and Logic*. Strangers gave us unsolicited and misguided advice on how to transform a child who came to us nearly feral into a bourgeois wunderkind. Any problems with our child surely must be our fault, those around us reasoned. After all, we were "older." We probably focused too much on work and didn't give our son the attention he needed. Conversely, because he was an only child we surely must have adopted in desperation, we doted on him, spoiling him rotten.

"Hogwash," said our colleague Mark Durand, a psychology professor and author of *Optimistic Parenting: Hope and Help for You and Your Challenging Child*. "Listen," he told me, "when any kid graduates from high school with no addiction, jail, or pregnancy issues, the parents should be turning cartwheels."

Optimism remained a challenge. In high school, our son slipped into an exclusive technology magnet program but quickly started a downward spiral of failing grades and daily tantrums. Near the holiday break, my partner and I found ourselves in the program's conference room, surrounded by a bevy of school staff for a mid-year intervention.

A harried-looking math teacher held up a paper filled with large circular scribbles that our son had submitted instead of homework. "Something is wrong with your child," she blurted out.

My partner and I exchanged knowing glances and nervous chuckles.

"This is *not* funny," the teacher barked. She slammed the paper to the table and crossed her arms.

Another teacher thought our son wasn't trying hard enough in school and needed tough love. He recommended a "tour of prison." He meant our son needed to go outside the magnet program's mostly affluent and white students to visit the school's mostly working-class and Black traditional program. The teacher's words shocked us, along with the blatant racism lying behind them. They also crystalized how the school-to-prison pipeline works: Students with resources get tracked toward future success. Those who struggle to stay on track, especially ones without economic means or vocal parents, get directed toward dead ends. Perceptions of those struggling students are made clear through the terms used to describe them. Most all schools in our county have special magnet programs. Students not enrolled in them are called "gen pop," or *general population.* The term comes from the prison system, referring to regular inmates that don't require special treatment or additional punishment.

The problem was that our son did need help that the intervention team could not process. How could a smart white kid from a stable home not be on the road to success?

The answer lies in seeing us as an at-risk family. In the high-pressure academic environment, adoption and ADHD created a toxic petri dish where our son's anxiety and meltdowns thrived. He craved attention and approval; he gave teachers who praised him hugs and A-level work. For those who talked tough, he put up the protective walls he began constructing as a toddler to keep rejection and difficulty at bay.

But "at-risk" does not mean destined for failure. The intervention team didn't know the boy who carefully guided his elderly grandparents' wheelchairs through nursing home hallways. They didn't see the boy who, when we hiked the Grand Canyon, reached out to take my hand because he feared I might trip.

"You know, Mom," he told me. "You're kind of clumsy, but it's okay. I'll keep you safe."

Ultimately, we chose our colleague's optimism prescription. We had faith that this boy would grow up to be a fine young man, no matter what happened in school. So we did what at-risk families do: we put our son in gen pop.

Technically, he chose it. We gave him options: try to stick out the magnet, enter traditional high school, or go to private school.

"I'm a Spartan," he said, referring to his school mascot, "and I want to be in regular school."

OUR DECISION SHOCKED the parenting set and the magnet teachers. *How would he ever get into a good college*, they wondered, as if that was the only available and rational life path. It turned out that the gen pop side of the school had the right playbook to help a troubled teen navigate the system.

We have now reached our son's senior year. He's scheduled to graduate and has a part-time job he enjoys. He stays away from drugs and alcohol, and he has never been in any real trouble at school. We still struggle with the potty mouth, the angry outbursts, and the ever-broken house—but our home remains intact.

I told our son about my plan for May, when he walks across the stage to get his diploma.

"Mom, please don't attempt a cartwheel." He patted my arm tenderly. "You're way too old."

I knew there were two paths after her death: one led to bitterness and despair; the other toward healing.

From Grief to Joy
VICKI BREITBART

They say the death of a child is the greatest loss by far. They're right. I have lost parents, grandparents, and other family members, but the loss of my daughter was by far the most painful. *Disastrous, crushing, overwhelming*—these words can hardly describe it. When you lose a parent or grandparent, you mourn the past. When you lose a child, you grieve for the future that will not be.

I lost my twenty-four-year-old daughter Lela in 1995, the same year my father died. Her death was very sudden and unexpected. Of course, I thought she was special; I knew no one like her. She had enormous potential but was an amazing person at almost any age. I remember everyone remarking on how much "presence" she had at all her dance recitals.

We had a deep connection, so much so that when she was in college, she became a family-planning counselor and went on to work in a reproductive health center after college. I had been working on women's issues for years, specifically reproductive health. She was working in an abortion clinic as a counselor when she decided to take off on a cross-country trip with a college friend to figure out her future. She knew reproductive health was the field she wanted but wasn't clear as to the role she wanted to play. Her cross-country trip would be a time to think about what work she wanted to do and what graduate program, if any, she would pursue. This trip would be her time to explore and think about her possibilities.

It had been a very wet summer; when she and her friend arrived at Glacier National Park, it finally had stopped raining after several days of bad weather. She was hiking on one of the most scenic trails in the park when she stopped for a break and was struck unconscious in a rock avalanche. Her friend later told me how difficult it was to watch park attendants trying to resuscitate her for a long time before they declared her dead. Her death is listed in *Death & Survival in Glacier National Park: True Tales of Tragedy, Courage, and Misadventure*, a book about tragedies in the park; she was only one of ten who had died this way in over a hundred years of recorded history. For me, it was unimaginable. My grief was devastating.

I knew there were two paths after her death: one led to bitterness and despair; the other toward healing. I chose the latter. I quickly became immersed in several efforts to heal from the trauma. I set up a fund in her name dedicated to making grants for young women doing important reproductive health work. I quit my research job and began to work more directly with women again. I went to work in a reproductive health center, much like the one where she'd held her last job.

Soon after Lela's death, I went to a fundraiser given by a woman working on climate change. She mentioned that she'd lost her son and talked about how adopting a child had helped her to heal. The lecture was about climate change, but all I heard about was her trip to Costa Rica with her son she'd adopted after an earlier child's death. This made perfect sense to me. My quest began.

I remember when I expressed the idea of adoption for this first time. I was fifty-three. It had been over a year since my daughter died. I was at dinner with my husband, Dan, and two of my lifelong friends. They'd all been there the night I learned of my daughter Lela's death. When the conversation came around to how I was doing, I told them I wanted to adopt. I had mentioned it before to my husband, who had responded cautiously. My friends indulged what they imagined was my fantasy and politely smiled at the thought. I was the only one who took it seriously.

I soon learned of the many hurdles involved in adoption. First were the questions about my motivations. Was I looking at an adoption to deny my loss? Was it a way to bury my grief? As an educated, early childhood specialist and psychotherapist, I carefully looked at my reasons for wanting to adopt. As a parent, I'd learned to treat my son and daughter as distinct individuals, not to compare them to each other or to my image of what a child should be, based on my own past or dreams for the future. Both Lela and her brother, Josh, had taught me I could never make a child a reflection of my own unrealized self. It's impossible, and I shouldn't even try. I believed the words of the Sweet Honey In The Rock song, "On Children:" *You can strive to be like them / but you cannot make them just like you.* I expected to learn to love my adopted child in this same way. This would be my promise to Lela: I was not starting over. I was starting a new beginning.

Many of the questions about adoption dealt with my age. *Was I too old to adopt? Could I handle an infant? Was it fair to a child to have old parents?* My son, Josh, was the most honest and up-front with his reservations and questions about my taking on this responsibility. He asked for a three-way meeting with him, my oldest friend (who also happens to be a psychotherapist), and me. He was concerned about what the adoption would mean for him, our relationship, and what it would mean for me. He was very challenging, and my friend helped me listen to all his piercing questions.

In the discussion, we talked very frankly about future possibilities. Was he really ready to be an older brother or a caregiver if something were to happen to me? If anything should happen to me, he would not be the only person to raise his new sibling.

We also had his stepfather; my sister, who was living close by; and several family members and friends. He would not be alone.

Was he concerned about how adopting a sibling would affect his relationship with me? Yes, it would change our connection, but it didn't come from any lack in our relationship. My love for him would never be lessened by a sibling, as it had not been lessened because of Lela. Josh's questions came from a very compassionate and caring place. Would I have the energy it would take? Did I have the resources? Would I have the support I needed? He helped me remember that his dad and I hadn't figured everything out before we had his sister and him.

No, you figure it out as you go.

I never wanted to adopt because my son wasn't enough. I wanted to adopt because he was everything. In fact, I realized that parenting him and his sister was and is literally at the heart of who I am. I love parenting; watching an individual evolve into their true self is the most exciting, creative activity I can imagine; it's the most important, hopeful, and successful thing I have ever done. When I raised him and his sister, his dad and I had to find the resources and support to make it work—and my son agreed that it turned out really well. He helped me see that although it would be difficult, I had a lot of support in my life that could make it work.

Then there were questions about why I wanted to adopt a girl. This was never a question for me—from my first feeling about adopting, I wanted to adopt a girl. I had raised a magnificent son who clearly embodied the best of what a young man could be. So why a girl? I had worked so long, trying to ensure that girls could realize their own power, that I believed I had a lot to offer a girl. Seeing a young girl become an independent, loving, powerful person was a significant part of the future I'd lost and the future I wanted to have.

Though I took all these questions very seriously, they never changed my feelings about wanting to adopt a girl at fifty-three. Nonetheless, while I thought I was going into the process with my eyes wide open, I was not prepared for the reality of the adoption process. I had worked with adoption agencies as a social worker in a hospital and had been involved with helping women who chose this option. I felt I could trust an organization that had adoption as their main area of work; I never thought of hiring a private lawyer. I had no idea how complicated this was going to be.

As almost all families who want to adopt, my husband and I were put through a rigorous interview process. We had to construct a book about our family, about the world in which this child would live. We met with other families to discuss the process. I remember our group included another heterosexual couple who'd had no previous children and a single woman planning to raise the child on her own. That was the only time we met those people. Our past experiences were very different, but they'd led us to the same place, with similar wants and dreams. I've always wondered how the process went for them.

The most rigorous part of the adoption process was the one-on-one interview, where our social worker grilled us for hours about our past to see if we were fit to raise an adopted child. Having lived half a century, there was a lot to discuss. When we said we wanted to adopt an infant, the agency social worker suggested we choose an international adoption. She raised additional questions about how prepared we were to raise a child from another culture and most likely of a different race. We assured the social worker we would be mindful of these very serious concerns, but I wish we had been better prepared for this. We attended a workshop about cross-racial, cross-cultural adoption, but we only learned the real significance of these issues over time.

The adoption process seemed endless, and we were kept busy with many of the details in the process. This included fingerprinting and having the FBI check into our history—because of my activism in the sixties, I had an FBI file. I had been arrested with Lela when she was two years old in a demonstration for expanding day care in New York City, so I had to retrieve the final decision in that case before we could proceed any further. I was scared this arrest and my activism, though nonviolent, would be reason enough for the adoption to be canceled. In the end, I wonder if the adoption could've proceeded if my case hadn't been reduced to a misdemeanor.

Once we were accepted by the agency, we had to wait until a child was born and available to be adopted. I knew someone who adopted a girl from China, but we were told that it was out of the question because of our age—my husband and I had the combined age of over one hundred, which was the cutoff for adoption from China. It took a while to find another country where our age wouldn't be an obstacle. We waited two years from the initial contact with the agency until I got a call from the social worker that they had found an infant boy from Bulgaria we could adopt.

Two years had gone by from our first encounter with the adoption agency, and I wasn't going to doom my chances for a child. Not what I had planned, but I didn't say no. I'll always wonder if this was some sort of test of my motivation to adopt, because the next day, the same social worker called to say a girl had been born in Guatemala. Was I interested? I immediately said yes.

I was fifty-five years old and my husband was fifty-three when we flew to Guatemala City to meet our daughter, who was already five months by the time we could visit. Every moment of this trip remains vivid to me, especially when I opened the door of my hotel room to see Olga, my daughter's foster care mother, holding a baby wearing a frilly, light-blue dress.

The first evening was my introduction into what it would be like to raise an infant at my age. The three of us spent a lovely day in the city. I remember being somewhat cautious walking an infant past the young soldiers who seemed to be on every corner with machine guns, but the day was wonderful.

We were exhausted when we got back to the hotel. From the moment we got to our room, our daughter started to cry without stopping. Having had children before, I tried every trick I knew, but it wasn't until I turned on the TV and she heard Ricky Martin singing "Livin' La Vida Loca" in Spanish that she stopped crying and was calm. After bathing her in the hotel sink, feeding her by bottle—though I had breastfed my other children—and putting her to bed that evening, I knew this would be challenging, but I never doubted our decision to adopt. I felt that that my age had given me the experience I would need to parent our daughter, whom we named Mya. I knew we were in store for many hurdles, but we felt prepared to love her unconditionally.

The adoption procedure in Guatemala takes several months to be finalized, so we had to leave Mya with her foster care mother, Olga, and return to New York. While we were in New York, Mya and her biological mother, whom I had not met, underwent tests to confirm they were actually mother and daughter and they were healthy enough for the adoption to go forward. In the few short days Mya and I spent together, we had developed a clear bond that would never waver. The months apart were agonizing. I left her a teething ring, which she still had when we went back several months later to bring her to New York for the final step in the adoption process.

Perhaps the most difficult thing about being an older parent has been confronting my own mortality; I didn't have to face this with my other children. My daughter Mya was less than two when I received a diagnosis of colon cancer. Catching it early and being able to get the best medical care in the world certainly helped; I had to stay positive and focused on getting better, but I'm sure it took a toll on my daughter. And then, when Mya was sixteen, I was in the hospital for a month after I was hit by a car as I was crossing the street. It was difficult for her to visit me in the hospital, but she has witnessed me survive and come home. She has seen what resilience looks like, though I'm sure it was a frightening experience.

These events weren't necessarily a function of my age, but they made me more aware of the shortened amount of time I will have with Mya, compared to what I will have with my son or what most younger mothers have with their children. I am sad that I may not get to spend much time, if any, with Mya's children—she has told me she might adopt—compared to Josh's children. I think Lela's death and my age may have made me more overprotective than I was with my first two children, but I also believe it has made me appreciate the time I do have so much more. I never cease to be grateful for the gift of parenting at this stage in my life.

Several years after my daughter Lela died, I planted a tree in Prospect Park in her memory. As many of my friends gathered around for the ceremony, I wanted to say something to those who'd had so many doubts about my motivation and decision to adopt after this traumatic event. I felt I needed to address their concerns about whether the adoption would mask my grief or diminish my love for my first daughter. A friend who was there recently reminded me what I said as we stood around the tree: "If Lela taught me anything, she taught me you could never bring enough love into the world."

My daughter Mya is twenty now and has evolved into her own amazing person. She and the daughter I lost are so different and exceptional in their own ways. I have talked with Mya about how being Latinx and adopted are part of her identity, but I'm not sure I will ever completely know how adopting her from Guatemala later in my life has affected the person she has become. I am sad when I think about how I will miss some of her life's milestones because of my age. Yet I also know that parenting her has given me some of the most meaningful and wonderful moments in my life. She is living proof that grief can be turned into joy.

As the thirteenth-century poet Rumi wrote, "Grief can be the garden of compassion. If you keep your heart open through everything, your pain can become your greatest ally in your life's search for love and wisdom."

If one person in a similar situation reads this and feels like they can step in and do the right thing, I'm here to say it's worth it.

Twins? Are You Crazy?

PAMELA PITMAN BROWN

June 2013 was chaotic even before we got the call from Mobile, Alabama, that my daughter, Layne, was in labor, two months before her due date. My husband, Wayne, and I were in the middle of moving from Missouri to my new teaching job in North Carolina, so we drove to Winston-Salem, quickly unloaded our U-Haul, and took off for the hospital in Mobile. As preemies, Ava and Audrey were in the NICU (neonatal intensive care unit), but we were able to see them.

We had been in Mobile a week when Layne's husband yelled at me to stay out of their business—I had suggested they clean their once-nice, now-filthy rental, which we were paying for—so we headed back to North Carolina and began preparing our new home. After three weeks, Ava was released from the NICU, but poor Audrey had to stay in the hospital for another month. The state of their home was one foreboding sign, but when Layne and her husband neglected to visit Audrey in the hospital even *once* during those seven weeks in the NICU, I was pretty shocked. I guess I knew they weren't going to be able to care for the twins then, but it would take two more years of nibbling at the edge of the problem before Wayne and I took decisive action.

Some background: my son JT was born in 1987, when I was twenty-four and married to my first husband. Four years later, we had Layne and we divorced the next year. We were amicable and shared custody, but my thirties were a special kind of hell, one reserved for single mothers in the Deep South. Life was just survival: in and out of relationships, struggling to raise two kids, feeling judged by everyone, including myself. I had a college degree, but I couldn't find a job better than contract work—car salesperson, waitress, bartender. I received very little child support because A) it's Alabama and B) it's Alabama.

I HAD VERY LITTLE support in general. One year, I made five dollars an hour. My take-home pay was one hundred and twenty dollars per week, but childcare was fifty dollars per week and health insurance another fifty a week. This was during "welfare reform," when you couldn't get state-subsidized healthcare if you owned a car. My parents wouldn't help, either, because, as Southern Baptists, it was a "sin" to be divorced.

I was struggling to survive and I was constantly told that I was to blame for my struggles. I had been raised in a comfortable middle-class home and there I was, in a one-bedroom in a crappy neighborhood with a crappy school district. My ex-husband was remarried and had a nice house in a good school district. JT was already with him, so in 2001, when Layne was ten, I called him and said, "Listen, when she comes to you for summer break, she's got to stay and live with you." For a long time, the kids really hated me for doing that, but I was desperate.

On a date soon after, I ran into a nice, attractive man I'd known for years, someone I'd set up with my friends in the past but assumed saw me as a dumpy failure. Brazenly, especially given I was out with someone else, I asked why he wouldn't date me. He replied that he hadn't known I was interested.

A few months later, Wayne and I eloped, and I started piecing my life together. My undergrad GPA was too low to get into graduate school, so I went back to undergrad with Pell Grants to attend the University of South Alabama, where I got a 4.0. By 2007, I was accepted to six PhD sociology programs with funding. I hadn't even known that I could be paid for getting an advanced degree. I clawed my way into a career in academia—sociology and gerontology—and I've been teaching since 2008.

FLASH FORWARD TO September 2013: once the twins were both out of the NICU and living with my daughter and her husband, I hired one of Layne's high school friends to help her clean the house. The friend called me later, horrified. There was cat and dog excrement on the girls' cribs and the carpets, roaches all over the house, and black mold in the tubs and toilets. The twins were rolling around this mess, hungry and crying. At the end of this litany, the friend said, "I smell drugs."

Until that point, I hadn't understood that my daughter, like so many people, was addicted to meth and opioids. My denial gave way to panic as I tried to care for Ava and Audrey by proxy. I sent diapers, clothes, laundry detergent, baby food—anything to help our daughter care for the twins with minimal effort. If I had a three-day weekend, Wayne and I would hop in the car and drive to Alabama to take the girls to a motel for baths, feeding, and love. Fortunately, Layne and her husband were always happy to hand over the responsibility.

My heart would sink at each handoff of the twins and a dirty diaper bag filled with too-small clothes. We routinely threw out what they were wearing and bought new clothing at Walmart, and even their little bodies felt grimy, like they'd gone weeks without a bath. They often sat for days in the same soiled diapers, causing painful skin rashes. Once, when they were about a year old, we discovered them with diaper rash and yeast infections so severe that we had to take them to the emergency room. The police and child welfare services were called in and we filed a report with both. We began documenting the neglect. On a work trip to Dallas, we met an old friend who worked as a child therapist and could evaluate how the girls were doing. She noted the twins were small for their age and behind on every developmental marker, from speech to eye contact to motor skills.

It was clear we had to get the girls out of that home before they could remember too much and before they wound up in the system. (I was adopted out of foster care as a baby, and I knew that my relatively positive experience was by no means the norm.) Wayne researched the process for obtaining custody, including what it would cost, and started gathering documents like their birth certificates, which we'd need for the first step: a grant of temporary custody.

In August 2015, when the twins were two years and two months old, I learned Layne and her husband were going to be evicted from the rental house. This was the moment to act: I called her and said that given the eviction, we should take care of the kids for a while. She agreed right away. I told her they needed to sign some paperwork so we could take the girls across state lines and scheduled a notary to meet us at their home on a Sunday afternoon. The notary was in the middle of explaining the documents to make sure they understood that they were signing over temporary custody when Layne's husband interrupted with a rude, "Are we done here?"

The notary paused, looked at the two of them, and said, "Yep. We're done."

As Wayne carried Ava out to the car, I saw her put her head on his shoulder, pat his back, and let out a huge sigh. Although she had never slept in the car before, she was out in less than five minutes. I think she felt safe. That night, as we bathed and dressed them for bed, I noticed Ava had a huge knot on her head and Audrey had a sort of rug burn, as if she had banged her head on the carpet. I didn't have a visceral reaction to these obvious signs of abuse until I looked at photos later, when I had the time and space to feel sad. We met our lawyer before heading back to North Carolina with the twins. As we left, he said, "These girls need you."

Our temporary custody order meant we could secure health insurance for the twins via Medicaid, as well as schedule doctor appointments and vaccinations so they could attend daycare. At the hearing for permanent custody in 2016, our daughter and her husband showed up late. Layne tested positive for drugs. We were granted permanent custody.

Generations United, a non-profit that supports intergenerational collaborations of all kinds, gathers census and other data regarding "grandfamilies." Their 2018 report states that more than 2.4 million children are currently being raised by their grandparents. Some 66 percent of these grandparents are white, 19 percent are Black, 20 percent are Latinx, 4 percent are Asian, and 2 percent are Indigenous. Nearly 60 percent are in the workforce and grapple with childcare conflicts, just as younger parents do. Because they are grandparents, they don't have legal rights to access resources on behalf of the child, such as IEPs, and often don't get the financial support that a non-relative foster parent would. It was clear that we needed to be parents if we wanted to fully support the twins.

In 2017, we moved to Georgia to be closer to our extended family and support and we filed the petition to adopt. At first, Layne and her husband pushed back, saying they wanted visitation, but when they didn't show up for the adoption hearing, their parental rights were terminated.

Our actions provoked intense reactions from friends, family, and strangers. When a friend whose daughter had tragically died of an overdose learned we were adopting the girls, she responded with, "You are *ruining* Wayne's retirement and your future as a professor." That basically ended the friendship. The rift was painful—and loaded, because she had left her grandchild to stay with her drug-addicted husband, a decision that I judged.

As a mother, I wanted to protect Layne, but once we took on

the responsibility of the twins, protecting them meant I had to create a boundary. This shuffle in our family dynamic is bittersweet, to say the least. Wayne and I have moved from *grandfather* and *grandmother* to *daddy* and *mommy*; my son now has three sisters. Wayne's children, both in their early fifties, are now the girls' half-siblings. People have wondered why we didn't just stick with the original labels, but my view is that once you adopt, they are your kids. I say this as an adopted child myself. Relationships change with adoption, legally and emotionally, and it's easier to use the correct terms. It's like using the correct terms for body parts.

When we first brought Ava and Audrey home, they were shell-shocked and nonverbal. They would scream hysterically if their bottles ran out of milk because they thought that was all there was; food had meant scavenging spilled Cheerios off filthy carpets in Layne's home. Over time, they learned to trust the daily routine: the bellyful of food, going outside, getting a bath, learning to play tennis and golf.

Now, I'm happy to report, you can't shut 'em up—they fill our house with their giggles and questions. They tell us how glad they are that we're their mom and dad and that they wouldn't swap us for a car, house, pool, horse, new puppy, kitty cat, or a gazillion-trillion dollars. They sing "You Are My Sunshine" every morning. It's wonderful to see my husband, who's in his mid-seventies now, embrace his role as the go-to parent, just as I have embraced my role as breadwinner.

My father died recently. I texted Layne to tell her. That might sound cold, but we haven't spoken in six years and it is hard to know how to build a relationship at this point. The girls, who are almost eight now, had never been to church, much less a funeral, but they handled themselves beautifully during the service. I can't tell you how many people praised us for being "such good parents."

THE AFFIRMATION IS a far cry from all the unsolicited and angry comments the exact same people made over the years about how much money this venture was going to cost us, and how we had "no right to take the children from their God-given parents," and how we were "bailing our daughter out of her responsibilities," as if teaching Layne a lesson wasn't also leaving two toddlers in extreme danger. That criticism stung, but many other people have shown up for us and the girls over the years by sending gift cards, toys, and clothes, or just offering a few words of support for what we're doing. Adopting was a huge financial and emotional decision, but if one person in a similar situation (and there are *so* many of us) reads this and feels like they can step in and do the right thing, I'm here to say it's worth it.

At the adoption hearing, the judge asked Wayne to describe what the girls' life would be like if our request was denied and they were sent back to their parents. "I can't even imagine," Wayne began, and then to my shock, my usually Clint Eastwood-type husband choked up. "I love these girls," he said, tears flowing. "I don't know what *my* life would be like without *them*."

To me, it was a moment that solidified that Ava and Audrey are ours. And we are theirs.

*For more than eight years,
I was tasked with balancing
the needs of both my mother
and my daughter.*

Life in Balance
LAURA BROADWELL

My daughter, Eleni, is twenty-one now, but I distinctly remember a day when she was two and I was desperately trying to convince her to put on her shoes so we could go out to play. Eleni was running around distractedly and wouldn't listen, and while I was chasing after her, my mother, then seventy-five, was repeatedly asking me unrelated questions—something about a neighbor and what we would like for dinner. I answered my mother's questions, but she would ask them again because she was hard of hearing. For what seemed to be an eternity, I found myself caught in a cycle of speaking louder and louder to a two-year-old who wouldn't listen and a seventy-five-year-old who couldn't hear. To a bystander, the scene may have seemed comical, but I was not amused.

In retrospect, though, that particular day was golden. The sun was shining, my father—also seventy-five—was out for a run, and my Athens-born mother was still able to cook the foods of her native Greece. Though I was an exhausted, older single mother, I found immense joy in (eventually) taking my daughter out to play, and, as an only child, I reveled in the fact that my parents had finally been granted a grandchild. My family now felt whole and intact.

In a few years' time, things would change.

Ever since I was a child, I dreamed of becoming a mother; as I crept toward forty and remained unmarried, this dream, this ambition, didn't fade. And when I was forty-one, a confluence of factors arose that made motherhood seem possible. I had an unusually sizable Brooklyn apartment, a steady job I loved, supportive parents who resided within fifty miles of my home, a solid group of friends, and a surprising ally in the Chinese government. Though things have since changed, there existed a window of time, a fortuitous opening, when the Chinese government would allow a single woman over forty to adopt a healthy infant—in most cases, a baby girl. (For me this was a bonus, since I intended to raise a child on my own.) On top of that, the adoption process in China was fairly straightforward, though laden with paperwork. With some luck, it appeared I could be in China within eighteen months, a new mother to a baby daughter. After much thought and reasonable trepidation, I decided to pursue this option.

On August 16, 1999, I arrived at a dimly lit registrar's office in central China, where I was handed an eight-month-old baby. At the age of forty-two, I suddenly became a first-time mother. I named my daughter Eleni in honor of my own mother, who had waited patiently for her first and only grandchild. Nine days later, we flew home to New York, where my parents and friends greeted us at the airport with vivid pink balloons and welcome-home signs. Eleni and I were set to begin our new life together.

Our first two years in Brooklyn passed quickly. Eleni was a happy child, a curious child, an active child, a child who never slept. By extension, I was always exhausted, holding down a full-time job, caring for my daughter, having few spare moments to myself. But as an older mother, I viewed this juggling act and ever-present fatigue as a small price to pay for the joy of raising a child. As a parent over forty, I'd had countless years of "me time," during which I could travel, see friends, build a career . . . so spending a Saturday afternoon or evening with my parents and

Eleni was more than enough to make me happy. It fulfilled me to have my mother prepare Greek meals and bring them to our house or see my dad play so energetically in the park with Eleni. I was grateful for my job, grateful to reside in a neighborhood with other adoptive families and little girls from China, and grateful for the multicultural city in which I lived. By some divine stroke of luck, everything seemed in order.

But to paraphrase the poet Robert Burns, the best-laid plans often go awry. On September 11, 2001, when Eleni was almost three, the World Trade Center was hit by terrorists, which brought trauma and devastation to our city. Several weeks later, the magazine at which I'd worked for nearly a decade folded, citing a consistent loss of revenue. Then, in the spring of 2004, my seventy-nine-year-old father—the bedrock of our family, a man who ran marathons into his sixties and had boundless energy to play with Eleni for hours—was diagnosed with mesothelioma, a rare form of lung cancer. How supremely unfair it felt that a man who had never smoked and who had valued his health, worked hard, and had so much to live for would be struck with such a fatal illness. Within six months of his diagnosis, my father died, leaving me with countless business affairs to look after, a shocked and broken heart, and a mother and daughter who were beyond bereaved.

Eleni was young—five, almost six—when her grandpa died, so it was hard for her to comprehend how this vibrant man had left us. On the playground at school, Eleni would look up at the sky and see her grandfather's wispy, white hair in the cloud formation above her. In class, she described his spirit as coming to her "like a wind," helping her with her math problems. My dad was athletic, so in tribute to him, Eleni learned to play soccer and tennis. She went to baseball camp as one of two girls in attendance. She was fast on her feet and adopted my father's work ethic.

My mother, on the other hand, was seventy-nine when her

husband died. For years, her health had been faltering, first with coronary bypass surgery in her early fifties, then later with various vision, hearing, and other issues that caused memory loss and body pain. My mother was surprisingly strong, having survived not only these health problems but also the shelling of Athens during World War II, yet somehow, she liked to convince everyone that she was weak, a victim who needed constant care.

My father had been that primary caregiver, her rock—the man around whom she'd built her life, her financial supporter, her buffer, her lifeline to the world. When he died, my mother was understandably adrift. In order to protect her, my father had declined to tell my mother exactly how sick he was, perhaps believing he had more time to live than he did. But her lack of emotional preparedness and the relative speed of my father's passing sent my mother into a confused and anxious tailspin. There were days when she stubbornly refused to take her medication and her memory loss worsened. Then there were times when she became short-tempered with Eleni and me.

As the weeks passed, I tried to keep our lives in Brooklyn in balance. My daughter was in first grade now, attending a slew of birthday parties and learning to read, write, and socialize. I was working from home as a freelance writer and editor, which gave me flexibility in terms of time and workflow. But every weekend, Eleni and I would run out to my mother's house some fifty miles away to check up on her and a family friend who'd agreed to stay temporarily. My mother was sad, lonely, and increasingly confused, and it became clear that she would soon need a higher level of care. The turning point came a short while later, when my mother arrived at my apartment for an extended visit. As she bent to tie her shoelaces one day, she slipped and fell, fracturing a vertebra in her back. It was the last day my mother would walk independently. She would soon need a wheelchair.

Faced with this new set of circumstances and knowing my

mother could no longer live in her home—a house with three flights of stairs—I decided to move her to Brooklyn. Fortunately, my father had financially planned for a time when he and my mother would require nursing care by taking out a long-term-care insurance policy and making other investments. I tapped into these funds and found a sunny assisted-care facility within a short walk of my home. I hired loving professional aides to care for my mother and to clean her small, private room, and I visited almost daily. But although the logistics of having my mother nearby made life easier, I was still wracked with guilt. I knew my mom was suffering.

For one thing, my mother wanted to go home, and home meant her house on Long Island. Because of her deepening dementia and overwhelming grief, my mother couldn't understand why she couldn't live alone and why my father had left her. In an effort to comfort her and settle her nerves, I brought my mother some photos and personal belongings, including a painting she loved of Eleni and me. I also brought my six-year-old daughter to visit her room whenever possible. Sometimes Eleni would draw or play contentedly, and sometimes we would all sit together on the couch, watching *Dancing with the Stars* on TV. But on other days, both my mother and Eleni would vie for my attention while an aide was trying to talk to me. At still other times, Eleni found it too hard to visit. It was tough for her to reconcile the grandma she'd once known—the woman with whom she'd enjoyed meals and played cards—with the one now lying in a hospital bed. How could this be possible?

For more than eight years, I was tasked with balancing the needs of both my mother and my daughter. Early on, I decided it would be easier for me to see my mother on my own, preferably when Eleni was at school or at a friend's house. I could sit and hold my mother's hand or help feed her. I could take her to doctor visits within the assisted-care facility, check on her medication, and talk to her aides about her daily care without interruption. Eleni would come for shorter visits, after school or on the weekends.

My days with Eleni at home, soccer games, school, or in the world were cherished times and often proved to be the antidote, the needed balance, to caring for an aging parent. As a first-time mother—and an older one, at that—I loved every stage of Eleni's development. As Eleni grew, she played sports. She read and watched movies. She danced. She had friends. She did homework—more and more of it, as school demanded. She grew taller than me and at times her grandmother barely recognized her, instead remembering her as a smaller child. While my mother drifted in and out of reality and often in and out of hospitals and hospice care, my daughter found joy in real-life activities. She was thriving, and her curiosity about the world buoyed me.

Eleni also knew intuitively that I was doing my best in a difficult situation. From the time she was six until she was fourteen, Eleni watched as I cared for my mother as she edged closer to dying and bounced back again. She, along with family friends, helped me clear out our Long Island home with its more-than-fifty-years' worth of possessions, and she was there on the tearful day we sold it to help pay for my mother's care. Five years after my father's mesothelioma diagnosis, I was diagnosed with early-stage endometrial cancer and required a hysterectomy. Eleni was there to greet me at home with her godparents on the day I returned from the hospital. I was fortunate in that Eleni has always been a considerate child and a fairly easy one to raise. But as she grew older and into her teen years, she empathetically cut me slack when my conflicting duties got the best of me.

In hindsight, it's hard to say how I—we, all three of us—got through those challenging years. Sometimes things fell apart, such as when an aide, Eleni, and I took my mother to an off-site doctor's appointment and got stranded there when our wheelchair-accessible transport failed to arrive. Other times, I lost my patience; there were times when I completely lost my temper with everyone. Eleni had hard days of her own, too, and sometimes seemed inconsolable despite my best efforts to support her. But even in my worst moments, I was lucky enough to have a village to help raise my child *and* care for my aging mother.

At its center were the four loving aides who rotated shifts and worked as a team to care for my mom 24–7. Over time, we established a relationship with one another that was both personal and professional, and these women worked for our family for years as a result. Since they were there on a day-to-day basis to ensure my mother's well-being, I was freed up to make the big medical and financial decisions and to spend some quieter times with my mom. Their steady, reliable care also allowed me the space to work and to create a stable, relatively peaceful home life for Eleni, who had her own village of people around her. Her various teachers, coaches, godparents, friends, and parents of friends all stepped up when I needed them to, lending their support and an extra hand when necessary.

During those years, I thought often of my father and how he had run marathons later into life, driven by a will of steel. When he died, it felt as if I'd followed in his footsteps. My marathon, however, was of an emotional nature, a very long race that would call for a great deal of energy, determination, and grit in order to reach the finish line. But because I was an older parent in my late forties and fifties during those "sandwich" years, I was able to draw on decades of my own life experience and find wells of strength I never believed I had.

I was also willing to refocus my priorities on both my mother and daughter, knowing I had one shot to get this right. (As a result, my career and personal life were indefinitely put on hold.) It soon became clear that I couldn't help my mother get "better," but I was dedicated to helping her find some measure of comfort and peace. She became less verbal over time, making it hard to know exactly what she needed and why she held on for so long. But as one of her nurses once told me, "She has too much love. She's not going anywhere." As for Eleni, I had waited so long to become a mother that I wanted our experience together to be memorable. I wanted to soak up all the time we had at each stage of her journey, whether it was big things, like going to Disney World when she was nine or London at thirteen, or the small things, like watching *Harry Potter* movies on repeat, chatting away as we walked to soccer practice, or laughing together at night. Her joy, happiness, and sound emotional development was at the top of my to-do list each and every day.

In the end, my mother chose the time and place of her passing. On February 15, 2013, on what would have been my father's eighty-eighth birthday and one week short of her own, my mother died in the Brooklyn hospital where I was born more than fifty years earlier. In another act of perfect symmetry, she was holding the hand of my daughter, a child who was then fourteen and had been named after her, years earlier.

It was an emotional walk home from the hospital that night. But when we arrived back at our apartment, I pulled out my mother's wedding ring, a simple, silver band with tiny, twinkling diamonds my dad had given her more than sixty years earlier. That ring had symbolized their commitment, their union, through fifty-two years of marriage and eight years of widowhood. I slipped the ring onto my hand thinking I might wear it, but it just didn't look right on me, so I offered it to Eleni. By some stroke of magic, it fit perfectly on her long, slender ring finger, and I joked that my mother's ring chose its wearer, just like Harry Potter's wand chose him.

Eleni has worn my mother's ring religiously since that night. It traveled with her and protected her on the subways she took to high school. It swam with her and glistened in the turquoise-dappled waters of the Aegean Sea. It accompanied her to college and to a semester abroad in Italy. And it has been given new life and a new set of adventures in a modern world. I loved and admired my mother's ring during my own childhood, and it's a ring my daughter now wears proudly in memory of her namesake. It's a symbol of the time that my mother, Eleni, and I all spent together—a symbol that we all made it through.

PART IV
PARENTING AFTER FORTY

Ellen was okay, John was okay, and I felt not only relief, but a rare joy. I was okay too.

Never Too Old to Be a Father—Again
ROBERT BENCE

I was forty-two when my second child, John, was born. Prior to his birth, I'd had major doubts about whether I had the energy and commitment to once again be all I thought a parent should be. Because of a very contentious divorce that happened when my daughter, Chris, was eight, I struggled to get to see her, much less be consistently connected to her childhood. Fatherhood was often exhausting, painful, and emotionally draining. I was always uncertain what my role could or should be. What parental decisions should and could I make? When and where should I provide support and discipline? With no scheduled visitation days, I pathetically waited in phone-watching anticipation—often unsuccessfully—for last-minute opportunities to share at least an hour of being together.

While I dearly loved Chris, I seriously questioned my ability to be a successful father. Too often one's choices about the future are bound by the past, so I resisted my wife Ellen's strong desire to have a baby together. It was difficult for me to share her anticipated joy of parenthood. But after two years of difficult discussions, I reluctantly began to resign myself to a pregnancy. I wondered what life would be like in nine months.

The process of becoming a father again began to offer clues

that indicated history did not have to repeat itself. It was the '80s and not the '60s, so fathers were expected to—and did—become more involved during pregnancy. Birthing classes especially helped me connect more to both the reality and importance of my place in this shared parental experience. I had been far removed from my daughter's "mysterious" birth in 1968, which I spent in an uncomfortable chair in the isolated waiting lounge of West Virginia's Mon Health Stonewall Jackson Hospital. This time, I was beside Ellen in the delivery room of a hipper Massachusetts hospital when John first experienced daylight. Ellen was okay, John was okay, and I felt not only relief, but a rare joy. I was okay too.

It shouldn't have been a surprise, but fatherhood was easier this time, in large part a result of Ellen's trust in my parental skills. Due to her less flexible twelve-month, nine-to-five-plus work schedule, John was required to spend much of his early life with me. My stamina and energy were still high, and I bonded quickly with this large, quite active kid. Much like the rewarding hours I devoted to my daughter's early life, I almost always enjoyed attending to John's babyhood needs, trying to introduce and guide him through many of the activities we found valuable for his development. I steadied him on his first bike rides, read endless books, introduced him to outdoor and indoor sports, and shared my love of videos and TV. With this child I had the precious opportunity to be a full-time father after he turned eight, and the three of us camped, canoed, and traveled extensively, experiencing "normal" family dynamics for the first time.

I'm grateful that Ellen didn't defer to my extreme hesitancy about second-time fatherhood. My then-sixteen-year-old daughter, Chris, drove Ellen, newborn John, and I home from the hospital upon receiving her driver's license. Brother and sister went on to become quite close, and the four of us, later joined by a son-in-law and two grandchildren, have experienced many adventures together. One of my most treasured gifts is a framed photo of Chris and John together, which they surprised me with for Father's Day.

It was as if I didn't exist in his life, as if I didn't do homework with him, as if I hadn't shared my parental concerns.

Who is That? Becoming a Bonus Mom at Age Forty-Five

PAIGE AVERETT

I see my sweet boy, James, through the glass; he is in the midst of a pack of boys all hovering over a game. I'm excited to see him—it's been a week and I missed him. I rush in and hug him with a, "Hi buddy. Having fun?"

He smiles at me but says, "Aww, I'm not ready to go yet."

This is a common refrain when he's having too much fun and isn't quite ready to leave yet. As I sometimes do, I say, "Go ahead and play for a bit. I can hang out and wait."

All of the boys in his new pack of kindergarten friends are staring at me, a few with gaping mouths. I back away in an attempt to watch them play but give them space, and as I do, I overhear, "Who is that?"

My kiddo, James, glances up at me shyly to see if I heard the question. He hesitates, and you can see the thoughts rumbling around as he tries to land on the correct response. I hold my breath and instantly know the poor kid can't win: he either has to launch into a full explanation with multiple sentences, which isn't his style as an introvert and I'm not sure he even has the language for all of it yet, or he has to tell a little white lie, which he's been taught not to do and also doesn't resonate with his personality. The other option is that he has to say something that may hurt my feelings and is only part of the story, but it *is* true.

He's five, and it's not fair that he has to navigate all of that, so I feel sad for him. However, I can't help but involve my own ego as well, and his response will either make my day or sting a bit.

He goes with the response that's only part of the story, and says, "That's my dad's girlfriend."

I release my breath and try to smile through the small blow. I know it's not a criticism, but for the past year, it sure has felt like one. It creates distance; it says I'm not connected to him but rather to his dad. I don't have a title when it comes to James, and that hurts. Every time either of us is asked a question regarding our relationship or we discuss one another, it shines a glaring spotlight on the lack of definition. It's a reoccurring experience and question, one that I'm tired of having to explain awkwardly: Who am I to this child?

At age forty-five, I began an intense and quickly committed relationship to James's father, Mark. Mark and his soon-to-be ex-wife shared joint physical custody of James, then four years old. The custody agreement required James to be with each parent for an equal amount of time. After just a few months of dating, I moved in with Mark, and thus I had an equal amount of time with James as his mom and dad did.

I jumped right in and got involved in James's life. I took him to and picked him up from childcare. I bathed and fed him. I helped put him to bed. I guided, played, and was involved in organizing his life. I supervised homework. I arranged playdates. I hosted birthday parties. I became a parent, and it was primarily by choice.

I had been married twice (once at twenty-five and again at forty), and while I had tried to have children for a brief time when my first marriage ended at thirty, I was relieved I hadn't succeeded. I then made the conscious choice that I *would* not. I had long felt that I was too interested in pursuing my own goals—including international travel, getting my PhD, and being pretty free to come and go as I pleased—and that having a child would impede those goals. I was fearful I would resent a child and their needs and demands upon my time and energy. When I divorced, I wanted to be completely unencumbered, so children were not an option. I didn't even date people who had children.

Meeting Mark (and James) changed that. I fell so deeply in love with Mark that I was willing to try it. I was also in a much different stage of life; I was forty-five and had achieved most of my goals. I was more settled, successful, and secure. The first time I saw a picture of James, I thought, "We'll be great together," and the first time I met James, I fell in love all over again. He was so very easy to love—sweet, shy, affectionate, and well-behaved.

Once James was in my life half the time, I knew I wasn't a primary caregiver, but I *was* a parent. Some of that certainty was based on my past; I had watched and participated in my large extended family with its many blended parts, which embraced roles and labels of familial relationship even if they didn't exist legally or biologically. There were lots of (step)children and (step) grandchildren and cousins who weren't really cousins and uncles that weren't really uncles. My parents are called *aunt* and *uncle* by so many children they absolutely had no "real" connection to, but those children and my parents live and believe in those adopted roles. I have a cousin and godsister, and we call each other *sister* and act just like sisters. Taking on the label of *parent* wasn't problematic for me, but I was soon to find out it was problematic to others.

It is a constant challenge to be a parent who isn't legally or biologically connected to a child. These challenges are present in every level of interaction I have: personal, institutional, cultural, and social. Not a week goes by without the issue coming up. Every year at James's school, I have to reassert myself as his parent who's worthy of sharing information with and receiving acknowledgment. The schools continually send out forms that request only the father's and mother's information. Every year, I tell the new teacher how disrespectful this is to any kind of family diversity:

stepparents, queer parents, and grandparents raising their grandchildren, just to name a few family configurations that do exist in our school. I have shared my frustration with the administration and offered to do a training on it for all school staff with no response, and so, every year, I go through the same process and have the same talk with the new teacher.

Yet nothing changes. I recently attended a school meeting to discuss services for James's slight stutter. As an academic, I have an especially keen interest in his educational success. I met with several administrators, including this year's teacher, and we completed the documentation together. It was glaringly obvious to me and my partner, but no one else in the room seemed to recognize that I wasn't listed as being in attendance, nor were my spoken thoughts documented while both his mother's and father's were. It was as if I didn't exist in his life, as if I don't do homework with him, as if I hadn't shared my parental concerns. According to the school, I'm not important to this child I'm raising.

It's even more challenging when I meet another potential friend or acquaintance and I attempt to navigate honesty and clarity and assert my role while also trying to make a relational connection that can grow. Inevitably, I must go through an explanation of who he and I are exactly, or else be viewed as deceptive. As a result, it often feels like I'm overexplaining and defensive, no matter how many times I go through it. My mother once said, "Well, just don't explain. Say he's your son, period." I used to do that, but I've also had multiple experiences where I did just claim him, and then when the friendship or conversation went deeper and the specifics of our life came out, I had to backtrack and explain. In these instances, I ended up coming off as convoluted and possibly having boundary issues that disrespect his biological mom.

Recently, James and I were in the yard kicking a soccer ball around. He is now eight and I am soon to be fifty. I had my grandbaby on my hip because Mark's adult daughter (who is twenty-five) and her daughter (nine months) were visiting us for the weekend. As James and I played, a woman and little girl walked up and introduced themselves as our neighbors and as mother and daughter. The daughter wanted to play soccer with James. The mother began chatting with me about the yard and neighborhood. She was charming and friendly and I was excited and engaged, because while our neighbors are polite and cordial, they're typically not friendly.

However, it soon went downhill as she attempted to clarify our family structure. It began when she asked the age of "my daughter," the baby on my hip. I laughed and said, "Oh no, she's not mine! This is the grandbaby." I used the word *the* instead of *my*, trying to be honest while still honoring the relationship that does exist between us as well. Then I inhaled deeply; I knew what was coming.

She immediately looked at James, and then quickly looked at me, and then the baby, and back to James. She was wondering how I had both this eight-year-old and a grandbaby. She then asked in confusion, "So he *is* yours, right?" pointing at James.

And here we go. I tried to explain, "My partner has an adult daughter, and this is her daughter, our grandbaby. James is mine—well, not mine, but yeah, he is mine." I took a deep breath and continued, "He's my stepson." And there I went, lying. I felt trapped, awkward, defensive, as though I needed to cut it short instead of going on about who he is and isn't. I just said "step" because people know what that means, and then I could just shut up.

I inwardly groan, though. My internal dialogue begins, *Who cares?! Why do I have to explain all these things? He is mine!* But I know why I have to explain. I rarely have fellow mothers approach me—due to my age, I believe. I am forty-nine and most women who have eight-year-old children are in their mid-to-late thirties;

I get the sense that they don't think we'll have much in common. On the rare occasion a fellow mother approaches me—as occurred with this neighbor—I attempt to give an honest explanation and it all sounds like too much drama, too complicated, and no one wants to deal with that. I see potential friends immediately disconnect and lose interest. As a result of my age and position, I haven't developed a single mom-friend during the four years I've been a mother. All my friends who *are* mothers were so before I became one.

THE STRUGGLE TO FIT IN as a parent is overwhelming at times, doubly so because of my age. Yet it continues to surprise me that blended families go acknowledged, and alternate parent labels don't readily exist. According to a Pew study, today non-traditional family structures are more common than traditional ones (*traditional* being defined as having two biological, heterosexual parents). As women waiting to have children increases, so does the number of those becoming mothers for the first time at (or after) forty. And we know that millennials and coming generations are growing more and more skeptical of marriage and are more likely to have partners or significant others instead. Yet our society doesn't seem to acknowledge any of these shifts. We aren't getting with the times.

WHAT'S ESPECIALLY GLARING in my experience is our lack of terminology for non-traditional parents. Currently, *mom*, *dad*, *foster mom*, *foster dad*, *stepmom*, and *stepdad* are the only available, culturally understood terms. There isn't one simple label that defines who I am to James. I am not his mother; he has one who is very loving and involved. I am also not his stepmother, a term with roots in the law, a word which Merriam-Webster defines as "the wife" of one's parent "distinct from one's natural or legal mother." James and I have both struggled with what to say for years.

I finally ran across a show on Netflix called *Bonus Family*. Leave it to the Swedish to come up with the best new term. The family drama is about blended households, with a focus on non-married partners with three children between them and one on the way. There's also a single dad who lives with his lesbian mother and her partner (who gets upset when no one is respecting her role as bonus grandmother), and the grandmothers do as much caretaking as the dad. The show regularly uses *bonus mom* and *bonus dad* as terms for the non-biological parents.

Watching the show led to an "aha" moment for me, and I decided James and I would use these terms. The problem, however, is that he's not really my bonus son; he is my only son, and I still feel like I'm negating how unique he is to me when I add bonus to it. But I continually try to push past that and let go of my niggling academic mind.

I now introduce myself as James's bonus mom, but I do sometimes get a bit of condescension in response, as I received in the school meeting described above. One school administrator's response to my introduction was, "Cute. That's new. I haven't heard that term before." And then I wasn't listed as being present for the school meeting. I can only assume bonus mom wasn't considered a real parental category.

However, I believe I've had the resilience and determination to navigate these situations as a result of my age. Because I took on being a bonus mom at age forty-five, I've had the presence, skills, and esteem to press on and assert my role, even though it's awkward and challenging. I advocate at the school every year, every meeting, every email—not just for myself but for all the marginalized parents in the school. Because I am an "older mother," I also have a well-established support system that includes mothers, so the lack of new mother friends isn't a gaping hole in my life. I also have a family, as I said before, that's used to blended structures and the use of various family labels. I'm supported as much as I'm negated.

My plan is to keep pushing the bonus label out there as a cultural norm. I also have hope that as millennials give us a whole new catalog of terminology for sexual orientations (e.g., pansexual, queer, fluid); genders (e.g., genderqueer, gender-fluid, genderfuck); and pronouns (they/them, ze/zem); that once they really begin family formations (later than my Gen X generation typically did), they'll also give us more and more parental labels. Even more, I hope that as Gen Z rises, they'll keep pushing the idea of "Why do we need labels and definition at all?" and many of these ideas—and my struggles—will become obsolete.

I might not relate to the families in gay parenting magazines because even though we're same-gender parents, most of those magazines don't account for complex family dynamics like ours.

Old Life, New Life, and Parenting in the In-Between
ERIK MALEWSKI

If you were to ask me when it all began, this parenting at an older age, I'd tell you about Hurricane Irma—September 2017. I watched with great concern as Irma churned off the Atlantic Coast, slowly gained power and momentum, and headed toward two of my favorite US cities, Miami and New Orleans. Like many across the nation, I was hooked on the twenty-four-hour news cycle, which focused on potential pathways and categorical strength, when Irma suddenly turned north, moved up central Florida, and directly toward my home city of Atlanta. Atlanta is nicknamed "the city in the forest," and the winds from Hurricane Irma were enough to knock down scores of trees and cut off power to large swaths of the city, even when downgraded to a storm. The recovery took weeks. Hurricane Irma became allegorical for my life as an older parent.

Two days after the storm passed through the city, I received a phone call from the man who is now my partner, Rico. He and his four kids were without power, and they couldn't make it another night in the heat and dark. Rico's friends in the area were also without power. I told him my condo building had been spared, and he asked if they might come stay until their power was back on. Surely, Rico explained, it would only be a night or two.

I was unsure how to respond and told him I would call him

back in an hour. My mind spun with all I would have to consider: *Where would they sleep? Is my house childproof? What would they eat? Is there anything I have around my bachelor pad that they shouldn't find?*

As you read this, you might guess that they did come over, we did become a couple, and I did become a parent at forty-five. I often tell everyone that Hurricane Irma turned my life upside down, but not in the way most people initially think. Unlike those who lost a home or experienced devastation, I wouldn't change the chaos that Irma ushered into my life—that of becoming a parent to four children—for anything in the world.

My life has had two major chapters: B.I., Before Irma, and A.I., After Irma. Before Irma, I had what many might describe as a near-perfect existence as a successful, professional gay man who lived an exciting, fast-paced life in metropolitan Atlanta. I had worked hard to get a PhD, worked as an administrator, and had been awarded tenure at a well-known Research 1 university. After a sabbatical year, during which I taught graduate courses and conducted research as a visiting professor, I returned to my then-institutional home and applied to a few administrative positions. I had worked in a diversity unit for many years before becoming a faculty member; after tenure, I wanted to move into a senior administrative diversity role at a university. I accepted a cabinet-level position as chief diversity officer at Kennesaw State University and quickly established a professional network of friends and colleagues within the metropolitan area. While this new position required that I work hard on campus initiatives, the high rank and public-facing nature of the role meant I had ample opportunities to attend evening events, award galas, and professional conferences. My friends, colleagues, and family frequently remarked that my hard work had paid off—I had arrived.

It didn't feel like my arrival mattered much the first night Rico and his four kids stayed the night at my condo. Aged four, five, five, and nine, the kids didn't comprehend that the grape preserves from their peanut butter and jelly sandwiches would stain my white aniline leather counter stools, or that the hand-spun Peruvian pottery on my coffee table was delicate and would break if knocked to the floor. I quickly learned that my guest bedroom could handle not only the king-size fold-out sofa bed, but also two queen-size blow-up mattresses, and that the tall, slender lamps on the nightstands would not survive an impromptu pillow fight. The carefully curated furnishings in my condo—paintings, bowls, and figurines that reflected my taste and experiences—went from points of pride to reminders that I had not truly childproofed my home. I looked around for things that were durable and put them with the children; delicate items were quickly moved to the storage room. I didn't realize it at the time, but my life was already changing.

We settled in together for a total of three nights, and it was during this time that something transformative happened. We cooked, cleaned, watched movies, played games, read books, and little by little, all the material things that had symbolized my arrival began to matter less than the five people with whom I had been living for the last few days. This is not to say I gave up my career, colleagues, and friends—or my art—but rather, I began to envision a different future for myself, one that involved Rico and these four kids.

Hurricane Irma became an allegory for the crazy life that was about to ensue. In my mid-forties, I wasn't just preparing for the final stages of my career and beginning plans for retirement; I was also discovering what it might mean to co-parent four young children and build a relationship with their father. I found myself trying to figure out how I would retain some elements of my prior world, elements that provided purpose and meaning, while also moving into a new world where four little lives needed love, support, guidance, and motivation.

To say that I've transitioned well to this new life would be a lie.

Compared to the families in gay parenting magazines with their fresh smiles, bright eyes, and perfectly styled hair, I have permanent bags under my eyes, have gained enough weight to require a new wardrobe, and now have the attention span of a Labrador puppy as I juggle children, a move to the suburbs, and the demands of a faculty career. When I read the stories of the parents featured in these magazines, I don't relate, and their storylines are not my own, despite having a predictable pattern. In almost every one of these gay parenting magazines, the fathers or mothers felt unfulfilled or lacking in one or more ways, and then the individuals found each other, became a couple, adopted or birthed a child or children, and, almost like magic, they were happier, knew a deeper love, and better understood the ultimate purpose for their lives.

On the other hand, I was perfectly happy as a single gay man and wasn't looking for a relationship or to become a parent in an already-established family. I'm fulfilled and challenged differently now that I'm partnered and raising four children. The need to find time to put myself first is now my biggest challenge, whereas previously I lived my life as I wanted, with only my own interests driving my decisions. As I juggle carpooling, life as a faculty member, and figuring out lunches and dinners for children who sometimes have very different tastes in food, I can say with certainty that I've transitioned, but not that I've done it well or that I experience family life as making me happier or more complete. I would say it makes me differently happy, with its own set of rewards and challenges.

I might not relate to the families in gay parenting magazines because even though we're same-gender parents, most of those magazines don't account for complex family dynamics like ours. We are a multiracial, multigendered family that shares custody of our children with two other fathers—Rico's previous partner and his husband. While our children have different skin tones and many people assume the two brown-skinned boys belong to my partner, who is African American, while the white-skinned girl and boy belong to me, a European American, together they only know each other as brothers and sister. Our complexity raises eyebrows outside of gay, lesbian, and queer social networks, and as a result, we teach a lot of coping and critical thinking skills to our children. So common was the refrain, "Whose kids are those?" from outsiders in public settings that we taught our kids to respond that they're all family and nothing else.

This coping is the result of a heck of a lot of in-betweenness. I am in-between my old life and new life as an over-forty parent. Our kids are between homes as we share custody with two other fathers. We negotiate different racial and gender identities, as both sets of parents are interracial and our children are white, Latinx, and African American. Our shared experiences are always marked by third spaces that are intersectional, ever-evolving, and difficult to define; families like ours rarely make it into gay parenting magazines. Yet theories of third spaces, where we're halfway in and halfway out of different lives and identities, help to make sense of many of our experiences. Indeed, in-betweenness and third spaces are the shared sense-making strategies that bond us together. Our complexity, uniqueness, and contingency has become a source of family strength.

I have always been extremely motivated and successful in my career. Yet as a parent, I find I regularly fail, and I'm not sure if I'll ever get much of this parenting thing right. Ask me to comb my daughter's hair and make two equal pigtails and you'll see me struggle and likely make something my partner would describe as a hot mess. Ask me to dress my two youngest sons and inevitably, I'll put them in the wrong pants at least once a week, where the bigger one looks like he's in capris and the smaller one can't find his feet. Structure and discipline for our children is another challenge, and not a day goes by that I don't doubt my abilities.

Learning to parent in my forties means being comfortable with failure.

I try to balance the need to show them love and my genuine excitement that they're in my life with the sorts of direction and boundaries I think they need to understand prioritization, planning, and self-discipline. Unlike my career, where my successes are measured in publications, grants, and teaching evaluations, my parenting is more accurately characterized as shots in the dark. I came to their lives later in the game, and I can only hope I'm giving them what they need. The markers of parenting success are elusive at best.

This doubt regarding my parenting also carries over into issues of identity and identity formation. Just as our oldest son is and presents as a dark-skinned African American, our two middle children are twins with Latinx and white ancestries and present as white. Our youngest son is multiracial and presents as a light-skinned African American. To teach that race and gender are constructs and forces that *shape* who we are rather than categories that *reflect* who we are, works against our interest in providing foundational cultural knowledge so our children know their backgrounds and better understand themselves.

As with race, I both fail and succeed at teaching the construction of gender roles, how they can help and hinder human development, and how to grapple with them. Not long after I became a dad, my only daughter would exclaim during arguments with her twin brother that he should leave her alone because she's a girl and not as strong as him. As a feminist and critical education scholar, her plea startled me on multiple levels. At her current age of six, my daughter is both taller and more physically developed than her twin brother. What ensued was a lengthy conversation regarding gender construction and different forms of human capacity, from flexibility to muscle strength and coordination. I explained the importance of employing gender toward healthy development and not allowing others to stereotype or constrain our spirits and abilities based on narrow, toxic gender roles. The conversation seemed to help, as my daughter stopped associating her assigned gender with weakness. While we have complicated gender for our children, I feel less successful when it comes to teaching my children to cope with gendered structures and expectations that exist in society. My doubt is only further deepened by the fact that as an older parent, the generational divide between us is vast.

Two years into this parenting thing and I still find myself halfway in and halfway out of this life and my previous one. Weekly meetings with friends at what used to be my local bar have given way to monthly meetings I drive into from the suburbs. Now when we get together, we share stories from lives that no longer overlap. The connections with my friends are just as deep and we do remain a group of really good storytellers—years ago, it wasn't uncommon for three to five of us to meet and socialize as the Friday night crowd filled the bar all the way to last call. That dynamic has shifted some, and now, two years later, I'm typically the first one in our group to leave. When I was single and childless, my storytelling was focused on my own experiences—who I'd met, the places I'd eaten, the trips I'd planned—but the scope of my storytelling has expanded beyond my own interests and needs. As my friends continue to tell stories about their dates, boyfriends and girlfriends, and their roles in the celebrity culture that so often defines Atlanta nightlife, I more often than not pull up pictures of my children, tell funny stories about their lives, and talk about the recent repairs I've made on our house while my friends discuss their newest outfits and evening galas. The result is that our narratives seem strange—often intriguing, but not familiar.

In the end, as an older parent who had a long life as a single gay man, my experience is that I don't fully fit in either of the lives I've created. Immersion in one life leaves me longing and thinking about the other—life with Rico and our four children in our suburban home brings longing for the single life, for the excitement of dinner parties and late nights with friends at clubs and bars, but when I join my friends in the city for a night out, I wonder what's happening back home. Far from giving me a sense of dissatisfaction or disappointment, though, this sense of longing and desire for what is elsewhere provides me with a sense of purpose. Living outside the bounds of intelligibility in a world that wasn't made for us gives us profound insight into the cultural assumptions, beliefs, and conventions that shape human relationships and family dynamics. This outsider awareness forces me to move in and out of different social contexts with amazing agility— not fitting in any space fully, but seeking out and finding fulfillment from many different communities.

I might write more, but I just finished lunch with my friends in the city, one of whom who is off-the-charts excited because he'll be dressing an Atlanta celebrity for a big photo shoot. I'm sitting at a coffee shop, amazed at two new high-rise buildings that have come up since I was last here and how they've changed the look of this neighborhood. Now I have to dart out and get in the carpool line at our suburban Catholic school, where my four kids will be waiting.

I longed to be cared for, not to be a nurturer.

My Grandmother, My Mother, Myself, and My Son
JEAN Y. LEUNG

My son was born at noon on Halloween during my fortieth year. Later that night, I lay in bed and listened to the sounds of the famed Greenwich Village Halloween parade as it snaked its way past my hospital. How many times had I observed this parade—had even participated in it? And now I was about to embark upon a journey I once thought I didn't want. As a teenager, I'd sworn I wouldn't have a child after forty, yet here I was, doing exactly what I'd said I wouldn't do.

I was the last of six children for my parents, my mom being forty-four when I was born. Our timeline had stretched over two decades and three countries. They had first become parents as teenagers in a middle-of-nowhere village in southern China. After the third one, a boy who could bear the family name, was born, my father left for America. That was what the men in a subsistence farming village did: they went elsewhere to send money back. Frequently, they were only allowed to leave when they had sealed their ties to the village with children.

Generally, the men would come back after they'd made their fortunes. That's what happened to my mom's dad. He'd returned from the West Coast and had my mother. We're not sure how old my grandparents were when they had my mom, but she had siblings who were already married with children when she was born. Those siblings, like my mom, were probably married as teenagers.

THERE WAS NO MEDICAL CARE, never mind birth control, in the remote villages of southern China. When my father's brother fell ill, he just took to bed, then died there. There were no doctors, nurses, clinics, or hospitals around. Women had children until they went through menopause or died.

However, family support was plentiful because everyone lived in close quarters, often too poor to start separate households. When my father and his brothers married, they didn't move out. Instead, their spouses moved in. I've been in my grandparents' tiny two-room house, and it was hard to believe that at one time, this house contained my grandparents, my father and his four brothers, their spouses, and their children. My mother grew up in a similar setting. Even though she was very young when she became a first-time parent, there was always support—nor were children considered special. They integrated themselves into the family and village life of work, home, and community.

After my father left, the situation in China—though never stable—turned even more dire with World War II. Dad realized that the world he'd left was one he couldn't return to. He also knew how hard it was for Chinese migrants to bring their families to America. From 1943 to 1952, only about 105 Chinese people were allowed into the US. My father joined the army, got his citizenship, and started the arduous process of bringing over my mother. By the time she stepped off the plane and into my father's arms, they were grandparents twice over. Within four years, they managed to have two more children: my brother and me.

Unlike their first go-arounds as parents, this second time was lonely. My mother was adapting to a new country, a new language, and a new culture when my brother was born. Of course, all this was exacerbated by the fact that my parents weren't young, being in their forties. Back home, there were always people to help out with childcare. Now there was only the two of them, with no relatives nearby.

I saw the contrast between my family and other families. Friends and classmates reported going to Little League, dance lessons, movies, and parks with their parents, but I had no such experiences. Money was probably an issue for my parents, as was our work (our Chinese laundry operated seven days a week, even during holidays). But a bigger reason for the contrast, which I didn't realize at the time, was how my parents had grown up: they didn't know this way of life existed, so they couldn't act upon it.

I BLAMED THE AGE DIFFERENCE between my parents and the other parents, who all seemed much younger. *If my parents were a "normal" age*, I thought, *they would teach me how to throw a ball, ride a bicycle, swim, etc.* My parents' marriage was arranged, so they never dated. Without a courtship, they didn't know how to counsel me through the teenage angst of boy-girl attraction. They expected me to go to college but couldn't give me any guidance or support. Retirement loomed on the horizon, so they couldn't help out financially. *If only Mom and Dad were younger*, I believed, *things would be better.* I swore I'd never have a child late in life. *People over forty have no business having kids*, I thought.

By the time I reached my late twenties, however, my aversion to having children at a later age had morphed into dislike of the idea of motherhood itself. I had always believed that men and women were equal, and yet women were rarely treated that way from what I could see; instead, they were the underpinnings of society, their families, men, and children. I held jobs where I worked for men, but when I was the boss, I felt I never got the respect a man would have gotten. I longed to be cared for, not to be a nurturer.

Motherhood was not for me, I decided. I wanted to resist

the prevalent idea, which my own parents shared, that motherhood was a woman's only purpose. Practical reasons also held me back—I dreaded the sleepless nights, tons of diapers, lack of privacy, childcare, financial needs, and most of all, the eternal responsibility.

But as I watched other women start families in my thirties, something nagged at me. What if I was missing the boat? I envied men who, it seemed, didn't have this ticking internal clock. I knew the time would come when I'd pass the invisible line of being unable to conceive a child, and while I knew adoption was a choice, I wanted a biological child—not for egotistical reasons like passing along my DNA, but because I've always been a from-scratch person. If I was going to experience motherhood, I wanted to do it all the way: to feel the morning sickness, the swelling belly, the pain of a baby trying to push its way out of my body.

Because my mother was in her mid-forties when I was born, I held steadfast to the idea that I could easily have a child in my forties. But tales of women who had tried and failed to have children in their forties haunted me, so it was with great anxiety and trepidation that I looked at a pregnancy test at the age of thirty-nine and was greeted with a firm blue line.

My husband was elated. Unlike me, he'd always wanted to be a parent and was more aware of our fertility fragility, since he, too, was in his late thirties. To his credit, he was only been a gentle influence on my decision-making, due to his strong belief in a woman's ability to control her reproductive destiny.

If I had any doubt that I was an older mom-to-be, the medical profession quickly dispelled that thought, and the constant reminder of my age made me afraid of losing my baby. I was made to undergo genetic testing. I followed the doctor's orders religiously, took vitamins, ate better, exercised more, and even started talking to my belly. It felt silly at first, but a fluttering sensation made me feel better. Maybe the baby was listening?

During my pregnancy, I read and researched pregnancy and child development. Once I made the commitment to be a mother, I wanted to be the best parent I could be, and I could focus on this goal because I was older. I'd already established myself as an independent woman with well-paying jobs, even before I married. I'd already accomplished my career goal of being published. All the travel I'd done had sated my wanderlust. I could focus on someone else's life because mine was already so full.

The age difference between me and most of the other moms became more apparent when my son started preschool and we began to socialize with other families. Of course, most of the families we gravitated to reflected our own, with older, more affluent, educated parents. But many of Jacob's elementary school classmates had parents who were in their twenties. These families tended to be poorer and less child-centered than the families with older parents, I noticed.

I vividly remember an incident that illustrated the difference between being a younger and older parent. Another mother and I had agreed to take our children to a concert. On the day of the concert, though, the children balked at going. It had been the other mom's idea. When my son and his friend put up a big fuss, I knew it wasn't a good idea to go through with it. I took the long view—the band would probably play again, and we could make childcare arrangements in advance then. "Look," I told her, "I've been to many concerts, and it won't kill me to miss this one."

"But it'll kill me," she retorted. In the end, I stayed home with the kids and she went by herself.

The older parents I knew also tended to have smaller families like ours, usually with only one child. With fewer children, the older parents had more money to spend on resources for their children. The younger parents had more children or were more fragmented in their family configurations.

I recently asked my adult son how he felt about having older parents. What he remembered most was our lack of interest in sports. As he got older, however, he realized that this had more to do with us as individuals than our age. I had come from an immigrant family, and my husband was an immigrant. We both came from cultures that didn't emphasize American sports like baseball and basketball.

My son also complained about how he'd been overscheduled with after-school and weekend activities and how he'd been envious of friends who had more unstructured time. Jacob was right; this was a product of us being older. We had so many experiences that we wanted him to have, and I had a pressing sense of urgency that time was passing by. There were so many opportunities in the city he grew up in for enrichment in the arts and sciences—perhaps younger parents would have been more relaxed about this, or too busy. But did he suffer in the long run? I think he and I could agree that he in fact benefited from these activities, which gave him more possibilities to make friends, explore the world, and formulate his own likes and dislikes.

My grandmother and mother didn't have choices about having children. Since all of my grandparents had long passed away before I was born, I don't have a clue about how they felt about having children late in life. I do know that my mother tried to escape her predestined life. When she found out that a girl from a neighboring village was being sent to America to become the bride of a cousin, she begged the girl to take her along as a servant. It turned out to be impossible, as there was only one visa. Shortly thereafter, my mother married my father and moved into his village. She dreamed of America, believing life would be better here, and was bitterly disappointed when life turned out to be harder in many ways than what she'd known in China.

Still, my mother could never understand why a woman would not want children. Motherhood was what set women apart from men; it was what made them valuable. I disagree with that belief and know many women who have lived rich lives without children. But I'm glad I chose to become a mother, even later in life. It's been the most satisfying role I've ever had, full of unexpected pleasures, and the fact that it came to me later in life has made it all the more precious. Having taken care of myself, I could now nurture someone else. Instead of being rained upon, I feel like my parade is full of rainbows.

*I'm not finding myself;
I'm not struggling to make
a go of my career.*

His Old Man
ADAM BERLIN

My dad had me when he was twenty-nine. He was finishing his PhD in English Lit at UC Berkeley. He'd traveled with my mom through Europe for seven months. He'd been a Woodrow Wilson fellow. He'd served two years in the army under the G.I. Bill. He was born on the Lower East Side and had grown up a street-smart kid in Williamsburg, Brooklyn.

All of this is to say, my dad had been around a lot of blocks. When I was born, he was more man than young man—but he wasn't an old man, not by fathering standards.

I am. I was almost fifty when I had my kid.

My girlfriend, Katherine, is fourteen years younger than me.

My dad died two months before my son was born. Before that, though, he'd touched my girlfriend's stomach; I like to think he felt my kid kick, but at least his hand was only a few layers of skin away from my boy's almost-formed body. I'd hoped for a real bond between my son and my dad, but I knew, as my dad knew, that age might prevent this. And it did. And that's one grave downside to having a child at forty-eight, an age when many parents become grandparents.

Unless I live well beyond my life expectancy, I won't be in my son's life for as long as my father was in mine. It's hard to parse the different life lessons my father taught me in a chronological way—lessons I learned through his example, through talks we had at the dinner table (my family ate three squares together while I was growing up, and after I moved out, I frequently went home to visit my parents until my dad died), through letters and emails and postcards from abroad (my parents were big travelers). These exchanges sometimes recapped the usual but sometimes focused on important moments—my discontent as a camper, my move to New York City at seventeen, and the rejections and acceptances that marked my life as I tried to be an actor (getting my SAG card was a big day), a writer (getting my first novel published was another), and finally, the news that I was about to be a father. This was the final big email from my dad. Here's what my dad wrote:

Dear Adam,

I believe you may be feeling somewhat anxious about the inevitable changes in your life with the arrival of your son. Less freedom, more responsibilities, paying attention to things (both big and small) that you never had to think about before. Stated this way, it seems rather daunting. But then the boy will arrive and you will realize—I guarantee it!—that you have been given the magical opportunity to love someone who comes from you and Katherine, who allows you to see the world with other eyes than your own, who will grow and thrive because of your attention and love. Think of it. Your son! Life as you know it will change. But whatever your life has been up to now—and I see it as a life of real accomplishment, a life of many experiences (both good and bad)—the future with your son will add a freshness to your life. My wish, and your mother's wish, is that he will be as wonderful a son to you and Katherine as you have been to us.

I love you,
Dad

I don't know if my dad could have written this note if he hadn't known me for as long as he did. I was an older soon-to-be parent;

he was old. Our father-son relationship spread across many decades. There's wisdom and joy here, as well as sadness when I read his note over today—my dad never did experience that exclamation point after the simple, declarative *Your son!*

Chances are, I won't be around for at least some of the big milestones in my son's life; I won't be able to talk to him the way my dad talked to me at the end. By then, my dad was who he was: retired, content with his accomplishments, clear in what he felt was important in life and what was not. His solidity, coupled with the solidity I'd achieved as a forty-plus adult, made for eye-to-eye talks that were less about the lesson and more about the moment.

The upside to my later-in-life fatherhood resides in this solidity. My son is only three now. I'm not finding myself; I'm not struggling to make a go of my career. As a tenured professor, I'm not stressed about job stability or overly stressed about money. All the workday worries that young parents have—the details that steal much of our lives and get passed down through day-to-day interactions—will not be part of my son's young life. My parents worked hard to not let their stress touch me, and I never heard them argue until later in life, when they no longer needed to filter for my sake, but there *were* problems, problems related to growing up and growing comfortable, problems I now see from the safe distance of my adulthood.

My mom was depressed when I was a kid; the coldness of Montreal and the long hours my dad spent at McGill at the beginning of his career broke her down. She lost weight; she felt unappreciated; she was a young mother who'd put her career on hold. Her depression must have rubbed off on me, even if I didn't know what was happening at that time. In addition to being a nail biter, a nervous habit that started in Montreal, I was a kid afraid of changing the slightest routine, who refused to wear a jacket when summer was over and then, when I finally did, refused to take off my jacket when summer arrived. This behavior suggests a need to hold on, to keep stable, to maintain order—a need that once seemed an aberration for a kid raised in a loving home but now seems a plausible symptom of something that must have been happening around me. I now see other markers that showed my parents' tension rubbing off on me—usually gently because we were a close family, but with the residue of things not so gentle. The kind of growing pains my relatively young parents went through, pains I went through pre-child, are no longer part of me and haven't been for a long time. And so, the residue of many hard life experiences, experiences often exacerbated and complicated by the presence of a child, will not be part of my son's growing-up.

Solidity and self-confidence born from age now allow me to bring up my child using and trusting my gut. When I hang out in playgrounds and hear the usually inane conversations about child-rearing—young parents talking about what they've read or bought that will help their young children—I can't help but judge. There's a whole industry of how-to books and gadgets that prey on the desperation of the parental masses to do right by their kids and shame parents into thinking that if they don't use this method or buy that product, their kids will lose a competitive edge in the world and will be less likely to adapt. Too often, adapting, fitting in, and beating out is young parents' impetus for having a kid in the first place: the goal is to create a body to fulfill dreams, which, in a perversely self-destructive, catch-22 way, deprives young parents of fulfilling their dreams. My extra decade or two of experience has helped me see a bigger picture rather than getting caught up with too-easy theories-of-the-day or solve-all products.

Perhaps (Beckett's favorite word, my dad taught me) there was some selfishness in my decision to wait so long to have a child. I deprived my dad of years with his grandson; I'm depriving my son years with me. At the end of Hemingway's *My Old Man*, the narrator/son is called *old boy* right after his father dies, the son's "old" a connotative consequence of having to grow up too soon without a father. I could certainly argue with myself that the balance of spending more years with my son tilts heavier than my belief that these years will be full of a purer, fresher, less-cluttered joy. But again, I believe a solidity born from this selfishness will benefit my son. So many parents regret not having lived the lives they wanted before their freedom—or their perception of freedom— became limited by the constant attention to and demands of an infant and young child.

Before my son was born, I had lived my life to the lees, as Ulysses might say. I'd sowed fields full of wild oats. I'd traveled as much as I'd wanted. I'd been able to live low to the ground, choosing free time over money, renting illegal sublets for cheap, working part-time jobs, never having to answer to anyone. I had a kid when I was ready. No regrets—no coulda, woulda, shouldas that can create damage, even if they go unspoken. In moments when they're not smiling for the camera, I often see younger parents pushing or pulling their young kids with pursed lips, their dreams deferred because a kid came along, even if the kid created other dreams.

My only regret, and it's a selfish one, is that my dad never got to see me being a dad. I have never and will never receive the single compliment from him I now crave: that I'm a good parent. I'm sure younger parents get that compliment from their parents, who are alive and thriving and ideally engaged with their children's lives. It must be grounding and simultaneously elevating to hear those words from a parent: *You're a great dad.* It's a compliment founded in begetting that completes a natural, three-generation cycle—a compliment so simple yet so connected to the complexities of family, history, legacy, promise, and hope. It's a compliment I'll never get.

When I was a kid and my dad was closer to young man than old man, he used to joke, "I try to be a good daddy." I remember laughing at that, at the way he stretched out the words to sound like potential disaster, at the way he pulled a face that showed inept. I laughed because the opposite was so true. He was a great dad, no trying about it. But here's a fact my dad might have complimented me on: my kid laughs far more and more joyously than I ever laughed—and I had a mostly happy childhood. And in that laughter is me, an older parent who doesn't give a fuck about what's not that important, who has given my son the example and encouragement to fuck-it laugh.

And in that fuck-it freedom, I believe—biased though I may be, as an older dad—that my son will have more room to grow, unbridled.

I spent angry months working out how to accept being a less superhuman mom than those I was constantly reading about, those who had miraculously recovered their children.

If I Don't Laugh, I'll Cry

ELIZABETH NEWMAN

They say life is a roller-coaster. If not for the birth of my fourth daughter, this line would have remained a cliché to me. Instead, it's become a core theme.

As a young person, I avoided roller-coasters. I was never a thrill seeker; the rocketing ups and downs were not my thing. I preferred a slow, steady pace in entertainment—and in life.

Mia was born just after my fortieth birthday, and her diagnosis of epilepsy and autism shoved me headfirst onto a figurative roller-coaster. In my late forties, I chose to board a Disney roller-coaster for the first time. After all, how scary could it be in comparison to riding the Mia-coaster for so many years?

You see, life in Mia's world is much like life on the Kingda Ka strata-coaster. One of the world's tallest coasters, the Kingda Ka takes riders 456 feet above the ground, then drops 418 feet straight down and reaches speeds of 128 miles an hour. The ride lasts a mere ninety seconds, but it can feel like a lifetime. The precipitous highs, plunging lows, time-warping speed, and enormous cost—over $100 million to build—equate to life with Mia for me.

On a roller-coaster, some people are terrified; some are exhilarated. I was one of the terrified ones. So, my question became: How do I get from terror to exhilaration?

How indeed does one find joy in a ride that entails sewing on one-piece pajamas every night so your diapered six-year-old will not smear her feces all over her bedroom? A ride with a repetitively circling, endlessly banging, monotonously humming but otherwise wordless "autotron." A ride that means malicious attacks with baby teeth, nails, and limbs in moments that you least expect them, no matter how many times they occur. A ride that propels you into an eerie war zone, where any movement might lead to the explosion of some buried mine of a missed developmental milestone, morphing seizure activity, inexplicable meltdown, smashed china, unhinged doors, and walls pelted with holes. Our little roller-coaster conductor once even ran into my bathroom one morning, ripped off my bra, and bolted away. Inhabited by this china-shop bull, our world was constantly upended.

How would our family find a way back to any semblance of normalcy?

In the overwhelming aftermath of Mia's diagnosis, the first promising escape hatch we explored was labeled COMPLETE RECOVERY. We sprang into diagnostic reaction mode as we searched through nearly endless treatments to recover our Mia and our sanity.

I WROTE A PIECE of verse called "Categorical Panoply," which is about wading through all the therapy options. Though copious, it is by no means an exhaustive list. The word *panoply* means "all the arms and armor of a warrior," which is pretty much what we were seeking: all the ammunition to reach and raise our child and make sense of our lives.

Categorical Panoply

A categorical panoply of vast and varied therapies
to cure or combat ASD all swim before my eyes!
And every claim I've three times read,
each mixed and mingled in my head.
Which one shall be our daily bread? How am I to decide?

There's Melatonin and SCD, Vitamins and DMG,
Hormones, Gluten/Casein free, and that just starts the list!
There's Feingold, Enzymes, Stimulants, Anti-psychotics, Oxidants,
Prozac, and other Happiants,
such biochemical bliss!

There's Neurosensory Integration, Proprioceptive Stimulation,
Facilitated Communication, yet, oh, indeed there's more!
There's Therapeutic Dance and Art, Hippotherapy to start,
Joint Compression to impart.
What else could be in store?

Social Stories, Modeling, chairs to spin and chairs to swing,
Psychomotor Patterning, and still so much to know!
Psychodynamics, ABA, Son-Rise has found another way.
PECS and TEACCH and floortime play
each offer paths to go!

The options all just pile up. They fill and runneth o'er my cup.
Which shall I choose to greedy sup to reach my blessed babe?
For testimonies rich abound, each method has proponents found
and I am dizzy all around.
How will I find my way?

AS OUR FORTIES WHIZZED BY, my husband and I spent years—and our savings—questing for a cure, leaving no stone unturned.

While Mia made significant progress, she also experienced years of regression and serious medical challenges. As we entered our fifties, Mia began to lose her hard-won language skills, appetite, ability to emote, and general zest for life. She had a drop seizure at school and began to have panic-laced night terror seizures. These episodes occurred three to ten times a night for two and a half years, despite antiseizure medications.

Forever hardwired in my memory is the night these episodes were accompanied by vomiting. We woke to Mia's unearthly vocalizations as she scrambled out of bed and began scaling a wall to escape whatever demon was haunting her. My husband wrapped his arms around our daughter to keep her from hurtling herself down the stairs. Mia was incredibly strong, even at nine years old, and consequently not easy to keep hold of in the best of scenarios. As soon as she started vomiting, her slippery self was able to break free of his embrace. I attempted to snatch our little escapee and slid forcefully onto my bum in a thick pool of her partly digested dinner. My husband picked up the chase while I sat there in the middle of the night, marveling at the alter reality our lives had become. I remember thinking, perhaps even mouthing to myself, *Lord, I am too old for this.*

Throughout my forties, I fought against the possibility that complete recovery may not be in the picture for Mia, at least not in this lifetime. I spent angry months working out how to accept being a less superhuman mom than those I was constantly reading about, those who had miraculously recovered their children.

Then, quite suddenly, my struggle dissipated, and intellectualized wistfulness gave way to simple reality. As I entered my fifties, I squared my focus on who Mia was, rather than who I wanted her to be.

While our energy levels were dropping with age, a shift toward pragmatic reality was on the rise. My husband and I no longer pined like battered pups for what could be, but dealt head-on, like vigilant bullmastiffs, with what *was*. We embraced Mia's ways and made it our job to ensure everyone else did too. Due to Mia's aggression and developmental delays, we homeschooled her for several years.

EVENTUALLY, we took a chance on the public school system to help us educate our wild child. As I sat in the principal's office, I detailed once again all the reasons Mia would continue to need one-on-one paraprofessional support. The principal's tone was patronizing as she said, "Now, Elizabeth, you realize the goal for Mia is independence, don't you?"

Having grown accustomed to playing the what's-necessary-for-Mia's-success-versus-what-the-school-budget-can-accommodate-game, I didn't bat an eye, but answered with knowing conviction, "Actually, the *dream* is independence. The *goal* is keeping Mia and everyone around her safe." Luckily for all concerned, after the fourth clearing of the entire school in response to Mia's impulsive fire-alarm pulls, the necessity of keeping a "whirling dervish" protectorate posted with Mia at all times was firmly established.

Along with this pragmatic realism, we also began to champion laughter over horror. When Mia was initially diagnosed as permanently brain-damaged in the hospital emergency ward at three in the morning, I went into shock. Our older girls were somber, and my husband was tongue-tied. Yet our third daughter, Gabri, who was five at the time, started to laugh. When my husband recovered enough to ask her if she understood what was happening, she said "Yes, Daddy, I understand. But if I don't laugh, I'll cry!" Naturally more of a joker than I am, my husband quickly came to appreciate this wisdom from the mouth of our babe. But I, too, eventually came to see there was no way around it—it was indeed our choice to laugh or cry at every turn. Countless times in my pre-Mia life, I had found myself laughing so hard that I began to cry. Was it possible, then, to cry so hard that I could begin to laugh?

In my attempt to puzzle this out, I wrote some cathartic lines of poetry, which end with:

> For because we feel pain so often, so deeply
> we must also learn to feel delight more often, more deeply
>
> We simply must learn to explode
> bent over double with laughter, snorts, giggles
> lest we implode
> with grief

HOW TEMPTING IT IS to wear our grief like it is the whole of who we are and all of what we experience in life. But, praise the Lord, the scales have fallen from our eyes with maturity and we are more often than not able to see that it just isn't so. Along with sorrow, the world keeps offering up beauty and joy.

OUR LIVES WITH MIA have certainly given us ample fodder to bust a gut. On one occasion, my ten-year-old neighbor, Cydney, told me about a conversation she had with one of her friends, in which the friend said, "I think I have what Mia has."

Cydney, who had known Mia nearly all her life, strongly disagreed, but her friend insisted, saying, "Yes, really, I think I have autopsy!" Mia, who can outlast the Energizer bunny, is hardly an autopsy candidate, but I often wish I could get inside her racing body and understand just how her jumbled-up nervous system operates.

On another occasion, Mia was at the pool and ran by two little boys. She hit one of them as she sped by. One of the boys was familiar with Mia's impulsive behavior, but the boy she hit didn't know Mia. He looked quizzically at his friend with an expression of, "What's up with that?"

His friend brushed off the event, saying, "Oh, that's just Mia—she's authentic." Truly, with Mia, what you see is definitively what you get.

I have come to a new appreciation of this funny world, with all its odd creatures and comical occurrences. I consider my Mia to be among the oddest. Her ability to communicate was long in coming; now she is so verbose and repetitive, we often find ourselves thinking we should have been more careful about what we wished for. Fortunately, strewn amid the hundredth declaration that her "belly is hungry" and she is "starving to deaf," she also puts words and thoughts together in the funniest ways. Lately, she's taken to introducing herself by announcing, "I'm Mia Newman, I'm special needs and special forces!"

And a special kind of force she most surely is. On a recent excursion to the grocery store with her older sister, Mia noticed another shopper with an enviably full cart. As Mia loves food with a passion most people never experience, she was immediately impressed. Smiling broadly, she remarked to the shopper, "You got a lot of food in there. You a good man, probably." I can't imagine he ever expected to be so positively summed up by the contents of his grocery cart, but in our household, we have grown accustomed to Mia's verbal appreciation of food. As I made lunch one day, I let Mia know I was going to prepare her a sandwich. She broke out in song, exclaiming, "Mom is making lunch, Mom is making lunch, she just said something brilliant, she's making cheese and salami." If all I have to do is announce the slapping-together of a sandwich to be hailed as brilliant, consider it done.

Mia's language is also laced with appreciation, compliments, song, giggles, and a more-than-occasional *meow*. She tells me almost every day, "Mother-mom, you are so adorable." She has no agenda. She is the most authentic human being I have ever met and consequently calls me to greater authenticity.

NOW APPROACHING SIXTY, our peers experience the freedom of empty nests, but we continue to arrange babysitters and take turns at never-ending Mia duty.

WE REGULARLY REMIND HER to stop eating every plant that catches her fancy—an especially taxing exercise over the holidays, with an appetizing Christmas tree within reach. We manage her menses. Years past menopause, I never anticipated shepherding another woman's cycle, and my husband never imagined lining underwear with pads and counting down the days. Yet here we stand, always at the ready for the expected unexpected.

Along the way, we've learned a thing or two about overcoming exhaustion and dread. The answers we've found have a lot to do with practicing behaviors that support coping, as opposed to those that lead to the collapse of our joy, marriage, and family. However, there is no escaping that Mia's antics and escapades are often horrifying; we've been on the receiving end of many a burning look, which send a message of, "poor, pitiful child," "poor parent," and often, "you are a bad parent with an unruly child." Once, I was attempting to pull a stubborn grocery cart from its nested bunch when Mia scooted away to attack an unsuspecting shopper. My daughter's slaps and pinches were returned with vigorous swats, as if she was a pesky fly. Mortified by Mia's actions and astounded at her victim's response, I considered confronting this battered woman to defensively explain Mia's lack of control and indignantly demand an explanation for her own. But I passed on, suddenly seeing the lesson was for me. How could I expect this stranger to release her shortsighted, incriminating judgment of Mia while I still stood, paradoxically, in reproachful judgment of her?

Just as Gabri's five-year-old observation set me on a path to understanding the value of raw bliss, the trip to the grocer's inspired me to explore turning self-pity into an opportunity to offer the compassion I so desperately wanted from others. These moments schooled me to be the first to withhold judgment, the first to give what I want to receive, the first to look for hilarity in tragedy. It's taken me decades to internalize the lessons of laughter and compassion deeply enough to generalize them across our Mia-centered universe.

Now, as grandparent-aged parents of an "always-toddler," we have learned to look with better eyes, to be kinder than is necessary. While trips abroad, romantic dinners, quiet nights at home, and belongings found just where we left them still taunt me with delicious appeal, I wouldn't trade life with Mia for any of these empty-nester norms. After all, the truth I've come to appreciate is that every parent has, or will at some point in their lives, experienced life as a roller-coaster—maybe even a strata-coaster.

I didn't realize it when I named Mia, but the meaning of her name has the connotation of bitterness. It's tempting to think how fitting this name has been, but it is only half the story. The better half is that by her very nature, she transformed me and my husband into thrill seekers, for it is the breathtaking exhilaration of a mile-high, Mia-coaster view that allows us to endure the trials. So yes, our nest will be forever full, but when this otherworldly Mia-coaster plummets toward despair, our instinctual reaction is to fix our gaze on joy.

*I leaned on my friends—
and complete strangers.*

What Is Hard?

CATHERINE ARNST

In the twenty years since I adopted my daughter as a single, forty-five-year-old woman, I cannot count the times I have fielded comments—by casual acquaintances, close friends, and complete strangers—that run along the lines of "Isn't it hard, raising a child on your own?" or, "You are so [brave, noble, strong, generous, etc.], adopting a child on your own. It must be hard." The less-diplomatic remark might even be, "A child at your age! How hard is that?"

I usually smile politely and say, "No, it's not that hard." Sometimes, though, when I'm not feeling all that generous, I give an honest answer: "Watching someone you love die is hard. This is easy."

I did watch someone die: my husband, at age forty-two, of a brain tumor, just two years after we were married. That was unspeakably hard. Motherhood, not so much.

I met Peter Sleeper in Boston when I was thirty-three and he thirty-eight. Both of us were reporters. I was smitten with his wit, intelligence, and good looks. We shared an edgy sense of humor, a slightly unhealthy obsession with politics, and a love of journalism, movies, books, travel, and cats. We were each too cynical to use the word *soulmate*, but we would have if we'd dared. Within six months, we were living together, and in August 1988, we got married.

While on our honeymoon in Italy, Peter kept getting headaches. When we got back, he learned that a pituitary tumor at the base of his brain, which he thought had been successfully removed several years earlier, had recurred and was pressing against his optic nerve. He underwent brain surgery, then another brain surgery, then radiation treatment. Because his doctors warned him that the treatment could leave him sterile, he deposited his sperm in a sperm bank. Although we both wanted children, I thought we should wait for him to be cured before starting a family. A bad decision.

The tumor was in remission when I was offered my dream job as a European science correspondent with *Reuters*. We rented out our newly purchased house in Boston and moved to London in September 1989. Shortly after we arrived, Peter consulted with a leading specialist for pituitary tumors and discovered his was growing again. Still, this type of brain tumor is rarely fatal. He underwent brain surgery again, as well as an experimental hormone treatment that seemed to work miracles. We were soon traveling around Europe, biking in France, motoring about the Scottish Highlands, and entertaining a steady stream of visitors from the States. We refused to accept that we were living on borrowed time, but we were. Despite top-notch care from his medical team and our determination to try every possible option, Peter died in a London hospital in October 1990.

He died two months to the day after my mother died of an asthma attack at age sixty-three. My parents had been living on a sailboat for several years and were in Key West when she went into respiratory failure. She was in a coma for several weeks, and I was torn between staying with her and my devastated dad or returning to London to be with Peter, who was going through chemotherapy. I chose Peter, so I wasn't there for my parents when my mother died.

The deaths of Peter and my mother left me a zombie. I couldn't lean on my father, who was even more of a wreck than I was, and though my London friends were wonderful, I still felt alone and adrift. Back home, the US was mired in a recession sparked by a housing crash, and our Boston home was part of the collapse. Our tenants moved out, I couldn't find new renters or a buyer, and I couldn't manage the mortgage without Peter's income. Within months of his death, the bank foreclosed.

I was thirty-seven and completely, utterly shattered. In one year, I had lost the love of my life, become financially ruined, and found myself essentially without family. The sum of my experiences had not prepared me for any of this. I could see no way forward.

I sleepwalked through the next three years in London until I decided enough was enough. I accepted a job at a magazine in New York, a city where I'd once lived and still had friends. My plan was to get my head together, fall in love with someone new, and start a family. I got two out of three. Though not lucky in love a second time, I had learned from Peter the importance of love and family—so I decided to go for both, married or not.

At forty-two, I tried getting pregnant with Peter's banked sperm. Two failed attempts later, my fertility doctor recommended I use donated sperm. But I wanted Peter's child, not a stranger's. Since Peter and I had often said we would adopt if we weren't able to conceive, I decided to adopt the child we might have raised together. That's how I found myself standing in a courtyard in Yueyang, a small city in central China, in November 1999, meeting for the first time my eleven-month-old daughter Ba Yu-Si, soon to be Jesse Arnst. She took one look at me, started to scream, and kept it up for the next eight hours.

What had I done? How would I, a single, middle-aged woman, ever manage this ball of emotional need? My first parental lesson was that I couldn't do it alone. I went to China as one of eight families and had originally planned to travel without a companion. A few months before the trip, however, my good friend Nancy pointedly told me not to be ridiculous—she was coming with me. Thank god for Nancy. It quickly became clear that I had no idea how to care for a baby, but Nancy, a mother of two and one of twelve siblings, had seen it all. Once we got through that first stressful day, Jesse woke up the next morning smiling and was Miss Congeniality for the rest of the trip. She had no health problems, ate everything that was put in front of her, and fell asleep on any moving conveyance. With Nancy's help, China was quite fun.

I arrived home in Brooklyn two weeks later, jet-lagged and clueless. I had smugly assumed that I, an experienced journalist who had covered a huge range of stories in lots of different locales, would have no problem caring for a baby. Such hubris! The village around me was more sensible; they came to my rescue. My upstairs neighbor, Alice, who had two young daughters of her own, made sure I had everything I needed, including two extra hands. Friends visited regularly, referred me to a wonderful pediatrician right up the block, and introduced me to all the kid-friendly stores, restaurants, and resources in my neighborhood. I was invited over to dinner or for the weekend. I had multiple guides to the land of parenthood, and I was mature enough to know what I didn't know—which turned out to be a lot. I took advantage of all the help and advice. My three months of home leave were almost too easy.

Then reality bit. It was time to return to my demanding job as a senior writer for a weekly magazine. I'd read every disheartening article about how hard it is to juggle work and family and how women can't have it all, so of course I was anxious. The raised eyebrows I kept getting when I told people I was raising Jesse without a partner—and at age forty-five—didn't help. *Maybe this really is too hard*, I worried.

But then along came a miracle in the shape of Cheryl, the world's best nanny, Jesse's second mother, the woman who raised her up right. Cheryl and Jesse took to each other instantly; I stopped worrying about returning to work the first time Cheryl picked Jesse up and they laughed together. I immediately made one of my wisest decisions ever: to trust Cheryl completely.

Since I was the novice, I gave Cheryl carte blanche to care for Jesse as she saw fit, and she, in turn, took Jesse and our household well in hand. She soon had Jesse on a routine, got her to start walking (Jesse had shown no interest in doing so until Cheryl came along), made her healthy meals (with leftovers for me), and added nannies in the neighborhood to her already-wide circle of friends around the city, so Jesse had playdates almost daily. I, in turn, got to meet the parents of those playdates, some of whom became lifelong friends. Sometimes Cheryl took Jesse to her own home for a few days so Jesse could play with her own three kids and their cousins, and we now remain close to her and her family. And when Jesse was three, Cheryl took her to Newport for a weekend to meet one of her former charges. I admit I was jealous.

Nights and weekends, I leaned on my friends—and complete strangers. An example: when Jesse was two, I took her to the beach for the first time, the two of us on our own at Coney Island. But it hadn't occurred to me to bring snacks or water. A Guatemalan family nearby saw my dilemma and took pity on my poor girl. Despite a language barrier, they happily fed us food and handed Jesse juice boxes, instructed their kids to play with her and share their beach toys, even watched her while I went swimming. It doesn't just take a village; it takes the world.

Toddlerhood passed with a minimum of tantrums (though time may have dimmed those memories), and by the time Jesse started kindergarten at a public school around the corner from our apartment, she was a happy, healthy, outgoing kid. She knew how to pick up her room, behave in restaurants, make friends, and charm adults. What more could you ask?

The advantages of parenting while older were paying off. I was well-established in my career, so I was able to afford Cheryl, who worked for us until Jesse was nine. My friends were mostly older parents themselves, with kids the same age as Jesse or teenagers who found her adorable. I became close friends with another single mother in the neighborhood who was around the same age as me and had a daughter two years younger than Jesse. Both of us traveled often for work, and we quickly formed a partnership. When I was out of town, Phyllis took Jesse to her home, and when she travelled, I took charge of Lela.

I also had the benefit of years of hard-won experiences to fall back on, which gave me some perspective on the everyday problems that might have caused me to worry obsessively when I was younger. And I was extraordinarily lucky. Terrible things can happen to children—illness, violence, drug addiction, teen pregnancy, depression, bullying. Life can throw things at kids that bear no linear relation to the parent's child-rearing choices or age—I would caution against a glib assumption that the age or lifestyle of an unmarried mother can set the stage for cataclysm. My own experiences and those of close friends prove such assumptions are nothing more than biases.

I don't want to imply that Jesse and I faced no challenges or that I have no regrets about how I parented her. I wasn't energetic or resourceful enough to adopt a second child, which means Jesse doesn't have a sibling. I don't have an extended family to share with her. I'm the opposite of a "digital native," so I wasn't on top of any social media pressure or internet dangers she might face. When Jesse hit puberty and I was in my late-fifties, hormonal swings and growth spurts were accompanied by terrible grades and discipline problems. Overwhelmed during those few years, I'd fantasize about a path not taken, one where I was drinking wine in Italy with sane adults, instead of drinking wine in Brooklyn to calm down from our latest screaming match.

Then again, you can only spend so much time in Italy before you come home alone. I would have missed the adventure of a lifetime: watching Jesse grow into a wonderful young woman. The terrible tween years were mercifully brief, and by high school, we were mostly back to normal. Today, she is a senior in college, majoring in dance. She is funny and kind and dedicated to her art, and a delight to spend time with.

She will be graduating soon and I will probably be retiring, so with luck, there will still be time to drink wine with friends in Italy, Brooklyn, or wherever else, while we brag to each other about our now-grown kids. I don't feel like I sacrificed anything by starting parenthood later in life. Considering the alternatives, it's been pretty easy.

"But I can get a new dad, right?"

Being All the Things
KATHERINE C. RAND

It's five-fifteen and my eyes open of their own accord from an active dreamscape. I am all the way at the edge of the bed, about to fall off, and my son's head is nestled into the crook of my shoulder. I gingerly lift it off my arm so I can extract my body and hopefully get to writing. Suddenly, it occurs to me that I left a load of laundry in the washer, thinking I would get up to transfer it to the dryer after I put Maurice to bed, but I was too tired and slept right through. Before I can even stand up, though, he notices the warmth of my body is gone and says, "Mommy, come back and lie down with me." I oblige, hoping he'll drift right back to sleep, but when I get in on the other side of the bed it's cold and urine-soaked—no wonder he'd pushed me so far to one side of the bed! Exasperated, I return to the other side and snuggle in.

As I lie there, I begin to try and work out the logistics of the laundry, calculating how I'm going to get the bed linens washed and transferred to the dryer before we go to sleep tonight. The process is made more complicated by the ones sitting in the washer now. I wanted to wake up early to write, but childcare and running the household takes over. I am grateful I have a washer/dryer in my apartment, but I'm also looking for a new place to stay, as we need to downsize, and I don't know that I'll have this convenience wherever we go next, even though it's essential to my ability to continue pursuing my writing and scholarship outside of my other commitments. Renting in Los Angeles is expensive, and renting for a family on one measly educator's salary is hard.

When Maurice seems sufficiently asleep, I try and sneak away again. I begin to deal with the laundry and realize I have to unload the laundry basket before I can unload the dryer before I can move the wet clothes. My shuffling around in the bedroom to put away the clothes wakes my son again. "Is it wake-up time?" I tell him no, and he sits up straight as an arrow and loudly says, "What did you say?"

I tell him it's not wake-up time and miraculously, he puts his head back down on the pillow, and that's the end of it. Forty-five minutes after I first tried to get up to write, I finally manage to get my fingers on the keyboard, the dryer running in the background and the early sun pouring in the living room windows.

I SHARE MY STORIES of mothering as a way of exploring the intersection of various identity markers—especially age and class, since my experience of being an older parent is inextricably linked with family culture, social location, and the expectations that accompany both. I certainly don't pretend to write for all older parents; I speak from my limited perspective and the incredible privilege that comes along with being a highly educated, American-born white woman, whose long-retired parents are comfortable enough to provide significant financial support to me and my child, even if their age and geographical distance precludes them from helping out in other ways.

THE IRONY IS THAT I ended a pregnancy when I was seventeen, feeling certain there wasn't a soul who would support me in making a different decision; at the time, I understood my parents' response to mean they would not provide me any financial or material assistance and that I quite literally would be on my own. But I don't think it's a huge stretch to say the challenges I face as a single, forty-three-year-old with a PhD are not all that different from the ones I would have faced had I been a single parent earlier in life. Now there are varied roles to balance, which complicates things, though parenting is certainly made easier in that I have a significant safety net I can count on—in a way I at least thought I couldn't, twenty-five years ago.

This easy access to wealth seems wildly inequitable to me; it's also what allowed me to pursue higher education without having to maintain a day job. And it makes me wonder if the experience of becoming a parent after forty is reserved only for those with social and economic privilege. Many older parents take on the expense of fertility treatments or international adoption, and, if single, add that to the burden of being a sole income-earner raising and supporting a child.

My journey to parenthood involved a period of intense grieving tied to my adolescent abortion and centered around the impending loss of my fertile years. I had no committed relationship to leave open the possibility that pregnancy might happen in the context of a partnership, and I wasn't interested in adopting or exploring IVF. I had settled into real peace around having a life without the experience of parenting. Then, not long before my thirty-ninth birthday, I became pregnant the old-fashioned way and happily welcomed a child into my world. The other party took the same risks I did, which led to the pregnancy, but wasn't the least interested in becoming a parent. For the most part, it's just been me and my son ever since.

"YOU'RE MY BEST MOMMY," Maurice says at bedtime as he snuggles his head into my shoulder, what he's long called his "nest." I wonder how long it will last. I'm already fearing those tiny losses, as he becomes too big to call me *mommy* or want to spoon as he falls asleep.

"I'm your only mommy," I deflect, as I often do.

"And you're my best mommy." He pauses briefly. "My dad isn't."

I ponder these words, knowing that he's thinking about Dad and family more as Father's Day approaches and they spend an inordinate time on this arbitrary commercial holiday at his preschool, which is more a glorified daycare. In LA, public, subsidized schools are reserved for very low-income families, and many preschools in Los Angeles have multiyear waiting lists and price tags to match. Whether or not they'd be more desirable to me—embodying antibias and culturally responsive pedagogy, inclusive language, and the like—is questionable, and they'd most definitely be far whiter, which wouldn't be appealing at all.

Before I can respond, Maurice continues, "Remember at the train playground? With my dad? I dropped my thermos and he wanted me to pick it up. That was a long time ago."

It was six months ago, in fact, when we last saw his dad. And to him, it must feel like an eternity. I tell him as much and add that it's really too bad that happened. Then Maurice says, "But I can get a new dad, right?"

"Well, we'd have to meet someone and decide we really like them and they really like us, and maybe they start hanging around a little more often and we see what happens—just like with any of our friends."

"Maybe I could get a dad and two moms!" Maurice adds enthusiastically.

"Maybe," I respond warmly, so enamored of my son and his openness to different family arrangements, his ability to question the norms presented to him at school. Still, there is ambivalence, as there may always be for me—a kernel of wishing for something else, something that looks more like what I've been conditioned to believe is the proper family structure, of wishing his biological father could have a meaningful relationship with my son (and perhaps me, too), no matter how difficult it actually is to be in relationship with him.

I COULD HAVE a near-twenty-five-year-old, had it been a socially acceptable choice to continue a pregnancy when I was seventeen. It wasn't. That could-have-been child could ostensibly have their own child by now, and I could be a grandmother; I certainly have the gray hair and the physical exhaustion to prove it (bending over to tie my child's shoes is a loathsome exercise). So I really shouldn't be surprised when people ask if my now-three-year-old is my grandchild. I certainly don't blame them. While it may be at least vaguely normal for people like me to become a parent for the first time at forty, in many cultures both outside and within the United States, having a child at this time in life would only really happen at the tail end of one's childbearing, not as a first-timer.

HONESTLY, I'm more startled when strangers ask if I'm my son's therapist (yes, this actually happened), or the babysitter, or when they say, "Where did you get him from?" or, "He can't be yours, you must have adopted him" (yes, people actually say this too). These sorts of comments probably have less to do with my age and more to do with his and my skin color being quite different, but they have a similar effect, as far as imposing a particular norm of what family is supposed to look like. I try and receive these comments with a hermeneutic of generosity, but it's difficult. People may just be curious, but their lack of imagination and implied judgment is unwelcome.

In addition to the challenges that come with being a one-parent, multiracial family, the challenges I face as an older parent are particular to my social location. It's daunting, to say the least, to complete a dissertation while single-handedly raising a young child and determining how to effectively chart a postdoctorate career path in my early forties, knowing I want to be around for my child while also earning enough to provide for him, yet also being overlooked by many potential employers for either lack of teaching or publication credentials (I was parenting!) or for being out of the nonacademic workplace for so long (I was pursuing higher education!).

The PhD was a labor and birth as significant as having a child, and, these days, this society values that time, emotional commitment, and intellectual stewardship about as much as it does reproductive labor. It makes me question how much second-wave feminism really did for us. We have the option to pursue a career and higher education, but only at the expense of becoming a parent. We have the option to become a parent, but it is far more difficult if we try and do that outside of a traditional family structure, where there is at least one high-wage-earning member of the parenting dyad. However we end up managing parenting and our career, we are virtually on our own, and the person who assumes primary childcare responsibilities during the especially intensive parenting years will be penalized in terms of earning potential and career development. We need a personal safety net if we want to parent alone.

People are becoming parents at an older age through various means and in various family constellations, but at what cost? Is it only an option available to people who have access to significant income and/or wealth? As older parents with the power and privilege that come with delaying parenting in the first place, how can we use that power for good? What can our own experience of marginalization—the burden of which we may feel in only some small way, as compared to other parents with fewer resources—do to help us better respond to the oppressive cultural narratives and public policies at play? I don't have the answers to these questions, but I navigate them in my everyday interactions, where we bump up against some of the complex realities attached to identity and the values I hope to instill in my child.

MAURICE IS ASKING ABOUT when he can come see me at my school. I don't really know. He says, "Who's your teacher, Mommy?" And I tell him I don't have a teacher, per se; I *am* the teacher.

"Are you all the things, Mommy?"
    I nod my head.
    "Why?"
    "Because that's what mommies do, my love."
    "Are daddies all the things too?"
    "Sometimes they are, yeah."
    "What about Ceces and Papas [what he calls his grandparents]?"
    "Maybe sometimes they are too. But mommies almost always are all the things."
    "Why?"
    "Well, think about it. Who takes care of you? Me. Who feeds you? Me. Who makes sure you have clothes that fit you? Me. Who takes you to the doctor when you're sick? Me. Who brings you to school every day? Me. Who makes money and pays the rent?"
    By now, Maurice has caught on and enthusiastically announces, "You do!" Then he adds, "Mommies really *are* all the things."
    Being a single parent is not easy. We have to be all the things. And that's with the wisdom and experience of my age and the resources that come with my social privilege. Women still bear the brunt of reproductive labor in this society, and we have not tried to ease that burden in ways that could further equity. To me, this should be a high priority in the contemporary feminist agenda, so that it's not just those of means who have the option to become an older (single) parent, and so that the efforts of our forebears to create more educational and professional opportunities for us can be more fully realized.

Michael consolidated our family life for the better and presented his parents with opportunities for self-fulfillment we would have otherwise never known.

Better Late Than Never
DANIEL E. HOOD

Sometimes parenting after forty is a necessity. Well, parenting is never a necessity, really. But in our case, if we wanted to be parents, which we did, fate decided that it would have to be after forty. Married at twenty-six and just short of twenty-one, respectively, Linda and I decided to put off kids for a while because we had pending educational goals—grad school for me, and two years for Linda to finish her BA. Over the next five years, I finished an MA and began a PhD, while Linda finished her undergrad work and began to build a career in classical flute performance. It seemed too soon; we were too busy for a family.

As we approached our tenth anniversary, Linda had become an office manager and software trainer; my doctorate had stalled and I was working at a research firm. We looked at each other one day and asked, almost in unison, "You think it's time now?" Three of my five younger brothers had already started families and her younger sister had three kids, so we threw out the birth control devices and waited for nature to take its course.

And waited, and waited, and waited. After a few years without results, we began to suspect something biological might be amiss.

We consulted fertility professionals and learned that the impediment—whatever it was—rested on the distaff side of the equation. The professionals began testing and probing Linda every which way, with few immediate results.

After a year or two, with no confident diagnosis, we nevertheless became pregnant. It was a happy day. But should we tell the world? The doctors were cautious. Linda's mother had had several miscarriages before giving birth to her; Linda's only sister was adopted. We decided not to tell our families until we had passed the third month, when, the doctors said, we could have more confidence in the viability of the pregnancy. We told a few close friends who had been following Linda's medical adventures, which had included three trips to the OR for two D&Cs and an exploratory laparoscopy, as well as other procedures.

In the middle of our third month of pregnancy, my family held a reunion in Michigan; we had all grown up in Detroit and its suburbs. Linda and I attended, and although it was almost two weeks shy of our completed third month, we told the assembled family—my parents, five brothers, three sisters-in-law, and assorted nieces and nephews—that we were expecting. The family was excitedly flabbergasted. We had been married nineteen years, I was forty-three, and Linda was thirty-eight—they all had given up hope of our producing any offspring. Two happy days later, we drove to Indianapolis to visit Linda's father, who had no idea what was in store. Nor, as it turned out, did we.

Linda's father was disturbed by the news that she was pregnant. He, of course, was intimately familiar with her mother's miscarriage history. (Linda's mother had died five years earlier, and he was now remarried.) His concern was prescient. Two days later, Linda woke me to say she was spotting. Later that day, I drove her to Indianapolis's IU Health Methodist Hospital, where she was examined and rushed to the OR by a surgeon who had coincidentally studied with one of her New York doctors. The exam revealed a cervical pregnancy and lifeless fetus. Another D&C ensued.

After a long wait, the doctor told me they were having difficulty stopping Linda's bleeding and he wanted to perform a hysterectomy. I asked if there were any alternatives. (I had worked in an OR for six years while in grad school; I had read the feminist literature about male surgeons and uteruses; I knew how desperately Linda wanted a child.) He said, "Well, we could pack her uterus off overnight and hope the bleeding stops. But I don't advise that."

I said, "Let's do that." He was not happy; this decision meant having to resupply a surgical room in the morning, an extra procedure for the surgeon, more cost for the insurance company, and additional anesthesia for Linda if he was right. But, of course, he had to follow my wishes.

I spent a restless night. My father-in-law assured me they were praying for Linda and that God would do what was best; I relied on the six-pack I had picked up on the way back from the hospital. We arrived at Linda's room early the next morning to learn that her bleeding had stopped during the night and she was being discharged. Two days later, she and I drove sadly back to New York City.

Naturally, Linda was upset by the whole process, but after several months, and with help from her former therapist, she decided to see the fertility doctors and try again. They suggested she see an endocrinologist, and the tests showed she had a thyroid insufficiency.

Two months of medication produced a pregnancy that, despite her dad's distress, resulted in a beautiful ten-pound boy who became the central focus of our joint lives. After all those years, Michael's birth was a small medical miracle. It also cemented our marriage, which had never been entirely solid prior to his "advent," and thus was something of a connubial blessing, as well as a neonatal one. Linda and I were still in love, even after nineteen years, but passion is rarely enough to sustain a relationship over the long haul. Michael's addition to our lives gave Linda and me a shared purpose beyond ourselves, which we hadn't had since courtship.

So, I became a father for the first time at forty-six years of age. Linda was two months shy of forty-one. After nineteen years of married life, our son was the result of several years of medical investigation and intervention, as well as our desire and persistence—though I still harbor guilt that Linda's body had to bear all that medical "manipulation" before it got to bear the burden of a nine-month pregnancy and painful delivery. His birth—his broken collarbone and twenty-plus stitches to Linda's birth canal notwithstanding—was the best thing that ever happened to us. I still have that in black-and-white, in her handwriting.

MICHAEL WAS A MARVELOUS CHILD. The most indicative anecdote I enjoy telling is how after a taxi ride home from the hospital, he started crying the minute the apartment door shut behind us and did not stop for four hours. We tried everything the books recommended; nothing soothed him. Linda and I looked at each other and asked, almost simultaneously, "Have we made a terrible mistake?"

THEN HE STOPPED, as suddenly as he had begun. The number of times he cried seriously over the next twenty-five years can be counted on one hand. We wondered if he'd figured out how old we were and decided to take it easy on us. He was indeed an ideal child in many ways.

Michael was not perfect, of course, and neither were his parents, but he was an easy child, a cooperative adolescent, and a successful high school student and athlete. The only serious trouble he got into was in college, which was as much the fault of the school as it was his and his friends' behavior. And he recovered quickly to graduate with multiple honors, becoming the third and final family member to graduate from the same city university system. The photos from outside Radio City Music Hall, the graduation venue, show all smiles all around.

Before our quest for conception, my academic career had stalled at the ABD level, like so many others. I was flailing about, trying to find an alternative career I did not want. Michael's arrival provided me with the opportunity to restart—and finish—my doctoral studies. As we awaited his birth, Linda and I agreed that I would go back to grad school, continue teaching—both part-time—and arrange my schedule to include significant primary childcare time. This plan allowed us to avoid leaving Michael with a full-time nanny, something neither of us wanted.

ONCE LINDA'S six-week maternity leave was up, we started a pattern of care that lasted at least until middle school. Linda did her nine-to-five-plus job and took major responsibility for Michael's care on evenings and weekends; I typically did weekday mornings until I had class as either student or teacher, which was when I would hand him off to a hired caregiver for the bulk of the afternoon. When school started, I walked him to his local elementary school and Wendy, his nanny, would pick him up and tend to him until Linda or I got home in the evening.

This schedule meant that Michael spent much of his "playground time" under Wendy's care—except, that is, for the weekends, when Linda was in charge. This often meant that Michael was the one to introduce Linda to the other playground parents and a variety of other neighborhood regulars, including some local merchants, and it wasn't unusual for adults to greet Michael and exclaim, "Are you with your lovely grandmother today?" This social *faux pas* occurred more often when a younger woman—Linda's niece or cousin—accompanied them, but as this crowd got to know Linda, that mistake largely stopped occurring. However, it never failed to ruffle her feathers, and she made sure each misperception was promptly corrected.

Well before Michael was born, Linda had abandoned her musical career to climb the corporate ladder in software management. She continued to pursue music recreationally in ecclesiastical and community settings—choirs, by and large—with few opportunities for vocal or flute solos. Michael's arrival changed this in ways that heightened Linda's sense of musical fulfillment and enjoyment of life in general. From the age of ten, Michael spent most of his Sunday mornings engaged in organized baseball or soccer, almost always with both of us in attendance. As a result, Linda chose to give up her longtime participation in Episcopal Church choirs, as well as her attendance at Sunday morning services, but she wanted to continue attending church for both herself and Michael.

Because of Michael's sports schedule, we (re)discovered our local Mennonite church. I had gotten my BA at a Mennonite college and we were married at a Mennonite church in Indiana, and we had maintained many connections with Menno friends when we moved to New York City. The local Mennonite congregation met at five in the afternoon on Sundays. The timing was perfect for us: no morning services. We all began attending regularly and were involved in the life and operation of Manhattan Mennonite Fellowship over the next decade. I eventually served as congregational chairperson and Linda very quickly assumed responsibility for the musical direction of this small congregation.

While only some of the talent was professional, all Mennonites have a well-earned reputation for their musical abilities. Linda could spread her musical wings in ways never before possible with the Episcopalians. She directed and sang with choirs and performed flute and vocal solos and ensembles at her own discretion; she also played piano and led congregational singing for Sunday afternoon services as necessary. All because Michael's sports enthusiasm prompted her to leave the Episcopalians and rediscover the Mennonites.

Around this same time, I abandoned my quasi-weekly Sunday rock climbing outings in upstate New York and exchanged them for voluntary umpiring for Michael's Little League, which eventually morphed into a career as a high school umpire that I continue to enjoy to this day, thanks again to Michael.

Michael's second contribution to Linda's musical life came in 2003, when we were casting about for an exciting place to vacation. The two of us couldn't settle on a location, so we asked Michael where he'd like to go. He said Ireland; he was taking a course on the history of Ireland. It was a lovely trip, but the best thing about it was Linda's discovery of Irish traditional music. She was entranced and interviewed musicians at every *seisun* (the Gaelic term for an informal performance) we visited all over Dublin, Cork, and Drogheda.

When we returned to Manhattan, Linda began seeking out Irish trad venues and was performing regularly with a couple of groups by the next year. It was a more welcoming and mutually supportive environment than the competitive music circles she'd encountered years before, and groups were plentiful and varied enough in Manhattan's numerous Irish pubs that she could find sessions that welcomed newbies, as well as more accomplished venues as she improved over the years.

I had never seen her more excited about a new music venture. Her longest, most intense involvement was with the Washington Square Harp and Shamrock Orchestra (WSHSO) in their Saturday afternoon sessions at Lillie's Victorian Establishment and other New York venues, like the Irish Consulate, St. Patrick's Cathedral, and WFUV's local Irish radio. As a result of her immersion in Irish music, Linda realized a lifelong dream: she performed a vocal solo on a New York stage—at Symphony Space—and recorded the solo with WSHSO on a professional CD, the sales of which benefit a children's AIDS charity.

When Michael was twenty-five and Linda six months from retirement, our lives took a tragic turn. He was poised to move out and begin his career as a paramedic when Linda collapsed one morning and died on our kitchen floor. Michael was with her and performed CPR until the three ambulance crews arrived, but to no avail. There was a blood clot blocking her pulmonary artery, which was attributable in part to a localized estrogen treatment she used to ease postmenopausal symptoms. It may also have been related to whatever had caused her and her mother's multiple miscarriages; the autopsy report listed multiple contributing factors. At that point, nothing could have saved her.

It is impossible for me to convey in print how happy and productive Linda was in this last decade of her life as a result of our return to the Mennonite tradition and her discovery of Irish traditional music. Neither would have occurred without Michael's "tardy" arrival, nor would I have finished my doctorate and received two university appointments or become a high school umpire. Michael consolidated our family life for the better and presented his parents with opportunities for self-fulfillment we would have otherwise never known. Michael, now an accomplished rescue paramedic with the FDNY, was and is by all measures a godsend—absolutely better late than never.

Two Poems
ELIZABETH ACEVEDO

When You're Born to Old Parents

Who'd given up hope for children
and then are suddenly gifted with twins,
you will be hailed a miracle.
An answered prayer.
A symbol of God's love.
The neighbors will make the sign of the cross
when they see you,
thankful you were not a tumor
in your mother's belly
like the whole barrio feared.

When You're Born to Old Parents, Continued

Your father will never touch rum again.
He will stop hanging out at the bodega
where the old men go to flirt.
He will no longer play music
that inspires swishing or thrusting.
You will not grow up listening
to the slow pull of an accordion
or rake of the güira.

Your father will become "un hombre serio."
Merengue might be your people's music
but Papi will reject anything
that might sing him toward temptation.

"So how old are your parents?"

Opening Up
OLIVER ARDILL-YOUNG

What's it like having older parents? Well, most of the time you don't notice it. They're your parents and you love them—it's as simple as that.

And then there are the times when you feel it keenly, and these moments are far from simple. The first time I can remember becoming aware that my parents were older than normal was playing football in the park—for me, having older parents has always been secondary to having lesbian parents, so when my friends played football with their dads, it was much more noticeable that I played with my mum. One afternoon, when I was seven or eight, my mum announced it was time to head home after only a short play. I pleaded for another five minutes, but she said she was just too tired. On the walk home, I was lost in thought. It wasn't because she was a woman, nor did it have anything to do with being a lesbian—it was because she was older. I felt a strange, aching sadness at this, and a little bit guilty as well. I didn't want different parents, but I also didn't want my mums to be suddenly old and tired—for their sakes, as well as for mine.

Come secondary school, I faced the first real pressure to fit in. Having fifty-something lesbian parents was not the easiest hand to be dealt. I vividly remember a musical performance night in year seven, during which a friend of mine joked that his dad was soon going to be "so old" at fifty. My biological mum was fifty-five at the time, and his joke, though not directed at me, put me at a distance. From about thirteen to fifteen, I was nervous each time someone from school met my parents—not because of the lesbian scenario, as this had been explained beforehand, but because I thought they would think my mothers were old.

However, the extent to which this surfaced was usually in conversations along the lines of:

"So how old *are* your parents?"

"Fifty-five and fifty-three."

"That's pretty old."

"Yeah, I guess so."

Coincidence or not, some of my closest friends now also have at least one parent around the same age as mine. While there are times when we talk and joke explicitly about the fact that our parents are older, and sometimes have very tender moments where we think about how lucky we are to have them while we have them, there are also some small nuances that I think mark us out. For one, we seem to be more open to conversations with people of any age—not in an appropriating "living history" way, just as a connection to another human. We also seem to share an understanding that life is not a clearly mapped-out route that stops being interesting after forty. Most enjoyably, though, we spend most of our time hanging out in each other's kitchens with our parents making fun of us.

At some stage, you do realize that because they're older, they won't be around as long. It's not something that's on my mind *all* the time and I'm often half-aware that it's on their minds far more than mine, but when it hits me, it's hard. Yet I can't say that having older parents feels unfair, because now that I'm a bit more grown-up (I'm twenty), I can understand that having older parents isn't embarrassing—it's lucky.

As a younger child, they were involved with me in a reassuring, comforting way. This isn't to say that younger parents aren't like this, but by the time my parents had me, they were relaxed enough in their lives and themselves that they wanted to be there *with* me. As a younger teenager, I was occasionally embarrassed by their sense of humor or how bemused and inordinately interested they were in some trend, but I'm pretty sure this would have been the case regardless of what age they were. By about seventeen, I started to realize how great it was that I could talk to them about anything. For example, when talking about drugs, they were considerate and honest—they weren't so young that taking drugs was a normal part of their lives like it might once have been, but they were older than the point at which they might have deeply regretted it and been reactionary. As a result, I didn't feel that not taking drugs would mean missing out or that drugs were the worst thing in the world—I heard about their experiences, both good and bad, and felt I'd been given a comprehensive picture to make a sound judgment for myself.

I recently held a summer job working on an organic farm. The farmer was forty-two, had a toddler, and was pregnant with her second baby. I was curious about how she felt as an older parent, just like my mother. She told me she slightly regretted not having kids younger because she could feel herself growing more uptight and wished she could be more open.

It's true; I seem to spend a considerable amount of time helping my parents look for their glasses while they swear furiously, but I disagree with the idea that because they're older, they're less open. I don't think being open means being less irritable; I think it means being honest and deeply involved in your child's life and their way of seeing the world—an engaged kind of open-mindedness. I've always felt this open-mindedness from my parents, and this may be because they've developed a greater capacity for it the older they get. I also think it's because of this open-mindedness that we're so close. I love them so much.

PART V

BUILDING COMMUNITY AND CHANGING THE NARRATIVE

Our kids were on the move and we were huddled over them, supporting their shaky steps with our bent backs.

Finding Our Way Together
SARA ELINOFF ACKER

Sixty or seventy years ago, if you had a gathered a group of frumpy, gray-haired, middle-aged ladies for a social occasion, they might have been getting together for lunch or tea, political organizing, or a game of bridge. In the '50s and '60s, these were the women of my mother's generation: married at twenty, with three kids (or more) by thirty, and by the time they turned forty-five, they were either on the verge of an empty nest, planning their children's weddings, or already proudly showing off photos of their newborn grandchildren.

Fast forward five decades. The frumpy, middle-aged, gray-haired women were in my living room, running after their toddlers. One of them was me.

It was a Thursday morning in rural Franklin County in western Massachusetts, and our mother's group was meeting at my house. We were eight women who all became first-time mothers after the age of forty. Our wild posse of eight children—six girls and two boys, all under the age of two—were shrieking madly and running around my living room in various states of undress. As usual, my own daughter, Sophie, was completely naked.

We watched our children while gulping down mugs of coffee and black tea. We were tired, bone-tired, more tired than we ever imagined possible. Having children after forty was a particular lunacy of our generation. We were all daughters of the feminist movement of the 1970s; we strived to "have it all": fulfilling work, meaningful relationships, the ability to change the world and parenthood. We delayed and delayed starting our families until our biological clocks practically shrieked with alarm. Now, here we were, with deep, dark circles under our eyes as our kids ran amuck.

Though exhausted, we were also deeply grateful. Everything we did in our pre-mothering lives could not have prepared us for this, our rambunctious offspring delivering daily doses of chaos and joy. We were totally in love with our children, our late-in-life miracles.

Loving them was the easy part. Dealing with the seismic changes to the lives we had before was difficult—thus, the mother's group. It wasn't just a playgroup for our toddlers; it was a survival strategy for us. It was a group that saved all our lives at different moments and, as you'll soon see, saved some of our children as well.

I CAME OF AGE in a world of possibilities for women, with rights and privileges fought and won by a generation of activists that came before me. As a teenager, I had access to low-cost, safe birth control, and I had the freedom to explore my sexual orientation, to figure out who I wanted to be in the world, and to delay my decision about motherhood for a long, long, long time. I spent many agonizing years trying to decide if I wanted to be a mother. I was wary of motherhood; I saw what had happened to earlier generations of women, women who had given up their dreams and independence to raise families, often without the support of an engaged partner. I had read Freidan, Steinem, and Rich and had witnessed much bitterness about motherhood, the sacrifices and price so many women made and paid.

But after years of living out many dreams; traveling; and working as an activist, journalist, and social worker, motherhood was calling me. I was headed toward forty, and my biological urge to procreate had become surprisingly insistent. I found a supportive and nurturing partner who wanted children and was ready to roll up his sleeves for the nitty-gritty work of raising a child.

Getting pregnant was not easy, between hormone injections, ultrasounds, and a devastating miscarriage. When I finally did become pregnant, I refused to feel pathologized, though all my medical charts labeled me as having an "advanced maternal age." I was triumphant, grateful, and only a little bit scared of what was ahead.

One month after my forty-third birthday, after twenty-eight hours of grueling labor, I was holding my healthy baby girl, Sophie, in my arms.

WOMEN HAVE ALWAYS raised children in extended families. But in early twenty-first-century America, many women in my generation lived far away from our closest relatives, and our communities of friends became our support system.

AS SOON AS I WAS PREGNANT, I knew I needed a mother's group. I'd spent the last two decades of my life in all kinds of women's groups: consciousness-raising, political activism, therapy, spirituality, a women's health collective, a domestic violence survivor organization. I knew a mother's group would be an essential part of my emotional well-being, especially coming to motherhood so late in life.

I was excited and anxious about the huge changes in front of me. I'd had more than twenty years as a child-free adult, and I relished my freedom. I wanted to be with other women who had also delayed motherhood. Luckily, I didn't have to look far. One of my closest friends, Ruth, was pregnant with twins. She was forty. Another dear friend, Taica, who was in her late thirties, was one trimester further along than me. We had all taken extraordinary measures to become pregnant: Taica, a lesbian, had enlisted her brother's best friend as her sperm donor. Ruth, after several years of trying to conceive, had turned to fertility drugs and ICSI to conceive her twins. I had endured multiple nights of hormone injections with the hopes of increasing my odds by increasing the number of my eggs. It was a miracle that all three of us were successful; we knew we had beaten the odds for women our age.

We got together over tea, talked about our hopes and dreams, and compared our bulging, different-sized bellies while crafting our birth plans. Taica planned a home birth that her own mother, an experienced midwife, would attend. I was looking at a birth center with an emphasis on natural childbirth, and Ruth, with two babies growing inside her, was hoping just to make it past the thirty-sixth week and give birth vaginally in her nearby hospital birth center.

A few months later, all of our babies arrived safely: three girls and one boy. We each had to let go of our "perfect birth" dreams: Taica could not finish her labor at home. Ruth, who'd had to go on bed rest in her third trimester, went into labor at week thirty-five and was rushed to a hospital an hour away and her twins, Jack and Chloe, had to spend two weeks in the NICU. I was so exhausted from my twenty-eight hours of labor that I couldn't push anymore, and my daughter was extracted from my vagina by a miraculous suction machine.

None of this mattered. We had our babies. We cooed and rode maternal waves of oxytocin and watched in awe as Ruth managed to nurse her twins simultaneously, one on each breast.

Before long, word spread, and we were joined by other late-in-life mothers. Deborah had used IVF to conceive her daughter, Sadie. Barbara had adopted Violeta from Guatemala. Michelle and Amy's daughter, Emma, had been conceived using Michelle's egg and a sperm donor and then carried to term by Amy; their donor, a "yes donor," had agreed to be contacted by Emma when she turned eighteen, if she wanted. Nan was the only one in our group who had conceived her son, Thor, without jumping any hoops or receiving any special assistance.

We met at each other's homes one morning a week. In the early months, we sat in a circle while nursing or holding our babies and talked about the joys (there were so many!) and the difficulties we were having with sleep or feeding or colic. We cooed over each other's babies and passed them around to be held. We laughed a lot and cried occasionally. As the weather warmed, we brought our babies out into the New England spring and took short hikes with them in backpacks. We posed the babies for pictures, lining them all up on a couch and laughing hysterically when the younger ones, unable to sit up on their own, started toppling into each other. When the babies started to crawl, things got a little more hectic, but that was nothing compared to when they started to walk. We gave up on ever finishing a conversation. Our kids were on the move and we were huddled over them, supporting their shaky steps with our bent backs.

The day it happened, our mom's group was meeting at my home. It was June. The kids were hungry, and we started setting up the snacks on the coffee table: cookies, pretzels, applesauce, and an enormous bowl of fruit salad. No utensils or plates, just a massive free-for-all of ravenous eating. Chloe, Jack, Luna, Emma, Thor, Sadie, Violeta, and Sophie practically took a nosedive into the fruit bowl. Their chubby little fingers grabbed slippery pieces of melon, clementine, blueberries, and grapes with a feverish intensity. All the moms stood nearby, chatting in pairs while keeping a watchful eye.

Suddenly, Sophie turned toward me, a strange expression on her face, her eyes filled with alarmed tears. She gagged. I knew right away: she was choking on a piece of fruit.

A wave of dread overtook me and . . . I froze. It must have been only a couple of seconds, but it felt much longer—my frozen body, unable to move.

But then, from my left, Michelle sprang into action. She scooped Sophie determinedly into her arms and whacked the space between her shoulder blades—and out flew a three-quarter-inch piece of cantaloupe. It landed on the hardwood floor.

Sophie took a breath and started to cry. I scooped her up and comforted her. Thirty seconds later, she was squiggling out of my arms, happy to be back in the throng of toddlers. I looked at Michelle, tears in my eyes. "Oh my god, thank you. I just froze."

"No worries." Michelle flashed me her broad smile. "Happy to help!"

I hugged Michelle hard and looked up. The other moms had all been holding their breath. We let out a collective exhale together, backing away from the precipice.

We each knew that with these children, our hearts would be forever outside our rib cages, vulnerable in a way we never thought possible. We learned to be vigilant of danger. Protecting our children became as instinctual and necessary as breathing. We taught our children to hold our hands before crossing the street; we double- and triple-checked their car seats.

But sometimes, danger crops up in the most innocuous and ordinary of moments. In that moment, I froze, but Michelle saved Sophie.

Maybe other moments weren't quite as dramatic, but truthfully, our mother's group saved each of us regularly. We consoled each other over our fatigue, our feelings of inadequacy, and the overwhelming changes we experienced after so many childless adult years. How the hell were we supposed to go through menopause, deal with hot flashes, and stay up all night with a sick child, all at the same time? There was no guidebook for this. It was completely new territory. My own mom became a grandmother at forty-five, and here I was at forty-five, with a two-year-old daughter. My gray hairs were sprouting by the second as I drove her from gymnastics to music group to doctor's appointments. Sex with my husband? Forget about it. He was in his forties too. Exhausted, we were in bed by eight.

Now all the moms are nearing or over sixty. Our group disbanded when our children were four. We had a reunion a few times when our kids were in elementary school, but it became more awkward as they got older; they don't remember their time together and don't feel connected. Not so with the moms—we're always overjoyed to see each other, even if it's infrequent. Our bond is unshakable.

I AM LUCKY to have stayed close to the two women I started the group with. We watch what is happening around us bemusedly— our friends are starting to retire, but we're just gearing up to pay for college. One recent night, I collapsed on the couch, exhausted from college visits. "I'm too old for this," I complained to Ruth on the phone, who was also collapsed on her couch after three days of college visits with her twins.

"Maybe we can rest after we turn seventy," we joked. If we live that long! And grandchildren? Would they even arrive by seventy-five? Would we be alive to meet them and watch them grow?

Recently, Sophie and I were driving through the center of the college town that borders our home to the west. The local Lions Club was sponsoring the Spring Carnival, as they have for decades. It didn't seem that long ago that Sophie rode her first mini-coaster there, the "Dragon Wagon," at the age of four. Now she's studying for her SATs. We both gaze longingly at the fair and remark on how much fun we had there when she was little.

Suddenly, my nostalgia turns to grief. I look at my daughter in the passenger seat, my eyes filling with tears. I've often told Sophie that the best thing that's ever happened in my life was getting to be her mother. I've loved all the stages and phases, and soon she will be launching into her own life as a college student and young adult. But how many more phases of her life will I get to be part of? Will I see her become a mother? (I've begged her not to wait as long as I did to have a baby.) Will her children and I get to have a relationship when I'm still capable of getting on the floor with them to play? Will I have a chance to see their bar and bat mitzvahs? Is hoping to make it to their high school graduations a pipe dream?

I've always believed that being a late-in-life mother had many advantages. I had an amazingly full life in my twenties and thirties; I had my chance to figure out myself, my work, and my relationships. When the time came for the selflessness of parenthood, I was ready. But what doesn't get acknowledged very often, in all the triumphant stories of women becoming mothers after forty, is this: I will have less time on earth to be here for my daughter and her life. There will be many things I'll never get to see, many experiences she won't have me around for. The grief of this thunders through me, making me catch my breath.

My heart is bursting with a wild mixture of love and sorrow. I reach over and rest my hand on Sophie's thigh. Fortunately, she's texting a friend and doesn't notice my tears. A typical teenager, she's often embarrassed when I cry. I take a deep breath and continue driving.

I learned later that a single mom can never be too anything to ask for help.

The Single, Most Important Community
ALIA R. TYNER-MULLINGS

When I was in college, I worked as a research assistant for my mom when she was compiling her volume, *On Our Own Terms*. Though various books, such as *The Second Shift* by Arlie Hochschild, have explored women's double day (working outside and inside of the home), my mother's work adds a component that is critical to understanding the lives of Black women. Her work explains how African American women also undertake a "triple day" by engaging in transformative work—the tasks of creating, cultivating, and activating community among friends, family, and neighbors, and producing the social mechanisms for their survival. My focus was generally on the first part of the triple day: my work. It was only later that the transformative work of community would become meaningful for me.

While I maintained my focus on work, I created general plans for different aspects of my life. My plan for dating had five steps: meet someone in places I enjoy, meet someone in places they might enjoy, try online dating, leave the state to date, and finally leave the country. I did think briefly about having children on my own and actually created a list of four potential donors. But I was focused on school and work, and as I began to teach, the steps in the dating plan slowly receded from mind until only the first one remained. Once I started full-time work, I no longer had time for even the first step.

After receiving my degree in sociology, I became part of the 2 percent of Americans (and the much smaller group of Black women) with doctoral degrees. I was also one of the 40 percent of Americans dating online and of the 30 percent of childless women between thirty and thirty-four. As I started my job as an untenured assistant professor at a brand-new school, I left behind the idea of having a child. I knew I was a fabulous aunt, and whenever having a child entered my thoughts, I worried it would disrupt my role as an aunt. I had firmly moved into the "don't need a child" camp.

But, as there was still a space in my life—and on my calendar—reserved for it, I began to wonder: Was I really worried about losing my auntieness, or did I hate the idea of dating? Was I worried about my career advancement and had thus convinced myself that childlessness was what I wanted? As I began to explore connecting with that second prong of the triple day (the home), a new idea began to form. Once I was able to disconnect dating from children, an entire world opened to me. I added that dimension to my plan.

After making the decision to decouple dating from having a child, shortly before my thirty-seventh birthday, I informed my gynecologist that I wanted to get pregnant in a year and I inquired whether there were any tests or preparations I should make before trying to become pregnant. She asked why I wanted to wait a year, and I explained that I was waiting to see what would happen with my job but didn't want to wait too long.

She asked whether I would consider freezing my eggs. I wasn't there yet. She suggested that I see a specialist now before making a final decision. A month later, I visited a fertility specialist, who also inquired about why I was waiting. I shared the same answer, and I asked whether there was a test that could tell me the likelihood of pregnancy in the future. He showed me a graph of fertility, which peaked at eighteen to twenty years old. The curve remained high until the thirties, and then dropped.

When I came back to his office about a month later, he shared the results of other tests. Apparently, my follicle count was not such good news, and neither was the level of my anti-mullerian hormone (AMH), which contributes to the formation of eggs. At my age, the average level is 2.3; mine was at .41. I was in the 5th percentile, the lowest quartile. It was low enough that the fertility specialist didn't even ask what I wanted to do; he went right to hormone treatments and freezing my eggs.

"No one gets more eggs over time. If you want to do this, it should have been done yesterday."

The woman who was always early for everything was late— really, really late.

My initial reaction was total devastation. I was a failure as a woman, and I would never be a mother. It had never occurred to me to bring someone with me to this appointment. I had made the choice to do this on my own, and I didn't want to bother anyone with my problems. I didn't cry on the street. I didn't even cry when I visited a friend that afternoon and explained the situation. I didn't cry until I got home.

I cried for seven nights. Once I stopped crying, I began to research alternatives, such as fostering and adoption, though I was still determined to keep trying.

A fertility specialist I consulted suggested in vitro fertilization, a process through which the egg is fertilized outside of the body. "I'm not there yet," I explained to him, "and neither is my insurance." The alternative was intrauterine insemination; the sperm would be placed in the uterus by the doctor.

It was then that I began to seed a community. I gathered my family and friends and asked them to help me find the perfect donor for my new family. They each had access to my online cryobank account and had the opportunity to select their favorite person. I was first inseminated the Friday before I worked as a greeter for the only Super Bowl held in the New York metropolitan area. The process was a roller-coaster, and I was inseminated for the third time on the fifth of May that same year. So began the making of my first child.

I WAS A PREGNANT, Black, thirty-seven-year-old single woman professor. Like so many, I struggled to think about which of those characteristics should be listed first in that sentence. They each had a role in who I was and would become, including in my new role as a mother. As in many things, the intersectionality of my race, gender, and class have their own unique place in my process.

THE SOJOURNER SYNDROME, a concept also developed through my mother's research, focuses on how the intersection of these three elements leads to disparate health outcomes for Black women—specifically infant mortality—and the strength we must maintain to survive. *Weathering*, a concept developed by Arline Geronimus, explores the physiological ways that chronic strains and stressors degrade the health of Black women over time. This theory suggests that it may be safer for Black women to have children when they are young, because as they age, all the stressors they've been barely surviving begin to take their toll.

Lifelong stressors manifest in the disparate health outcomes of Black and white women. Black women are "22 percent more likely [than white women] to die from heart disease, 71 percent more likely to perish from cervical cancer, [and an astounding] 243 percent more likely to die from pregnancy- or childbirth-related causes."[1] Serena Williams put a familiar face on the issue when she described what happened after her C-section delivery in a 2018 *Vogue* article. She stated that hospital staff refused to take her seriously when she tried to explain to them what was happening with her body; she almost died from blood clots in her lungs. Given the research on the physical and emotional strain of living as a Black woman in this country, and the way the health care system treats Black women of all ages and socioeconomic statuses (as evidenced by Williams's experience), I worried about my own health and that of my child through the rest of my pregnancy.

Many of the Black women I know had fibroids. They are not only more common in Black women than white women, but they also start in Black women when they are younger and grow faster than in white women. When my fertility doctor found uterine fibroids that were "normal for Black women" and concluded they were too small for concern, I still worried. I know women who've had to have surgery to remove their fibroids and were therefore given a small window within which they could have children, as well as women whose miscarriages and premature labor were caused by fibroids.

I worried constantly about everything.

My first trimester was difficult, as it is for many moms. I was lucky that the bulk of it occurred over the summer, so morning sickness kicked in right around the end of the semester. Though I started to notice how smelly my beloved city actually was and had to swear off bacon for a few months, it wasn't until I stayed up for twenty-four hours to get my grades in by deadline that I threw up for the first time. It got progressively worse over time until I was surviving on a diet of green tea lemonade and gluten-free pretzels. As I spent more and more time in bed, I ate less and less and threw up more.

By the time I entered the worst part of my morning sickness, I could barely leave my bedroom. As I sat in bed, hardly eating and trying to talk myself off my mattress, I reminded myself that I had chosen this and worked hard to get it. I knew it would be hard to do alone. I kept telling myself, *You're an adult. You can do this without anyone. You* have *to do this without anyone.*

I must also admit that I also had the image in my head of Black women giving birth in the fields and being forced to go back to work. If I couldn't get through this with all the resources I had, what kind of woman was I?

I sucked it up (and threw it up) for a month and soon began to realize I needed some support. I needed some community. A few weeks before the end of the first trimester, I moved in with my mom.

When I began to think about writing this article, I looked up the effects of age on morning sickness. I was sure it was my age that made it so bad. The research was inconclusive at best—in fact, there were a few studies that showed age actually has a positive effect on morning sickness. I eventually concluded that psychological, rather than physical, issues had affected me most. I didn't want to ask for help because I was too old for that. I learned later that a single mom can never be too anything to ask for help.

A week after my due date and thirty-eight-and-a-half years after my own birth, I gave birth to a healthy baby girl. We moved back into my apartment. Now that I was home alone with a baby, the four flights in my walk-up had never felt so long. Not only did I feel I couldn't leave, but I also didn't know what to do when I was home. In those first few months home, the days were so long, but the months flew by. I often compared this to my awesome auntieness and realized how much I'd missed in my niece's life. First my niece wasn't mobile, then she was crawling, then walking, and then talking. Despite my fabulousness, I didn't get to experience the six to eight months between those milestones. The afternoons at home were especially tough, as the mornings were highly scheduled. There was no plan for us in the afternoons, no events to break up the monotony of entertaining a three-month-old. All my attempts at a schedule fell flat.

Pushing though this was difficult for me. I'm not someone who puts herself out there. I had always been part of communities but never really had to do much to engage them. Following the model set in my mother's book, *On Our Own Terms*, I had written a paper in college about college-aged Black women's triple day: their schoolwork, relationship work, and community work in a predominately white university. I joined clubs, handed out fliers, and attended meetings. But I was not an entirely proactive group organizer.

Things began to change when my pediatrician suggested I join our neighborhood parents' listserv. On it, I met a family that needed a nanny share. Childcare was one area where my planning had failed me, so I saw a nanny as a quick fix to a potentially large problem. As we interviewed a potential nanny who said she couldn't work with us because the combination of hills and stairs were a little too much for her, I got a bit of advice from other parents: strap the child into a carrier and roll the stroller down in front of you, then drag it up behind you with groceries, laundry, or packages from the mail. Now we were free to go out and experience a change of scenery.

I was also able to use the listserv to connect with different communities. One of the things you miss out on when you're parenting alone is conversation. Early on, I asked around to find out if there was a group for new parents, and when I found out there wasn't, I collected email addresses and decided to create one. It got me out of my head and into the park, and it was the first group I'd encountered in which I could bounce ideas around. No one was going to judge me and tell me why what I was doing was wrong and how what they did was right. These were just other people with the same questions and their own answers. In a small neighborhood, these people became my first community, and some of them remain our friends. I also took a tummy time class once a week, which provided me with something to do, someplace to go, and again, people to talk to. You can only spend so much time walking . . . to nowhere. These parents and children were another part of building community.

Via social media, I created a broader community of the family and friends who had helped me choose my donor, the people who'd supported me during my ups and downs of miscarriage and pregnancy, and those who'd held me up as a feminist because of my choices. It allowed me to engage with them and allowed them to watch Lilli grow up. Within those fifty people, I had a smaller group of friends—my "circle of moms"—who had children within five years of my daughter's birth. When my daughter almost fell off my lap because I fell asleep while rocking her, I emailed them immediately. When I couldn't figure out weaning or potty training, they were there for me.

My longest-lasting community (beyond my family) emerged from Lilli's "school." She started in childcare at seven months, and on the very first day, we met someone from our new parents' group who became her best friend. As everyone began to move on when their children reached two, Lilli went to a new daycare with someone from our tummy time group. Another best friend moved with her to her final daycare, and finally to pre-K.

I'VE SETTLED INTO my life as a mom. My daughter's gregariousness contributed greatly to the development of our community, and we've established a routine of regularly interacting with local friends, family members, and neighbors. While I haven't used my circle of moms in two years, most of them are in the social media group I created for my daughter, and they see her at events and meetings. With the past as a narrative and the present under control, I have begun to look to the future.

AS LILLI PREPARES to attend primary school, I have become much more aware of the lack of African Americans in our neighborhood. Though our neighborhood has always been predominately Latinx and is now even officially designated Little Dominican Republic, it was only in exploring the demographics of the school that I came to realize that my neighborhood, though predominantly people of color, is only 15 percent African American. The student body of the school she will attend is between 10 and 12 percent African American, a proportion that seems almost invisible in a city like New York, where we make up 25 percent of the population.

It remains important to me to connect with African American parents, to connect with others who experience the world in similar ways while also understanding how experiences might be different. I've searched them out in person and on the listserv and collected contact information, but we've never had a good opportunity to develop and build that community. I return often to my idea of connecting with African American parents and making sure Lilli gets to connect with African American children within her community of color, and we recently had a picnic with a few others with similar interests.

I have moved into a new arena, but like so many strong, Black, single women, I didn't do it alone. The creation and cultivation of community—the kinwork that feels as though it is part of my birthright—took time and energy, but community is how I have been able to continue to move forward. By gathering friends and family, I've created a community for my daughter, and through her, I've created a community for myself.

Forget midlife. I'm beginning to realize I face a late-life crisis.

Reparation
SUSAN ARDILL

t's 2016. I'm sitting in my parked car, listening to a psychologist on a radio program talk about midlife crises. Listeners are invited to call in with their own accounts of midlife turmoil and change— relationship breakdowns, new marriages, empty-nest syndrome, changes in careers. I begin to notice the callers are mostly in their forties, occasionally early fifties.

From my point of view, they have plenty of time to reinvent themselves. When I turned fifty, I was studying for a second degree in history and literature, immersed in mothering a young child, and enjoying a child-oriented social life with other parents I'd met through his school and through lesbian mothers' groups. I felt shielded from the shock and emptiness of aging. Now I'm sixty. I'm stuck in an unhappy job, my son is in his final year of high school, and I have a strong sense that I'm on the edge of a crevasse. Within a few years' time, he'll have moved out of our home, just as the economic and physical options for reshaping my own life narrow considerably.

Forget midlife. I'm beginning to realize I face a late-life crisis, and there are few signposts—and few fellow travelers—for the track I find myself on.

I didn't set out to become an older mother. I didn't delay pregnancy in favor of a career or wait for the right person to do it with or change my mind at the last available moment. Instead, in my thirties, I spent nine years straining toward pregnancy with the support of my partner, going through five helpful donors, countless rounds of self-insemination and clinical insemination, and two investigatory surgeries and one major surgery to remove a dermoid-enclosed ovary and deal with endometriosis—not to mention years of psychotherapy. When I finally sat opposite an IVF specialist who told me that none of that really mattered, that the advanced age of my eggs—now forty-one—was the most important factor, I felt disbelieving.

I HADN'T KNOWN I needed my mother to die before trying to have a baby, but virtually no thought of fertility had crossed my adult mind before her death when I was thirty-one. A year later, as I swam in a canyon on a visit to central Australia, I was seized by the idea: *I want to have a baby.* It can't have been a coincidence that the same thing happened to my much-older sister. Almost as soon as our mother died, my sister, then thirty-eight, embarked on a series of miscarriages before finally giving birth to her son at forty-one. She'd terminated a pregnancy just a few years earlier. I felt proud of her attempts to get pregnant at her age, while simultaneously not really registering that the miscarriages were connected to age. It seemed to me that her baby had been an inevitability who would have arrived sooner or, as it turned out, later.

My sister conceived easily, but it soon became apparent that I was having difficulty with that first step. I was a lesbian using donors outside the medical system, which had worked for many of my friends, but when I ran into trouble, the system couldn't "see" me. One general practitioner outright rejected my self-diagnosis of infertility after twenty-five unsuccessful cycles at home, telling me I'd have to have twelve "proven" attempts before she would help me.

When I first started self-inseminating with the help of my

partner, we were living in England. A few years later, we moved to Australia. Both countries have strong, wonderful public health systems, which means social regulation; there isn't a free market for reproductive technology. There are ethics committees for each IVF clinic, governed by the public health ethos of the day. In the early '90s, the system was still considering its options when it came to providing treatment for lesbians. It would provide donor insemination and treat clear-cut medical problems with surgery, but it put limits on the use of reproductive technology for everyone and would not yet spend public money on IVF for lesbians. (It now does.)

Not that I thought I needed IVF. In some part of my imagination, I still thought I was going to be barefoot and radiantly pregnant and have a home birth. Instead, there were years of repetitive failure, years of desolation, years of investigations and surgical interventions, years of tension and distress as my friends had babies. I turned forty.

Then a lucky thing happened. In early 1996, I connected to the infant internet to do some distance study. I browsed through what were known as listservs, or email discussion groups. I joined one devoted to our dog breed, then I joined one about group behavior in cyberspace. Then, in an electrifying moment, I found Fortility, a group for women over forty having trouble conceiving. I plunged in.

I underwent a rapid education. Here were the women having multiple miscarriages. The women who'd finally met the right partner only to find themselves "too old." The women with infertile male partners. The women using surrogates or donor eggs. And the women like me, who had years of nonspecific infertility behind them. As I inhaled all these stories, all this shared information, all this helpfulness between members, I gradually jettisoned the last vestiges of hope for a "natural" pregnancy and realized I should do IVF.

In another chance discovery, I was browsing in a bookshop when I came across a book called *Getting Pregnant* by an Australian fertility specialist. Toward the end was a chapter on the philosophical dilemmas created by new, sophisticated reproductive technology, including whether to offer IVF to lesbians. Unlike some other clinics, including the one I'd been attending, his had no qualms about doing this.

That's how I ended up facing the doctor who told me my age was now the decisive factor. However, he was prepared to see how an IVF cycle would go. As I pored over the clinic's website, I saw that I had a 7 percent chance of having a baby from IVF with my own eggs at age forty-two. The first cycle went well, and I was briefly pregnant for the first time ever. After that, I had a D&C and a polyp removed.

On the second cycle, I was pregnant again. My luck held. Despite a precarious pregnancy, despite preeclampsia, despite an emergency preterm delivery and a severely underweight baby who spent his first month in NICU, I emerged into middle age as a mother.

ALTHOUGH MY SON is now twenty, I've been his mother for less than half my adult life. The novelty, surprise, and sense of sheer good fortune I feel about this turn of events has not dimmed with time. The striving and failing to conceive was so protracted, it became deeply embedded in my sense of myself. It's the shadow I carry around with me. As a lesbian, I was used to feeling out of sync with the mainstream (and enjoyed aspects of falling outside convention). But add to that the loss of my mother at a young age; the loss of my first great love to drugs before turning thirty; a move to the other side of the world, where the seasons were back to front; and then trying for ten years to do something that seemed to come more or less easily for everyone around me—by then, my sense of alienation from general assumptions about the natural order of life events was profound. To have that feeling overturned at the last possible minute imbued my life from then on with a sense of almost magical realism.

FINALLY, I HAD A CHILD. I had stopped hoping for or imagining this future, so it was like unexpectedly gaining entry to a new and fascinating country. A relief—but also an immediate torment. The first year of my son's life was difficult for me. Looking back, it seems inevitable that it would be, after all the trouble it took to get there. I was hypervigilant, unable to relax, anxious, unsure of my own capabilities, certain that everyone else and everyone else's babies were better at this than me and mine. I even had a day when he was a few weeks old of declaring to my partner that I'd made a terrible mistake (it was the sleep deprivation talking!). That first intense period held a strong undercurrent of self-consciousness about my age and a sense of unworthiness due to my experiences with infertility.

Somewhere around this time, Fortility sprouted a new group for those of us who'd been fortunate enough to become mothers through adoption, surrogacy, or birth and were communicating privately so as not to upset those still trying. This group became the Vintage Moms. (I'm a "mum," but the majority of the members were American.) I think the solid bond we developed was based on that sense of tremendous relief after perseverance, of rare good luck, of, "Oh, wow, I'm getting to do this after all." We relished sharing stories of our children, mutually appreciative of how hard-won even the mundane experiences of motherhood were. We were conscious of our ironic status: yes, we'd been successful at having babies in our forties, but it hadn't been easy. We wanted other women to know that it could be done, but not to assume it could be done at will.

I think being older meant I had a strong awareness of how quickly time passes, that this part of my life would all too soon become the past. The long experience of infertility gave me the strong impulse to savor every moment with my little one, to live without allowing any occasion for regret to arise. Maybe this was a terribly traditional version of motherhood, to put the child at the center of my life; I sensed that older friends who'd had children in a different era and under different strictures didn't understand why I would do this. Yet during my son's all-encompassing pre-school years, I quickly became aware of how ready I was to devote time to motherhood. I'd had my fill of clubbing, eating out, love affairs, constant travel, a hectic social life, and lying awake at night, feeling angst about work relationships. I'd parked my career in a cul-de-sac, secure in a part-time job that required nothing of me outside of working hours but was interesting enough while I was there. I felt no pull sideways—I wanted to explore being a mother in all its dimensions.

I couldn't have said what drove my quest to have a child. I grew up in a big, unhappy family with a distant, depressed mother. As a Catholic child, I'd seen many very large families close-up; I was intimate with the domestic drudgery demanded of women. As a young feminist, I'd worked in an abortion clinic and pored over the ambivalent anthology *Why Children?* in the early '80s. Yet undoubtedly, I was driven in my pursuit of motherhood, pro-pelled by forces that would not let go of me despite the failures and disappointments, and this translated into a very active, attached motherhood.

In retrospect, I see that this was the need to make amends to myself for my own emotionally deprived childhood. It was the drive toward reparation.

For me, this is the true meaning of being an older mother: I've had the time and motivation to work out what went wrong for me, what was missing in my own relationship to my mother (just about everything!), and how to do it differently. Although on paper this could sound like a recipe for an overindulged, overregarded only child, I see this in practice as an entirely positive drive, which has had nothing but beneficial consequences for my son.

Recently, a friend I'd known since I was nineteen died. She was sixty-eight, five years older than me. She felt like the first of my peer group to die of something approximating old age. My son, just out of his teens, sat at the very front of the Buddhist center, recording the funeral for friends in England. After the wake, he decided to go home early, saying he had a bad headache (he never gets headaches). Not much later, he rang me as he walked from the bus stop to our house, saying "I feel light-headed, like I might fall over."

I told him to slow down, take deep breaths, and lie down on the couch when he got home. That's where he was when we arrived an hour later. I sat beside him and took his hand. "I think you're feeling shocked and sad. It's frightening when people we know die. It's frightening to think of dying ourselves, to think your mothers are getting old and are going to die too."

I could see him relax with the naming and acknowledgment of his fears. This is what I can offer him, because I lived and thought as an adult in complex situations for years before he came along. I've been through the anguish of losing my parents, of losing lovers and friends to drugs and accidents, of dismantling my own unhappy childhood piece by piece to build up an alternative, happy home.

Being able to soothe him soothes me. And I can turn in a moment from the bleakness of grief to the enthusiasm of my son, who is always keen to argue about neurophysiology and linguistics and world soccer. I come home from work and he asks, "Have you ever heard of Joan Baez?" and my mood lifts.

It's 2019. I'm sixty-three, the age my mother was when she died. My son is twenty, a university student still living at home (the Australian way). A year after listening to the radio program about midlife crises, I suddenly get a new job in an entirely new field, with an array of much younger colleagues. A new world of ideas and relationships opens for me. I'm fortunate, but I'm also well-equipped for this. This is what being an older mother has meant to me—that life can go on offering profoundly new experiences, that I can still change and be curious and keep on learning in tandem with my son.

The personal and the wonky are intimately entwined in the late-onset phenomenon, as in all aspects of fertility management.

Late-Onset Motherhood: Many Stories, One Radical Plot Change

ELIZABETH GREGORY

Fifteen years ago, I began researching the trend of women starting their families in their mid-thirties and after in response to a lot of tick-tock news stories about just that. I knew why *I* had done it, but what were the wider causes and effects? What did it mean that so many women of diverse backgrounds (and their partners, both straight and queer) were making this fundamental life-plot change?

OVER THE NEXT FEW YEARS, one hundred and thirteen women shared their stories of delayed parenthood with me. All were fascinating, anomalous in the history of humanity, and, in their moment, entirely ordinary. It became clear that the pattern of delay was spurred by two structural causes: one technological and the other policy-based. The first cause was the emergence of reliable birth control (including hormonal contraception in 1960, backed up by safe, legal abortion in 1973), which introduced an evolutionary shift to giving humans the ability to control and time their fertility while sexually active. While birth control *allowed* people to delay the arrival of their first child until they felt ready, the second cause—the lack of social support that would allow women to work while raising kids—*pushed* them to delay until they could pay for good childcare themselves.

Additionally, many people didn't find or commit to a solid partner until they were older, an effect of both extended education (and resulting shifts in interests and expectations) and of public health advances that mean people live decades longer than they did one hundred years ago, allowing them to reschedule their life events. The increasingly acceptable social option of single motherhood also played a role in many women's decisions to delay, as did coming out—several of the older lesbians I interviewed couldn't imagine having kids early on but embraced them in the context of technological and social change.

The women I interviewed also pointed out that delaying parenthood allowed them the time to go to college—almost all did—and often graduate school, which then enabled them to get interesting jobs that paid decently and put them in positions of influence both as individuals and as a group. As more and more women entered the workforce, had money of their own to spend, and trickled up into decision-making roles, women's opinions and concerns took on greater weight in societal discourse.

Earning your own money—or even just having the *capacity* to earn money, due to your past work experience—meant that women no longer had to stay in crappy marriages in order to feed their kids. Over and over, women told me they had seen their moms stuck, unable to leave because they didn't have marketable skills. Their observant daughters delayed marriage and kids to the point where they could leave if they needed to. As a result, the power balance in their marriages differed from that in their parents' marriages from the start because it wasn't based in financial dependency. Dads also had it better, these women felt, because their wives' earnings meant the dads weren't burdened with all the fiscal responsibility and could spend more time with their kids.

Delayed parenthood has had enormous ripple effects in the sixty years since the invention of hormonal birth control. The trend of starting families later was already underway in some measure (my mother had me, her first child, when she was thirty in 1957 and my sister in 1960). But the real uptick in later births started in the '70s among women who had started taking the Pill ten or more years earlier, when they became sexually active in their late teens and early twenties. As a direct result of this delay, women as a group have an active voice in the polity. The push to deny access to birth control and abortion is at base an effort to stem the tide of this change.

Along with all these societal shifts, what about the personal? How does later motherhood play out in the experience of families? As many people I interviewed predicted, starting later has had cross-generational ripple effects. For example, late-onset motherhood also means late-onset grandparenthood. This plays out differently for different families: though my kids had a great relationship with my dad, they never really knew their grandmother without Alzheimer's, and both my parents died within five months of each other, when my girls were sixteen and ten. Their dad's mom died six years prior, and their one remaining granddad lives in another state. Down the line, if my kids start having kids when I did, at thirty-nine, it's likely that my husband and I will not be in our grandkids' lives for long. The nurturing role played by grandmothers, the original childcare, was essential to humanity's evolution (search "grandmother hypothesis"), so the possible disappearance of that bond deserves concern. One way to address that concern directly would be to make it more feasible for women to combine completing an education and finding well-paid, interesting work with having a family at a younger age.

My mom was fully present when my first daughter was born, but not by the time my second daughter arrived via adoption, when I was forty-eight. Nonetheless, she was there in spirit in every aspect of my life when I was the mother of young kids. For me, part of the attraction of motherhood involved reliving the core pleasures I'd shared with my own mom and dad (reading stories, running around, drawing pictures, baking and cooking, singing the same songs) and recreating the dynamic in the reversed role.

The personal and the wonky are intimately entwined in the late-onset phenomenon, as in all aspects of fertility management. On the small side: I colored my hair longer than I would have otherwise chosen to, so that my younger daughter didn't feel I looked too different from the other kids' moms (though many of them were dyeing their hair too). On the bigger side: I worry about getting Alzheimer's like my mom, while my kids are still young. As the sixty-two-year-old mother of a fifteen-year-old still at home as well as a twenty-two-year-old just out of college, I work at staying fit and take various supplements—always with anxiety that one of them might itself be reported as the next potential cause of Alzheimer's!

Embedded in the personal life details are big questions about the role we humans want family to play in our lives going forward. Pre-birth control, if you had sex, you had a steady stream of new family members, so all your life activities involved and depended upon them. Family was what people did. Now that children aren't the default, people are increasingly choosing to not just delay, but to not have them at all, so they have to invent new life plots and forms of connection. As situations shift over years, the decision not to have kids may morph into a desire for them after all, which may prove more complex or impossible by standard means at that point. Some give up while others seek ways around the problem via fertility technology or nonbiological means, including adoption, fostering, stepchildren or friend bonds, or by building alternative communities.

Late-onset motherhood is an unrolling phenomenon: as the Centers for Disease Control's annual birth reports document, there's been a twelvefold increase in first births to women over thirty-five, and almost a sixteen-fold increase in first births to women over forty between 1975 to 2018. And it's likely to increase markedly, as some of the many younger women who've currently put off kids (the teen birth rate fell 58 percent between 2007 and 2018) begin to have them later. Though all these women have their own stories, a key motive is a shared desire to combine motherhood with wider social and civic participation and financial independence. Gender has historically been a work-assignment system, with men doing most of the paid earning and women pushed into the unpaid care work at home. But now, with fewer kids per household, women are doing many of the paid jobs that would formerly have been filled by their sons, while men do more of the housework once done by daughters.

Women are moving into policy-making roles in a time of enormous environmental and technological risk, and many are raising big structural questions, like "Can we build a culture and economy of care instead of the model of exploitation based on gender and race?" and "How can we live in ecological harmony on our planet?" Delayed parenthood has played a big part in giving women a voice in such discussions; our contributions will be critical to saving the future. Bottom line, late-onset motherhood is rewriting the plots of all our lives, with each change spurring new twists in the wider human story.

Acknowledgments

FROM VICKI

The manuscript for this book was completed on the twenty-fifth anniversary of my daughter Lela's death. Her death was a turning point in my life; it was from then on that I realized how central being a mother is to my identity. I acknowledge Lela, my son Josh, and my daughter Mya as the most significant people in my life—they, as well as my grandchildren, Odysseus and Theda, have brought me the greatest joy and taught me what is most important in my life. I acknowledge them most for what I have learned about parenting, love, kindness, and the need for connection.

To Polly Howells and Eric Werthman, for getting me through the darkest time and helping me to heal; to the hundreds of people who showed up for Lela's funeral and marked the significance of that loss—thank you. People in my community still recall the longest line of cars they'd ever seen going to a cemetery.

To those who have helped with parenting: I am grateful to my husband, Dan Brady, my sister, Jini Tanenhaus, and to the community of people at the Park Slope Child Care Collective, as well as many close friends. I thank my son, Josh, and Kat Aaron for parenting my grandchildren with great love, attention, and caring.

I thank my mentor Kell Julliard for teaching me how to heal from trauma and helping me recognize my Buddha nature. I thank my dear friend and writing mentor, Bev Gologorsky; she has given me encouragement throughout the entire process. It was at her book reading that I met Elizabeth Strout, who gave me the title for this book. I thank the women in my aging women's group—Florence Tager, Lorraine Cohen, Carole Turbin, and Norah Chase—who encouraged me to transform a short draft of an article into a book, and my life-long friend and coeditor, Nan Bauer-Maglin, who helped turn it into a reality. This book is the result of a collaboration that made the experience—and the product itself—so meaningful.

Lastly, as a mother and woman, I am grateful to Mya's birth mother and acknowledge her loss.

FROM NAN

Many friends participated in the making of this book and provided the caring support that helped bring it to completion— a special thanks to all of you. And to my multiracial, patchwork quilt of a family made up of my adopted daughter, Quin, and her husband Anthony; my stepchildren Joshua, Heather, and Seana, and their partners, Angel and Jim; my grandchildren, Domenick, Nico, Lola, Layla, Luna, Amelia, Zane, Max, and Faith; my step-grandchildren, Willie, Eli, and Kara; and my great-grandchildren, Elize and Weston; I thank you. You all have nourished and embraced me in so many ways. Much of this large family was brought into my life by my late husband, Jon-Christian Suggs. I am so glad you are all nearby and a part of my life.

The final editing of the book took place during the COVID-19 pandemic, so for several months, Vicki and I could only work on the manuscript over the phone. We have known each other since college and are close friends; however, talking and thinking about family through this work brought us much closer together.

WE BOTH WANT TO THANK Dottir Press staff for shepherding this book along so smoothly. Special thanks to Jennifer Baumgardner for her smart reading of the original manuscript, Charis Caputo's skillful smoothing, and Larissa Melo Pienkowski's thorough copyedit. Deep appreciation to Drew Stevens, who designed the beautiful interior and took our author photo, and cover illustrator Ashley Seil Smith. Thanks also to publicist Kait Heacock, social media strategist Kayla Bert, and pearl-of-all-trades Pearl McAndrews.

Finally, it is to the writers to whom we owe the most thanks: their contributions fill *Tick Tock* with stories of the winding, fulfilling path to older parenting.

About the Contributors

SARA ELINOFF ACKER is grateful to still have two dogs and a cat to fuss over as she readies for her empty nest. Aghast at how eighteen years can flash by in a hiccup, she works as a psychotherapist and lives with her equally bereft husband in Pelham, Massachusetts.

ELIZABETH ACEVEDO is the *New York Times*-bestselling author of *Clap When You Land* (Quill Tree Books, 2020), *With the Fire on High* (Quill Tree Books, 2019), and *The Poet X* (Quill Tree Books, 2018), which won the National Book Award for Young People's Literature, the Michael L. Printz Award, the Pura Belpré Award, the Boston Globe–Horn Book Award, and the Walter Award. She is a National Poetry Slam champion and holds an MFA in Creative Writing from the University of Maryland. Acevedo lives with her partner in Washington, DC.

SUSAN ARDILL is an Australian writer and editor who lived in England for a formative decade in her twenties and early thirties, where she worked on the feminist magazine *Spare Rib* and the queer TV series *Out on Tuesday*. She now works in communications for an environmental organization.

OLIVER ARDILL-YOUNG is a psychology/linguistics university student who loves playing soccer, cycling, running, and ocean swimming.

JULIE BUCKNER ARMSTRONG is an English professor at the University of South Florida. She has authored and edited multiple works on the literature of segregation and the civil rights movement.

CATHERINE ARNST spent most of her career as a journalist covering health and science and now works as media director for a nonprofit in New York, focused on improving health care access. She lives in Brooklyn.

PAIGE AVERETT is a professor and associate head in the School of Social Work at North Carolina State University. Her research and writing deals with issues of identity, gender, sexual orientation, and social justice. A born storyteller, she believes in the power of personal narratives.

NAN BAUER-MAGLIN adopted a child from Colombia in 1977, at the age of thirty-five. Adoptive mother to one, stepmother to three, and grandmother to twelve, Nan's latest edited collection is *Widows' Words: Women Write on the Experience of Grief, The First Year, The Long Haul, and Everything In Between* (Rutgers University Press, 2019).

ROBERT BENCE was born in western Pennsylvania and now lives in Vermont. He has studied and taught political science in five states and Canada. For the last four decades, he has been a professor at the Massachusetts College of Liberal Arts. There is nothing he and his wife enjoy more than world travel, especially with their two children and two granddaughters.

ADAM BERLIN has published four novels, including *Belmondo Style* (St. Martin's Press, 2004, winner of the Publishing Triangle's Ferro-Grumley Award) and *Both Members of the Club* (Texas Review Press, 2013, winner of the Clay Reynolds Novella Prize). He teaches writing at John Jay College–CUNY and coedits the literary magazine *J Journal.*

JUDITH UGELOW BLAK is a single mom living in Aarhus, Denmark with her two boys, two dogs, and a cat. She teaches economics and chemistry to high school students. She intends to write and dance her way through retirement.

VICKI BREITBART has worked on sexual and reproductive justice for more than fifty years, as a program director, educator, researcher, and activist. Her writings on women's health have been published in several peer-reviewed journals. She has two adult children, one of whom she adopted at fifty-five, and two grandchildren.

LAURA BROADWELL is a writer and editor living in Brooklyn, New York. She was previously the editor of *Healthy Kids* magazine, the single-parent columnist for *Adoptive Families* magazine, and has contributed essays to ParentCenter.com, ThisIBelieve.org, and *If Women Ruled the World: How to Create the World We Want to Live In: Stories, Ideas and Inspiration for Change* (New World Library, 2004).

PAMELA PITMAN BROWN is an assistant professor of sociology at Albany State University and is the president-elect of the Georgia Sociological Association. She loves teaching, renovating homes (she is on house number twelve), yardwork, and playing golf with her husband and twin girls.

SARAH WERTHAN BUTTENWIESER is a writer and community organizer based in Northampton, MA. She attended Hampshire College and the MFA Program for Writers at Warren Wilson College.

LINDA CORMAN is a freelance writer working mostly in investing for social and environmental impact. She was a journalist for many years for magazines and newspapers. In her spare time, she has been working on a novel about her Russian grandfather.

PHYLLIS COX retired a quarter-century ago from teaching language arts K-12. Now she enjoys spending time with her family, which includes four grandchildren, as well as reading, cooking, and volunteering in the small college town of Oxford, Ohio, where she lives.

LAURA DAVIS is a professor at Kennesaw State University, where she serves as the associate chair of the Interdisciplinary Studies Department. Her teaching and research interests include digital pedagogy, queer studies, intersections of gender and the US South, ecofeminism, and the literature of William Faulkner.

SARAH DOUGHER is an educator and writer who lives in Portland, Oregon. She writes about girls, music, education, and equity. She has written fiction, made records, and now teaches college and high school. She is dedicated to the long haul of making higher education accessible and meaningful for historically underrepresented and disenfranchised people.

SALMA ABDELNOUR GILMAN is a writer and editor based in New York City. A former travel editor for *Food & Wine*, Salma published the memoir *Jasmine and Fire: A Bittersweet Year in Beirut* (Random House, 2012). Salma has written for the *New York Times*,

Tin House, and many other outlets, and currently manages editorial projects for media and nonprofit clients.

ELIZABETH GREGORY directs the Women's, Gender, and Sexuality Studies program and the Institute for Research on Women, Gender & Sexuality at the University of Houston, where she is also a professor of English. She is the author of *Ready: Why Women Are Embracing the New Later Motherhood* (Basic Books, 2007) and *"Apparition of Splendor": Marianne Moore Performing Democracy through Celebrity, 1952–1970* (University of Delaware Press, 2020), and she blogs at domesticproduct.net.

MARTINE GUAY completed a master's degree in nursing after a career in legal translation and management, and after raising three children, she had a fourth child through IVF and egg donation. She works as a fertility nurse at McGill University Health Centre in Montreal.

JULIA HENDERSON is an Age Studies and Theatre Studies scholar who resides with her husband and two children in Vancouver, British Columbia. She is currently doing a postdoctoral fellowship at Concordia University in the Department of Communication Studies and the Ageing + Communication + Technology Project, which is focused on creating theatre with people with dementia.

BARBARA HEREL is the founder, producer, and host of *Every Family's Got One*—a performance series, podcast, and blog devoted to family stories. Connect with her at EveryFamilysGotOne.com.

DANIEL E. HOOD is a retired professor of sociology. His last teaching position was at Otisville Prison for John Jay College. He has published two books that challenge standard drug treatments and has volunteered with harm reduction agencies, serving as a syringe exchanger, overdose rescue trainer, and board chair over the past few decades.

JEAN Y. LEUNG is a native New Yorker and received her master's degree in journalism from New York University and her bachelor's degree from State University of New York at Stony Brook. Throughout her career, she traveled extensively around the United States and abroad, but the journey she valued most was the one of motherhood.

ELLINE LIPKIN is a research scholar with UCLA's Center for the Study of Women and teaches for Los Angeles writing classes. She is the author of *The Errant Thread* (Kore Press, 2005) and *Girls' Studies* (Seal Press, 2009) and the former poet laureate of Altadena.

ERIK MALEWSKI is a professor at Kennesaw State University. He has served in various diversity administrative roles and held faculty appointments at Purdue University and Arizona State University. When he's not rushing to meet a writing deadline or folding mountains of laundry, he likes to spend time with his family.

LINDA WRIGHT MOORE is a retired journalist and communicator with four decades of experience as a newspaper columnist, public radio talk show host, television reporter, producer and anchor, mayoral press secretary, and tenured journalism professor. She enjoys travel, writing, photography, and dance. She's writing a memoir and resides in suburban Philadelphia.

ELIZABETH NEWMAN is the author of two books, *A Long Way from Shattered Glass to Mosaic: Living with Autism Spectrum Disorder* (2008) and *All In with The Almighty: Parenting Special Needs Children by Faith* (2018). Her books detail the challenges and joys of raising a daughter diagnosed with autism and epilepsy.

KATHERINE C. RAND is a relational educator, spiritual care scholar-practitioner, and older parent who supports people in telling their stories, being lifelong learners, coming into meaningful relationship with others, healing collective wounds, and fighting oppression. She is working on getting more comfortable telling her own stories in the process.

JIM SHULTZ is the founder and executive director of the Democracy Center. He lived with his family in Bolivia from 1998 to 2017, where he also led an orphanage that housed eighty children. His most recent book is *My Other Country: Nineteen Years in Bolivia* (2020). He currently lives across the street from his granddaughters in Lockport, New York.

ALIA R. TYNER-MULLINGS is an associate professor of sociology at Stella and Charles Guttman Community College–CUNY. Her areas of interest are education, communities, and popular culture. She also runs workshops on academic planning.

Notes

INTRODUCTION

1. Martin, Joyce A., Brady E. Hamilton, Michelle J.K. Osterman, Anne K. Driscoll, Patrick Drake. "Births: Final Data for 2017." *National Vital Statistics Reports*, 67, no. 8 (2018).

2. Brenoff, Ann. "Too Old to Adopt? Not the Case for These Parents." *Huffington Post*, July 3, 2012. https://www.huffingtonpost.com/2012/07/03/too-old-to-adopt-child-adoption_n_1606942.html

3. Friese, Carrie, Gay Becker, Robert D. Nachtigall. "Older Motherhood and the Changing Life Course in the Era of Assisted Reproductive Technologies." *Journal of Aging Studies* 22, no. 1 (2008): 73.

4. Rapp, Rayna. Interview. March 5, 2018.

5. Gregory, Elizabeth. *Ready: Why Women Are Embracing the New Later Motherhood*. New York: Basic Books, 2012.

6. Sussman, Anna Louie. "The End of Babies." *New York Times*, November 16, 2019. https://www.nytimes.com/interactive/2019/11/16/opinion/sunday/capitalism-children.html

7. "Reproductive Justice." SisterSong. https://www.sistersong.net/reproductive-justice

8. Sunderam, Saswati, Dmitry M. Kissin, Yujia Zhang, Amy Jewett, Sheree L. Boulet, Lee Warner, Charlan D. Kroelinger, Wanda D. Barfield. "Assisted Reproductive Technology Surveillance—United States, 2017." *MMWR Surveillance Summaries* 69, no. 9 (2020): 1–20. MMWR Surveillance Summaries 69, no. 9 (2020): 1–20.

9. Rothman, Julia, and Shaina Feinberg. "What They Paid to Make a Baby (or 2)." *New York Times.* February 7, 2020. https://www.nytimes.com/2020/02/07/business/what-they-paid-to-make-a-baby-or-2.html.

10. https://www.resolve.org/

11. Centers for Disease Control and Prevention, American Society for Reproductive Medicine, Society for Assisted Reproductive Technology. *2016 Assisted Reproductive Technology: National Summary Report.* Atlanta, GA: 2018. https://www.cdc.gov/art/pdf/2016-report/ART-2016-National-Summary-Report.pdf

12. Brandt, Justin S., Mayra A. Cruz Ithier, Todd Rosen, Elena Ashkinadze. "Advanced paternal age, infertility, and reproductive risks: A review of the literature." *Prenatal Diagnosis* 39, no. 2 (2019).

13. Gilbert, William M., Thomas S. Nesbitt, Beate Danielsen. "Childbearing beyond Age 40: Pregnancy Outcome in 24,032 Cases." *Obstetrics & Gynecology* 93, no. 1 (1999): 9–14. doi:10.1016/s0029-7844(98)00382-2.

14. Bayrampour, Hamideh, Maureen Heaman, Karen A. Duncan, Suzanne Tough. "Advanced maternal age and risk perception: A qualitative study." *BMC Pregnancy and Childbirth* 12 (2012).

15. Creanga, Andreea A., Carla Syverson, Kristi Seed, William M. Callaghan. "Pregnancy-Related Mortality in the United States, 2011–2013." *Obstet Gynecol* 130, no. 2 (2017): 366–373. doi: 10.1097/AOG.0000000000002114

16. Geronimus, Arline T. "Black/white differences in the relationship of maternal age to birthweight: A population-based test of the weathering hypothesis." *Social Science & Medicine* 42, no. 4: 589–597. doi:10.1016/0277-9536(95)00159-X.

17. McClain, Dani. *We Live for the We: The Political Power of Black Motherhood.* New York: Bold Type Books, 2019.

18. Dodge, David. "What I Spent to Adopt My Child." *New York Times,* February 11, 2020.https://www.nytimes.com/2020/02/11/parenting/adoption-costs.html.

19. Vandivere, Sharon, Karin Malm, Laura Radel. "Adoption USA: A chartbook based on the 2007 national survey of adoptive parents."

Last modified November 1, 2009. https://aspe.hhs.gov/report/
adoption-usa-chartbook-based-2007-national-survey-adoptive-
parents.

20. "Domestic vs. International Adoption." Adoption Network.
https://adoptionnetwork.com/types-of-adoption-options/domestic-
vs-international-adoption/

21. Solinger, Rickie. *Beggars and Choosers: How the Politics of Choice
Shapes Adoption, Abortion and Welfare in the United States.* New York:
Hill and Wang, 2001.

22. Roberts, Dorothy. "Feminism, Race, and Adoption policy."
In *Color of Violence: The INCITE! Anthology,* ed. INCITE! Women
of Color Against Violence, 42–52. Durham: Duke University Press,
2016.

23. Hall, Beth, Gail Steinberg. *Inside Transracial Adoption.*
Indianapolis: Jessica Kingsley Publishers, 2013.

THE TERRIBLE MATH

1. Toriello, Helga V. and Jeanne M. Meck. "Statement on guidance
for genetic counseling in advanced paternal age." *Genetics in Medicine*
10, no. 6 (2008): 457–460. doi: 10.1097/GIM.0b013e318176fabb.

2. Rabin, Roni. "It Seems the Fertility Clock Ticks for Men,
Too." *New York Times.* February 27, 2007. https://www.nytimes.
com/2007/02/27/health/27sper.html.

3. Harel, Monica Corcoran. "Baby, Please." *Los Angeles* magazine.
May 1, 2011. https://www.lamag.com/longform/baby-please/.

4. Vinciguerra, Thomas. "He's Not My Grandpa. He's My
Dad." *New York Times.* April 12, 2007. https://www.nytimes.
com/2007/04/12/fashion/12dads.html.

THE SINGLE, MOST IMPORTANT COMMUNITY

1. Gogo, Vickie. "The disturbing state of black maternal health in
the U.S." Last modified May 11, 2018. https://www.icf.com/insights/
health/african-american-maternal-mortality-rates.